# WorkingMother

# 29•MINUTE MEALS

*Edited by Carol R. Guthrie*

Library of Congress Catalog Number: 91-62448
ISBN: 0-8487-1070-3

Manufactured in the United States of America
First printing 1991

Published by Oxmoor House, Inc.
Book Division of Southern Progress Corporation
P.O. Box 2463, Birmingham, AL 35201

WORKING MOTHER magazine
    Associate Publisher: Susan Seliger
    Editor-in-Chief: Judsen Culbreth
    Art Director: Joan Ferrell
    Deputy Art Director: Marcia Maphis Jennings
    Food Editor: Carol R. Guthrie
    Director of Corporate Affairs: Jeri Sedlar
    Special Projects Manager: Susan A. Kesten

Oxmoor House, Inc.
    Executive Editor: Ann H. Harvey
    Director of Manufacturing: Jerry R. Higdon
    Art Director: Bob Nance

*29-Minute Meals*
    Senior Editor: Olivia Kindig Wells
    Senior Designer: Cynthia Rose Cooper
    Copy Editor: Diane Lewis Swords
    Editorial Assistant: Sue L. Killingsworth
    Production Manager: Rick Litton
    Associate Production Manager: Theresa L. Beste
    Production Assistant: Pam Beasley Bullock

*Cover: Sizzling Caribbean Pork menu (page 24).*
Photograph by Lisa Charles Watson.

*Back cover: (Clockwise from top) Sweet Onion Pizza menu (page 50), Skillet Steak and Peppers menu (page 8), A-to-Z Minestrone (page 225).* Photographs by Peter Johansky.

To subscribe to WORKING MOTHER magazine, call 1-800-525-0643.

# Contents

# Introduction

One of the givens of every mother's life is getting food on the table two and sometimes three times a day. It's not an easy task since time is tight, but that's why the editors at WORKING MOTHER created *29-Minute Meals*. Our goal is to provide you with recipes for fast, healthful, home-cooked fare.

We carefully developed each dish, avoiding those that seemed complicated or unappealing to families. (You'll notice the lack of liver, Brussels sprouts and tripe.) We also chose only recipes that fit our nutritional requirements. A registered dietitian double-checked our decisions and analyzed all the recipes for the amount of calories, fat, carbohydrate, protein, sodium and cholesterol they contain. You'll find an analysis following each recipe.

In addition, all the recipes have been tested in our own test kitchens to ensure that the instructions are easy to understand and the completed dishes taste great. Any that didn't meet our approval have been redone, fine-tuned and tasted again . . . and again, if need be.

These recipes were developed and tested by food professionals. All WORKING MOTHER recipe writers and testers have had extensive experience as food editors, test kitchen directors and freelance recipe developers. They are, in addition, graduates of certified culinary schools or food and nutrition programs.

With all this expertise, you can be sure these dishes not only look and taste wonderful, but that they also suit your lifestyle. When you're in a hurry to get supper on the table, rely on our "29-Minute Meals," the featured section of the cookbook. These menus—complete with game plans to help you get out of the kitchen fast—were timed during the testing, so you know they're quick to make.

The recipes in the "Relax While It Cooks" section are easy in a different way. Simply put the meal on to cook and forget about it. While supper simmers in the oven or on top of the stove, you can catch up with your family or enjoy some time to yourself.

Having a few friends over? Our "Easy Entertaining" section has seven special menus—from barbecues and picnics to elegant dinners and dessert buffets. Plus, you'll find loads of fuss-free serving ideas and make-ahead tips. There's plenty of room to modify each menu to suit your entertaining style—if you love preparing desserts, skip making the entrée and serve roast beef or smoked turkey from your deli. If you're short on time, save a step by serving purchased pasta or potato salads as side dishes.

*Chili Lasagna Roll-Ups menu (page 52).*

For family dinners, the real issue is not the side dishes or dessert—but the entrée. For inspiration when you get home from work, turn to our "Build-a-Meal" section. It's full of quick, terrific ideas for family-pleasing entrées like Tex-Mex Microwave Chili and Skillet Pizza Alfresco.

And for the picky palates in your family, we have a "Kid Pleasers" section: scrumptious meals and snacks for growing kids, delicious lunchbox ideas, adorable cookies you can bake with your child and recipes without "yucky" ingredients.

This cookbook would never have happened without the support of our Editor-in-Chief, Judsen Culbreth. Thanks also to Amy Biber Barr and Janet Charatan, associate editors

whose writing and editing helped make our recipes easy to follow and fun to read, too. And thanks to all the recipe developers, photographers, food stylists, prop stylists, and, above all, our art department for the splendid photographs in this book.

Families today may not sit down to a Sunday roast beef dinner as often as their parents or grandparents did, but they do strive to spend time together and create their own traditions. That's what this cookbook is all about—I hope you enjoy it.

*Carol R. Guthrie*

# 29-Minute Meals

*"What's for supper?" With this collection of quick-fix menus you'll have an easy answer to that daily question. A specially designed plan accompanies each menu, helping you work magic in the kitchen. In 29 minutes or less, you'll have a family-pleasing meal on the table. (Pictured, Curry-Glazed Lamb, page 20.)*

## Menu Plans:
Beef
Lamb
Pork
Chicken
Turkey
Fish
Pastas & More

# Beef Menus

## MENU
### *Skillet Steak and Peppers*
～～～
### *Broccoli with shallots*
～～～
### *Herbed Bread Knots*

*Here's a fast-fix menu that's full of bright colors and tasty flavors. First, preheat the oven and shape the bread knots. While they're baking, start the other dishes. Thinly slice some shallots and cook in butter or olive oil. Add broccoli florets and a little water; then cover and cook. Brown the steaks in a skillet and remove to a platter. Sauté peppers in the pan drippings; add a splash of sherry and a little mustard. Return steaks to skillet and warm through with pepper sauce.*

### SKILLET STEAK AND PEPPERS

2   tablespoons (¼ stick) butter or margarine
4   beef rib-eye steaks, trimmed, ½ inch thick
4   large red and/or yellow peppers, cut into 1-inch-wide strips
3   tablespoons dry sherry
2   tablespoons Dijon mustard
¼   teaspoon salt
½   teaspoon cracked black pepper

1. Melt butter in large skillet over medium-high heat. Add steaks and cook for 8 minutes for medium-rare, or until of desired doneness, turning once. Remove to a platter; cover and keep warm.

2. Reduce heat to medium. To drippings in skillet, add pepper strips; sauté for 10 minutes, or until tender, stirring occasionally. Add remaining ingredients; bring to a boil and cook for 1 minute, stirring to loosen brown bits. Return steaks to skillet; heat through.

Makes 4 servings.

*Per serving: 376 calories, 21 g protein, 29 g fat, 8 g carbohydrate, 89 mg cholesterol, 488 mg sodium.*

### HERBED BREAD KNOTS

1   package (11 ounces) refrigerated bread sticks
1   tablespoon butter or margarine, melted
1   teaspoon sesame seeds
¼   teaspoon dried oregano

Preheat oven to 350°F. Tie each bread stick in a loose knot; then place on baking sheet.

*Left: Skillet Steak and Peppers menu.*

Brush bread knots with butter; top with sesame seeds and oregano. Bake for 15 minutes, or until lightly browned.

Makes 4 servings.

*Per serving: 231 calories, 7 g protein, 8 g fat, 33 g carbohydrate, 8 mg cholesterol, 497 mg sodium.*

# MENU
## Sautéed Steaks with Watercress and Red Wine
~~~~~
## Parslied Orzo and Tomatoes
~~~~~
## Dinner rolls

*These mouth-watering steaks are simple, fast—and elegant enough for company! First, start cooking orzo. Meanwhile, brown steaks and remove to a serving platter. Add garlic and wine to pan drippings; then stir in watercress just until wilted. Top steaks with sauce and add final touches to the orzo.*

## SAUTEED STEAKS WITH WATERCRESS AND RED WINE

4 beef rib-eye steaks, trimmed, ½ inch thick
¾ teaspoon coarsely ground black pepper
½ teaspoon salt
1 tablespoon olive oil
2 large cloves garlic, minced
⅓ cup dry red wine
2 bunches watercress, stemmed

1. Sprinkle steaks on both sides with pepper and salt; press seasonings into steaks. Heat oil in large skillet over high heat. Add steaks and cook for 5 to 6 minutes for rare, or until of desired doneness, turning once. Remove to a platter; cover and keep warm.

2. Reduce heat to low. To drippings in skillet, add garlic; sauté for 30 seconds, stirring constantly. Add wine; cook for 30 seconds, stirring to loosen brown bits. Stir in watercress and any meat juices from platter. Increase heat to high; cook for 1 to 2 minutes, or until watercress wilts, stirring constantly. Spoon watercress and pan juices over steaks.

Makes 4 servings.

*Per serving: 284 calories, 30 g protein, 15 g fat, 2 g carbohydrate, 84 mg cholesterol, 402 mg sodium.*

## PARSLIED ORZO AND TOMATOES

1¼ cups orzo or other small pasta
1 tablespoon olive oil
1 can (14½ to 16 ounces) tomatoes, drained and coarsely chopped
½ cup chopped Italian parsley
½ teaspoon salt
½ teaspoon coarsely ground black pepper

1. Cook orzo according to package directions; drain and set aside.

2. Heat oil in same pot over medium heat. Add tomatoes; cook 2 minutes, stirring frequently. Stir in orzo, parsley, salt and pepper; heat through.

Makes 4 servings.

*Per serving: 263 calories, 8 g protein, 5 g fat, 47 g carbohydrate, 0 mg cholesterol, 442 mg sodium.*

## MENU
### Skewered Beef Satay
~~~~~

### Bangkok Salad
~~~~~

### Steamed couscous

*A quick marinating time in soy sauce and spices adds lots of zesty flavor to these beef skewers—they're served with a peanutty dipping sauce. Start marinating the beef cubes and onion wedges first. Meanwhile, steam some couscous and preheat the broiler. Then make the crispy iceberg and radish salad. Skewer the beef and onion and quickly oven-broil. The peanut sauce couldn't be easier— simply heat reserved marinade with some peanut butter and a little water.*

### SKEWERED BEEF SATAY

¼  cup reduced-sodium soy sauce
2  tablespoons packed brown sugar
2  teaspoons salad oil
½  teaspoon ground coriander
½  teaspoon ground cumin
1  pound boneless beef top sirloin steak, trimmed, 1 inch thick
1  medium Spanish onion
3  tablespoons smooth peanut butter
Chopped fresh cilantro (optional garnish)

1.  In large bowl, mix first 5 ingredients. Cut steak into 1 inch cubes; cut onion through root end into 8 wedges. Stir steak cubes and onion wedges into soy-sauce mixture; let stand for 15 minutes.

*Left: Skewered Beef Satay menu.*

2.  Preheat broiler. Alternate steak and onion on 4 skewers; reserve marinade. Place skewers on broiling rack 4 to 5 inches from heat source. Broil for 5 minutes for medium-rare, or until of desired doneness, turning skewers often.

3.  In small saucepan over medium-high heat, bring reserved marinade to a boil. Whisk in peanut butter and ⅓ cup water; heat through. Pour into serving bowl as dipping sauce for beef; garnish with cilantro.
Makes 4 servings.

*Per serving: 313 calories, 31 g protein, 15 g fat, 14 g carbohydrate, 76 mg cholesterol, 716 mg sodium.*

### BANGKOK SALAD

¼  cup seasoned rice-wine vinegar
1  tablespoon coarsely chopped fresh cilantro
¼  teaspoon ground ginger
¼  teaspoon crushed red pepper
½  medium head iceberg lettuce, thinly sliced
6  radishes, quartered

In medium salad bowl, whisk first 4 ingredients. Add lettuce and radishes; gently toss with dressing.
Makes 4 servings.

*Per serving: 28 calories, 1 g protein, trace fat, 6 g carbohydrate, 0 mg cholesterol, 10 mg sodium.*

### QUICK FLAVOR FOR PASTA
● Soy sauce is a staple of oriental cooking, but it also makes a good seasoning substitute when cooking vegetables. Try the reduced-sodium variety to season your next vegetables.

## MENU
*Glazed Steak Dijon*

*Savory Broiled Vegetables*

*Garlic French bread*

*Here, steak and vegetables cook in the same pan—which means less after-dinner cleanup! First, preheat the broiler and toss all ingredients for the vegetables in a broiling pan without the rack. Coat steak with the pungent mustard-horseradish topping; place on a rack set over vegetables and broil for about 16 minutes—the vegetables will cook in the time it takes to broil the steak. For a perfect go-with, pop garlic French bread in the oven alongside the broiling pan.*

## GLAZED STEAK DIJON

3  tablespoons Dijon mustard
1  tablespoon prepared horseradish
2  teaspoons salad oil
1¾  pounds beef top-round steak, trimmed, 1½ inches thick
Chicory or other lettuce leaves (optional)
Fresh marjoram (optional garnish)

1. Preheat broiler. In a cup, mix mustard, horseradish and oil; set aside.

2. Prepare Savory Broiled Vegetables (recipe follows). Set broiling rack over vegetables. Lightly score both sides of steak; place on rack over vegetables. Brush steak with some mustard mixture.

3. Broil steak 3 to 4 inches from heat source for 8 minutes; turn and brush with remaining mustard mixture. Broil for 8 minutes, or until steak is medium-rare and vegetables are tender-crisp. Let steak stand for a few minutes before thinly slicing on diagonal, across the grain. Serve steak slices with some chicory (if using) on top of garlic bread, if you like. Garnish with marjoram.

Makes 6 servings.

*Per serving: 204 calories, 30 g protein, 8 g fat, 1 g carbohydrate, 78 mg cholesterol, 284 mg sodium.*

## SAVORY BROILED VEGETABLES

12  small pattypan squash, halved
1  medium red onion, cut into thin wedges
½  pound shiitake or button mushrooms
2  tablespoons olive oil
1  teaspoon dried Italian seasoning
1  teaspoon salt
½  teaspoon cracked black pepper

*Left: Glazed Steak Dijon menu.*

In large, deep broiling pan without rack, combine all ingredients. Broil vegetables with steak according to preceding recipe.

Makes 6 servings.

*Per serving: 61 calories, 1 g protein, 5 g fat, 4 g carbohydrate, 0 mg cholesterol, 372 mg sodium.*

*Above: Chili-Spiced Beef Burritos menu.*

## MENU
### *Chili-Spiced Beef Burritos*
〜〜〜
### *Chunky Tomato-Avocado Salsa*
〜〜〜
### *Mexicali corn*
〜〜〜
### *Icy margaritas or lemonade*

*A Tex-Mex spice mix adds an almost char-grilled flavor to these speedy burritos. Here's the plan: First, preheat the broiler and make the salsa. Then rub both sides of steak with the spice mix and broil. Warm the tortillas in the oven while steak stands. Next, heat up a can of Mexicali corn. A pitcher of margaritas or lemonade completes the fiesta.*

### CHILI-SPICED BEEF BURRITOS

2  teaspoons chili powder
2  teaspoons ground cumin
½  teaspoon salt
1  beef top-round or flank steak, trimmed, ¾ inch thick (about 1 pound)
8  flour tortillas
1  cup (4 ounces) shredded Monterey Jack cheese
¼  cup sour cream (optional)
Fresh cilantro (optional garnish)

1. Preheat broiler. In a cup, mix chili powder, cumin and salt. Rub both sides of steak with chili-powder mixture. Place steak on broiling rack 4 to 5 inches from heat source. Broil for 8 minutes for rare, or until of desired doneness, turning once. Let steak stand for a few minutes before thinly slicing on diagonal, across the grain.

2. Turn oven control to 350°F. Wrap tortillas in aluminum foil; place in oven for 10 minutes to warm. Arrange a few steak slices on each tortilla; top with some shredded cheese and Chunky Tomato-Avocado Salsa (recipe follows). Fold sides of tortilla over filling. Serve with sour cream (if using) and garnish with cilantro.

Makes 4 servings.

*Per serving: 519 calories, 39 g protein, 17 g fat, 49 g carbohydrate, 96 g cholesterol, 908 mg sodium.*

## CHUNKY TOMATO-AVOCADO SALSA

1 large tomato, chopped
1 medium avocado, peeled, pitted and chopped
1 small onion, diced
1 tablespoon cider vinegar
1 tablespoon minced fresh cilantro
¼ teaspoon salt
¼ teaspoon hot-pepper sauce (optional)

In medium bowl, combine tomato, avocado, onion, vinegar, cilantro, salt and hot-pepper sauce (if using).
Makes 4 servings.
*Per serving: 92 calories, 1 g protein, 8 g fat, 6 g carbohydrate, 0 mg cholesterol, 143 mg sodium.*

# MENU
## *Stovetop Meat Loaf*
~~~~~
## *Orzo Parmigiano*
~~~~~
## *Peas and carrots*
~~~~~
## *Milk*

*Flavored with Italian seasonings, this skillet-made meat loaf takes half the time of oven-baked. Use preshredded cheese to save even more time. Start by cooking the orzo; then mix meat-loaf ingredients. Brown the meat-loaf patty in a skillet, and add ingredients for the tomato sauce. While meat loaf simmers, cook some frozen peas and carrots. Toss orzo with Parmesan, parsley, butter and a little pepper and top the meat loaf with mozzarella—dinner's ready!*

## STOVETOP MEAT LOAF

1 pound lean ground beef
2 slices whole-grain bread, crumbled
1 egg
1 small onion, minced
1 large clove garlic, minced
⅓ cup milk
¾ teaspoon salt
¼ teaspoon black pepper
2½ teaspoons dried basil
1 tablespoon salad oil
1 can (13⅓ to 14½ ounces) Italian plum tomatoes
2 tablespoons tomato paste
½ cup (2 ounces) shredded part-skim mozzarella cheese

1. In large bowl, mix first 8 ingredients and 2 teaspoons of the dried basil until well combined. Shape ground-beef mixture into an 8-inch patty.

2. Heat salad oil in medium skillet over medium-high heat. Add patty; cook for 3 minutes, or until bottom is browned. Using two wide spatulas, remove patty to a platter. Carefully return patty to skillet, browned side up.

3. Add tomatoes, breaking them up with a spoon; add tomato paste and remaining ½ teaspoon basil to skillet. Bring mixture to a boil. Reduce heat to low; cover and simmer for 15 minutes, or until meat loaf is cooked through. Sprinkle with cheese; cover and cook for 2 minutes, or until cheese melts. To serve, cut meat loaf into wedges and top with tomato sauce.
Makes 4 servings.
*Per serving: 466 calories, 29 g protein, 32 g fat, 15 g carbohydrate, 149 mg cholesterol, 901 mg sodium.*

## ORZO PARMIGIANO

1  cup orzo or other small pasta
¼  cup grated Parmesan cheese
2  tablespoons chopped parsley
1  tablespoon butter or margarine
¼  teaspoon cracked black pepper

Cook orzo according to package directions, but omit the salt. Gently stir in remaining ingredients.

Makes 4 servings.

*Per serving: 234 calories, 8 g protein, 5 g fat, 38 g carbohydrate, 12 mg cholesterol, 124 mg sodium.*

## MENU

*Po' Boy Burgers*

~~~~~

*Creole Onions and Peppers*

~~~~~

*Deli potato salad*

~~~~~

*Pickled okra*

~~~~~

*Cold beer*

*Here's a family-pleasing twist on a classic New Orleans sandwich. Start by sautéing the onion and peppers with a spicy seasoning mix; then combine burger ingredients. Shape burger mixture into ovals and brown in a skillet. Serve burgers on French bread, topped with sliced tomato and the onions and peppers. Team with deli potato salad, pickled okra and a mug of cold beer.*

*Right: Po' Boy Burgers menu.*

## PO' BOY BURGERS

1¼  pounds ground beef
3  tablespoons spicy brown mustard
½  teaspoon dried thyme
½  teaspoon salt
½  teaspoon cayenne pepper
¼  teaspoon dried oregano
1  small loaf French bread
1  large tomato, thinly sliced

1. In medium bowl, mix first 6 ingredients until just combined; do not overwork. Shape into 4 oval patties.

2. Heat large nonstick skillet over medium heat. Place burgers in skillet; cook for 5 minutes for medium-rare, or until of desired doneness, turning once.

3. Meanwhile, cut bread crosswise into 4 pieces to fit burgers (save any remaining bread for another use). Split each piece in half; stuff with tomato slices, burgers and Creole Onions and Peppers (recipe follows).

Makes 4 servings.

*Per serving: 516 calories, 30 g protein, 25 g fat, 41 g carbohydrate, 88 mg cholesterol, 875 mg sodium.*

## CREOLE ONIONS AND PEPPERS

2 tablespoons olive or salad oil
1 large Spanish onion, thinly sliced
1 large green pepper, thinly sliced
2 teaspoons Creole seasoning (see Note)

Heat oil in large skillet over medium-high heat. Add remaining ingredients; sauté for 10 to 12 minutes, or until vegetables are tender, stirring occasionally.

Makes 4 servings.

*Per serving: 110 calories, 2 g protein, 7 g fat, 11 g carbohydrate, 0 mg cholesterol, 425 mg sodium.*

*Note:* Creole seasoning is a blend of salt, red pepper and other spices. Look for it in the spice section of your supermarket.

# MENU

*Alphabet Sloppy Joes*

*Creamy Lettuce Slaw*

*Celery sticks*

*Alphabet pasta makes these sandwiches a surefire winner with the kids. The game plan: First, make the sloppy joe filling. While it cooks, make the creamy dressing for coleslaw— toss dressing with thinly sliced iceberg lettuce, carrots and green pepper. Then lightly toast kaiser rolls or hamburger buns. Spoon sloppy-joe mixture on top of rolls and sprinkle with a little cheddar cheese. Crunchy celery sticks are an easy accompaniment.*

## ALPHABET SLOPPY JOES

¾ pound lean ground beef
½ large green pepper, chopped (save other half for Creamy Lettuce Slaw, recipe follows)
1 medium onion, chopped
⅔ cup chili sauce
¼ teaspoon black pepper
¼ cup alphabet egg pasta, or other very small pasta
Salt to taste
4 kaiser rolls or hamburger buns, toasted
¼ cup shredded cheddar cheese (optional)

1. In large skillet over medium-high heat, brown beef with green pepper and onion. Drain and discard fat. Add chili sauce, black pepper and ¾ cup water; bring to a boil. Add pasta; reduce heat to medium. Cover and cook for 12 to 15 minutes, or until pasta is tender. Add a little salt, if necessary.

2. Spoon beef mixture over bottom halves of rolls; sprinkle with cheese (if using). Sandwich with tops of rolls.

Makes 4 servings.

*Per serving: 429 calories, 23 g protein, 14 g fat, 53 g carbohydrate, 53 mg cholesterol, 973 mg sodium.*

## CREAMY LETTUCE SLAW

¼ cup mayonnaise
2 tablespoons plain yogurt
1 teaspoon cider vinegar
½ teaspoon dry mustard
¼ teaspoon celery seed
¼ teaspoon salt
¼ teaspoon black pepper
½ medium head iceberg lettuce, sliced
2 medium carrots, grated
½ large green pepper, sliced

In large salad bowl, combine first 7 ingredients; stir until well combined. Add remaining ingredients, gently toss with dressing.

Makes 4 servings.

*Per serving: 135 calories, 2 g protein, 11 g fat, 8 g carbohydrate, 8 mg cholesterol, 238 mg sodium.*

*Above: Alphabet Sloppy Joes menu.*

# Lamb Menus

## MENU
### Maple-Mustard Lamb Chops
~~~~~
### Rosemary-Roasted Potatoes
~~~~~
### Steamed string beans
~~~~~
### Fresh pears
~~~~~
### Iced tea

*Glazed with a tangy-sweet sauce, these lamb chops are a snap to make. First, preheat the oven and put the potatoes in to roast. Meanwhile, steam some fresh string beans (we used a combination of wax and green beans) and prepare the chops. Succulent pears are an elegant dessert.*

### MAPLE-MUSTARD LAMB CHOPS

1   teaspoon salad oil
8   lamb rib or loin chops, trimmed, ¾ inch thick
1   medium onion, thinly sliced
⅓   cup maple syrup
¼   cup grainy Dijon mustard
4   teaspoons cider vinegar
½   teaspoon black pepper

1.   Heat oil in large skillet over medium-high heat. Add lamb chops and onion; cook for 4 minutes. Turn chops; continue to cook for 4 to 5 minutes for medium-rare, or until of desired doneness.

2.   Meanwhile, in small bowl, stir together remaining ingredients. Add maple-syrup mixture to skillet with chops; bring to a boil. Cook for 1 minute, or until sauce thickens slightly; turn chops once to coat with glaze.
Makes 4 servings.
*Per serving: 332 calories, 27 g protein, 15 g fat, 21 g carbohydrate, 90 mg cholesterol, 551 mg sodium.*

### ROSEMARY-ROASTED POTATOES

12   small red-skinned potatoes, quartered
2   tablespoons (¼ stick) butter or margarine, melted
1   teaspoon dried rosemary, crushed
½   teaspoon salt
½   teaspoon coarsely ground black pepper
Fresh rosemary (optional garnish)

Preheat oven to 450°F. In small roasting pan, toss potatoes, butter, crushed rosemary, salt and black pepper until well combined. Roast potato mixture for 20 to 25 minutes, stirring after 10 minutes. Garnish potatoes with fresh rosemary.
Makes 4 servings.
*Per serving: 144 calories, 2 g protein, 6 g fat, 21 g carbohydrate, 16 mg cholesterol, 341 mg sodium.*

*Right: Maple-Mustard Lamb Chops menu.*

## MENU
*Curry-Glazed Lamb*

~~~~~

*Autumn Fruit Sauté*

~~~~~

*Fluffy white rice*

*This main-dish recipe is easy and almost fool-proof—just be careful not to overcook the lamb. Start the rice first; then brown the chops and make the curry sauce. While sauce is cooking, slice apples and pears and sauté them in a little butter with crystallized ginger. (Pictured, pages 6 and 7.)*

### CURRY-GLAZED LAMB

1   tablespoon salad oil
8   lamb rib or loin chops, trimmed,
      ¾ inch thick
1   medium onion, chopped
1   tablespoon curry powder
¾   cup chutney, chopped
¼   cup apple juice or chicken broth
1   tablespoon cider vinegar
¼   teaspoon salt
Fresh mint (optional garnish)

1. Heat oil in large skillet over medium-high heat. Add lamb chops; cook for 8 to 9 minutes for medium-rare, or until of desired doneness, turning once. Remove to a platter; cover and keep warm.

2. To drippings in skillet, add onion; cook for 5 minutes, stirring occasionally. Add curry powder; cook for 1 minute, stirring constantly. Mix in remaining ingredients except garnish; bring to a boil and cook for

1 minute. Spoon sauce over chops. Garnish with mint.
   Makes 4 servings.
   *Per serving: 338 calories, 20 g protein, 13 g fat, 36 g carbohydrate, 64 mg cholesterol, 309 mg sodium.*

### AUTUMN FRUIT SAUTE

2   tablespoons (¼ stick) butter or
      margarine
1   large red-skinned apple, cored and
      thinly sliced
1   large pear, cored and thinly sliced
2   teaspoons minced crystallized ginger

   Melt butter in medium skillet over medium heat. Add apple slices, pear slices and minced ginger; sauté for 3 to 5 minutes, or until just tender, stirring occasionally.
   Makes 4 servings.
   *Per serving: 100 calories, trace protein, 6 g fat, 13 g carbohydrate, 16 mg cholesterol, 59 mg sodium.*

### ADD ZEST FROM THE REFRIGERATOR
● Chutney is a spicy-sweet Indian relish to use with curries or as a tasty glaze for grilled meats.
● Capers, a piquant Mediterranean condiment, provide a nice accent for salads, sauces or scrambled eggs.
● Fresh ginger is sensational in vegetable stir-fries and seafood, chicken or beef dishes. To keep it on hand, just peel, slice and place in a jar with sherry to cover—it will last for months.

## MENU
### Lamb Chops with Red Wine-Rosemary Sauce
~~~
### Honey-Orange Glazed Winter Vegetables
~~~
### Buttered noodles

*Shoulder chops are a delicious cut of lamb and less expensive than rib or loin chops. For this menu, put water on to boil for some noodles, and then start the winter vegetables. Parsnips and carrots are a wonderful combination, but if your family isn't fond of parsnips just use carrots. While vegetables are cooking, brown the chops and make the easy red-wine sauce. Just finish cooking the vegetables with a little honey, butter and orange peel—dinner's ready!*

## LAMB CHOPS WITH RED WINE-ROSEMARY SAUCE

2   teaspoons salad oil
4   lamb shoulder chops, ¾ inch thick, trimmed
½   cup beef broth
¼   cup dry red wine
2   teaspoons Dijon mustard
½   teaspoon dried rosemary, crushed
½   teaspoon black pepper
2   tablespoons (¼ stick) well-chilled butter or margarine

1. Heat oil in large skillet over high heat. Add lamb chops; cook for 7 to 8 minutes for medium-rare, or until of desired doneness, turning once. Remove to a platter; cover and keep warm. Discard drippings in skillet.

2. To skillet, add broth, wine, mustard, rosemary, pepper and any meat juices on platter. Over high heat, bring to a boil and cook for 3 minutes, stirring to loosen brown bits in skillet.

3. Remove skillet from heat; whisk in butter. Pour red-wine sauce over chops.

Makes 4 servings.

*Per serving: 229 calories, 21 g protein, 15 g fat, 1 g carbohydrate, 84 mg cholesterol, 311 mg sodium.*

## HONEY-ORANGE GLAZED WINTER VEGETABLES

4     medium carrots
4     medium parsnips
2     tablespoons honey
2     tablespoons butter or margarine
1½   teaspoons grated orange peel

Cut carrots and parsnips diagonally into 1-inch pieces. In medium saucepan over medium heat, in 1 inch boiling water, cook vegetables, covered, for 10 minutes, or until tender. Drain and return to saucepan. Stir in remaining ingredients; heat through.

Makes 4 servings.

*Per serving: 187 calories, 2 g protein, 6 g fat, 34 g carbohydrate, 16 mg cholesterol, 94 mg sodium.*

# Pork Menus

## MENU

*Ginger-Spiced Pork Tenderloin*

~~~~

*Chunky Apple-Pear Sauce*

~~~~

*Sautéed cabbage and kale*

*Pork tenderloin is a very lean, boneless cut. The size (one pound or so) is perfect for a family of four. For this menu, coat the pork with spice mix and put in a preheated oven to roast. Then start the quick-fix apple-pear sauce — it has a hint of lemon and cinnamon. While sauce simmers, coarsely shred some cabbage and kale and sauté in a little butter. Reserve a few uncooked kale leaves to garnish plates, if you like.*

### GINGER-SPICED PORK TENDERLOIN

2   teaspoons ground ginger
1   teaspoon fennel seeds, crushed
1   teaspoon salt
1   teaspoon black pepper
⅛   teaspoon ground cloves
1   pork tenderloin (about 1 pound), trimmed

1.  Preheat oven to 375°F. In a cup, mix first 5 ingredients; rub spice mixture over surface of pork. Place on rack in roasting pan.

2.  Roast pork for 20 to 25 minutes, or until meat thermometer inserted in thickest

*Left: Ginger-Spiced Pork Tenderloin menu.*

part registers 155°F. Let pork stand for a few minutes before thinly slicing.

Makes 4 servings.

*Per serving: 155 calories, 26 g protein, 4 g fat, 1 g carbohydrate, 83 mg cholesterol, 611 mg sodium.*

### CHUNKY APPLE-PEAR SAUCE

2   large cooking apples, cut into small chunks
2   large ripe pears, cut into small chunks
½   cup frozen apple-juice concentrate, thawed
1   teaspoon coarsely grated lemon peel
1   teaspoon lemon juice
¾   teaspoon ground cinnamon

In large saucepan over high heat, combine fruit and apple-juice concentrate; bring mixture to a boil. Reduce heat to low; cover and simmer for 10 minutes, or until fruit is tender. Stir in remaining ingredients.

Makes 4 servings.

*Per serving: 150 calories, 1 g protein, 1 g fat, 38 g carbohydrate, 0 mg cholesterol, 9 mg sodium.*

### STOCK THE CUPBOARD WITH FLAVOR

● Chicken or beef bouillon cubes (or canned broth) make a great base for sauces, soups and gravies. A fat-cutting hint: You can sauté meats and vegetables in a very small amount of oil if you combine it with a few tablespoons of broth.

● Sherry makes a rich, mellow addition to cream sauces or stir-fried dishes. It should always be purchased in a liquor store — supermarket cooking sherry is very high in sodium.

● Rice vinegar has a tart-sweet, delicate flavor that will brighten the taste of hot or cold vegetables and salads.

*Above: Sizzling Caribbean Pork menu.*

# MENU
## Sizzling Caribbean Pork
~~~~~
## Lime-Scented Rice
~~~~~
## Tropical fruit
~~~~~
## Juice spritzer

*For a bright taste of the islands, try this easy, elegant supper. Start with the rice; while it's cooking, cut up the vegetables and brown the pork. Next, remove pork from skillet and sauté vegetables with spices; return pork to pan and heat through. To finish, stir cilantro and lime into rice. Tropical fruit and a refreshing citrus-and-seltzer spritzer round out the meal.*

## SIZZLING CARIBBEAN PORK

2 tablespoons all-purpose flour
½ teaspoon salt
1 pork tenderloin (about 1 pound), trimmed, cut into ¾-inch cubes
2 tablespoons salad oil
2 medium cloves garlic, minced
1 medium onion, coarsely chopped
1 teaspoon ground ginger
½ to 1 teaspoon crushed red pepper
½ teaspoon ground cinnamon
¼ teaspoon ground allspice
1 can (14½ to 16 ounces) tomatoes
2 small green peppers, coarsely chopped
1 medium papaya or 2 bananas, peeled and cut into chunks

1. On wax paper, combine flour and salt; dredge pork in flour mixture, shaking off excess. Heat oil in large skillet over medium-high heat. Add pork; sauté until browned on all sides, about 8 minutes. With slotted spoon, remove pork to small bowl.

2. To drippings in skillet, add garlic, onion, ginger, red pepper, cinnamon and allspice; sauté for 3 to 4 minutes, stirring frequently.

3. Return pork to skillet. Add tomatoes with juice, breaking them up with a spoon; add green pepper. Bring to a boil; then reduce heat to low. Cover and simmer for 5 to 10 minutes, adding papaya during last few minutes of cooking.

Makes 4 servings.

*Per serving: 273 calories, 26 g protein, 10 g fat, 19 g carbohydrate, 74 mg cholesterol, 509 mg sodium.*

## LIME-SCENTED RICE

1 cup uncooked long-grain rice
1 tablespoon butter or margarine
½ teaspoon salt
1 small lime
2 tablespoons chopped fresh cilantro or
  parsley
Lime slices (optional garnish)

In medium saucepan over high heat, combine rice, butter, salt and 2 cups water; bring to a boil. Reduce heat to low; cover and simmer for 15 minutes, or until rice is tender and liquid is absorbed. Meanwhile, grate peel from lime and squeeze juice. Stir grated lime peel, lime juice and cilantro into rice. Garnish with lime slices.

Makes 4 servings.

*Per serving: 196 calories, 3 g protein, 3 g fat, 38 g carbohydrate, 8 mg cholesterol, 305 mg sodium.*

# MENU
*Quick Italian-Style Pork*
〰〰〰
*Spring Rice*
〰〰〰
*Fresh fruit with cheese*

*Stir-fry doesn't always have to be oriental! In this Italian version, the quick-cooking technique keeps the vegetables tender-crisp and the pork extra juicy. First, cook the rice with a little chicken broth for extra flavor and prep the vegetables. Next, stir together the wine-cornstarch mixture and slice the pork tenderloin. Stir-fry pork and vegetables; add wine-cornstarch mixture and cook until thickened. Just before serving, stir arugula into rice.*

## QUICK ITALIAN-STYLE PORK

⅔ cup dry white wine
1 teaspoon cornstarch
½ teaspoon salt
¼ teaspoon crushed red pepper
1 pork tenderloin (about ¾ pound)
3 tablespoons olive or salad oil
1 small bulb fennel, thinly sliced
1 medium red pepper, cut into thin strips
1 large clove garlic, minced
1¼ teaspoons fennel seeds, crushed

1. In small bowl, mix wine, cornstarch, salt and crushed pepper until thoroughly combined; set aside.

2. With sharp knife held in slanting position almost parallel to work surface, cut pork crosswise into ⅛-inch-thick slices. Heat 2 tablespoons of the oil in large skillet or wok over high heat. Add pork; stir-fry for 2 to 3 minutes, or until cooked through. With slotted spoon, remove pork to a plate.

3. Reduce heat to medium-high. To drippings in skillet, add remaining 1 tablespoon oil; heat for 30 seconds. Add sliced fennel, red pepper strips, garlic and fennel seeds; stir-fry for 4 minutes, or until vegetables are tender-crisp.

4. Stir wine-cornstarch mixture until smooth; add to skillet with pork. Bring mixture to a boil; cook for 1 minute, or until sauce is heated through and slightly thickened.

Makes 4 servings.

*Per serving: 206 calories, 19 g protein, 12 g fat, 4 g carbohydrate, 55 mg cholesterol, 369 mg sodium.*

### SPRING RICE

1  cup uncooked long-grain rice
1  can (13¾ ounces) chicken broth
1  bunch arugula or watercress, coarsely
   chopped

   Cook rice according to package directions,
using chicken broth and enough water to equal
2 cups. During last 5 minutes of cooking,
stir in arugula.

   Makes 4 servings.

   *Per serving: 184 calories, 5 g protein, trace fat,
38 g carbohydrate, 0 mg cholesterol, 444 mg
sodium.*

## MENU

*Thyme-Scented Pork Scallopini*

⌇⌇⌇⌇

*Steamed summer vegetables*

⌇⌇⌇⌇

*Peppery Corn Bread Bites*

⌇⌇⌇⌇

*Iced tea*

*Here's a garden-fresh menu that takes just minutes to make! First, prepare the cheesy corn bread batter and put it in a preheated oven to bake. Next, brown the pork chops in a skillet. While they're cooking, put some green beans and summer squash on to steam. Remove pork to a plate; add scallions, mushrooms, wine and seasonings to skillet to make the sauce. Return chops to pan; add tomatoes and simmer until done. Cut corn bread into squares and you're ready to serve!*

### THYME-SCENTED PORK SCALLOPINI

4  very thin pork loin chops with bone, trimmed (about 1 pound)
2  tablespoons all-purpose flour
1  tablespoon olive oil
1  tablespoon butter or margarine
4  scallions, cut into 1-inch pieces
¾  pound mushrooms, sliced
¼  cup dry white wine or chicken broth
¼  teaspoon dried thyme
¼  teaspoon salt
¼  teaspoon black pepper
1  cup cherry tomatoes, halved
Fresh thyme (optional garnish)

*Left: Thyme-Scented Pork Scallopini menu.*

1. Dredge chops in flour, shaking off excess. Heat oil and butter in large skillet over medium-high heat. Add chops and sauté for 10 minutes, or until browned and cooked through, turning once. Remove chops to a plate; set aside.

2. To drippings in skillet, add scallions and mushrooms; sauté for 3 minutes, or until tender, stirring occasionally. Add wine, dried thyme, salt and pepper; bring to a boil and cook for 1 minute, stirring to loosen brown bits. Return chops to skillet; add tomatoes. Reduce heat to medium-low; cover and simmer for 5 minutes. Garnish with fresh thyme.

Makes 4 servings.

*Per serving: 221 calories, 19 g protein, 12 g fat, 9 g carbohydrate, 56 mg cholesterol, 221 mg sodium.*

### PEPPERY CORN BREAD BITES

1  package (7½ to 12 ounces) corn bread muffin mix
¾  cup (3 ounces) shredded sharp cheddar cheese
1½  teaspoons cracked black pepper

Preheat oven to 425°F. Grease 8-inch square baking pan. Prepare corn bread mix according to package directions, adding cheese to batter. Pour batter into prepared pan; sprinkle evenly with black pepper. Bake for 15 minutes, or until golden brown and toothpick inserted in center comes out clean. Cut corn bread into squares.

Makes about 12 squares.

*Per square: 160 calories, 4 g protein, 6 g fat, 21 g carbohydrate, 27 mg cholesterol, 348 mg sodium.*

*Above: Pork with Chili-Corn Salsa menu.*

---

# MENU
### *Pork with Chili-Corn Salsa*
～～～
### *Cheese Tortillas*
～～～
### *Ice-cold beer*

---

*Pork cutlets topped with a warm, tangy salsa are ready in less than 20 minutes! First, preheat the oven for tortillas. Then prep vegetables for the salsa and sauté the pork. Cutlets are very lean and cook quickly—be careful not to overcook. Next, put tortillas in the oven to crisp. While they're baking, mix the salsa ingredients. Finish by melting cheese on tortillas and sprinkling them with olives.*

## PORK WITH CHILI-CORN SALSA

1  tablespoon salad oil
4  boneless pork sirloin cutlets, about ¼ inch thick
1  small green pepper, chopped
1  small onion, chopped
½  fresh jalapeño pepper, minced (optional)
½  teaspoon chili powder
1  can (8 ounces) whole-kernel corn, undrained
2  medium tomatoes, coarsely chopped
2  tablespoons chopped fresh cilantro or parsley
½  teaspoon salt
Fresh cilantro (optional garnish)

1.  Heat oil in large skillet over medium-high heat. Add cutlets; sauté for 5 minutes, or until cooked through, turning once. Remove to a platter; cover and keep warm.

2.  To drippings in skillet, add green pepper, onion and jalapeño (if using); sauté for 5 minutes, stirring occasionally. Add chili powder; cook for 1 minute. Add corn with liquid, tomatoes, chopped cilantro and salt; heat through. Spoon salsa over cutlets. Garnish with cilantro.
    Makes 4 servings.
    *Per serving: 398 calories, 22 g protein, 29 g fat, 13 g carbohydrate, 79 mg cholesterol, 475 mg sodium.*

## CHEESE TORTILLAS

4  corn tortillas, quartered
½  cup (2 ounces) shredded Monterey Jack cheese (plain or with jalapeños)
¼  cup sliced ripe olives

Preheat oven to 450°F. Place tortilla quarters on baking sheet and bake for 6 minutes. Sprinkle tortillas with Monterey Jack cheese and bake for 3 minutes, or until cheese melts. Top with sliced olives.
Makes 4 servings.
*Per serving: 135 calories, 6 g protein, 7 g fat, 13 g carbohydrate, 12 mg cholesterol, 192 mg sodium.*

## MENU
### Smothered Pork Chops
~~~~
### Smashed Potatoes
~~~~
### Garden vegetables

*Quick comfort food—this menu is simple yet sure to please. First, start cooking the onions for the pork chops and put the potatoes on to boil. While they're cooking, brown the chops and cook some vegetables (use your favorite combination of fresh or frozen veggies). Remove chops to a platter; make sauce in the same skillet. Spoon sauce and onions over chops, mash potatoes lightly with scallions and sour cream—dinner's ready!*

*Above: Smothered Pork Chops menu.*

### SMOTHERED PORK CHOPS

2  medium onions, thinly sliced
1  tablespoon sugar
2  tablespoons (¼ stick) butter or
   margarine
2  tablespoons all-purpose flour
½  teaspoon salt
¼  teaspoon black pepper
4  pork rib chops, trimmed, ½ inch thick
1  tablespoon salad oil
1  package or cube chicken-flavor instant
   bouillon
½  teaspoon dried thyme
Fresh thyme (optional garnish)

1.  In medium saucepan over medium-high heat, cook onions and sugar in butter for 15 minutes, stirring frequently.

2.  Meanwhile, on wax paper, mix flour, salt and pepper. Dredge chops in mixture, shaking off excess; reserve leftover flour mixture. Heat salad oil in large skillet over medium-high heat. Add chops; sauté for 6 minutes, or until cooked through, turning once. Remove chops to a platter; cover and keep warm.

3.  Reduce heat to medium-low. To drippings in skillet, add reserved flour, bouillon and dried thyme; cook for 1 minute, stirring constantly. Gradually stir in 1 cup cold water; cook until gravy thickens, stirring constantly. Spoon onion mixture and gravy over chops. Garnish with fresh thyme.

Makes 4 servings.

*Per serving: 248 calories, 18 g protein, 15 g fat, 9 g carbohydrate, 63 mg cholesterol, 763 mg sodium.*

## SMASHED POTATOES

1 pound red-skinned potatoes,
  quartered
⅓ cup sour cream
2 scallions, thinly sliced
½ teaspoon salt
¼ teaspoon black pepper

In medium saucepan over high heat, cook potatoes in water to cover for 15 minutes, or until tender. Drain potatoes and mash slightly. Stir in remaining ingredients.
Makes 4 servings.

*Per serving: 135 calories, 3 g protein, 4 g fat, 22 g carbohydrate, 8 mg cholesterol, 293 mg sodium.*

---

# MENU
### *Microwave Potatoes with Broccoli, Bacon & Cheddar*

*Crispy Carrot-and-Cucumber Salad*

*Milk*

---

*With the help of the microwave you can serve this hearty meal in 29 minutes. Don't worry if the potatoes aren't completely done after 15 minutes—they'll continue to cook during standing time. Here's the plan: Put potatoes in the microwave to cook; then make the salad and put it in the refrigerator. Next, prepare cheese sauce for potatoes; cover and keep warm while you sauté the broccoli with Canadian bacon. Split potatoes and top with cheese and bacon-broccoli mixture.*

## MICROWAVE POTATOES WITH BROCCOLI, BACON & CHEDDAR

4 medium baking potatoes
3 tablespoons butter or margarine
2 tablespoons all-purpose flour
¾ cup milk
1 cup (4 ounces) shredded cheddar
  cheese
2 teaspoons dry mustard
1 tablespoon salad oil
2 ounces sliced Canadian bacon, cut into
  thin strips
4 cups broccoli florets

1. Pierce each potato several times with a knife; arrange in circle on paper towel in microwave. Microwave on High for 12 to 15 minutes, turning potatoes over after 6 minutes. Let stand for 5 minutes.

2. Meanwhile, melt butter in small saucepan over low heat. Add flour; cook for 1 minute, stirring constantly. Gradually stir in milk. Increase heat to medium and bring to a boil; cook until sauce thickens slightly, stirring constantly. Remove from heat; add cheese and mustard, stirring until smooth. Cover to keep warm.

3. Heat oil in large skillet over medium heat. Add bacon; sauté for 3 minutes. Add broccoli and 3 tablespoons water; bring to a boil. Reduce heat to low; cover and simmer for 8 minutes, or until broccoli is tender-crisp, stirring occasionally.

4. Split potatoes. Top each potato with some bacon-broccoli mixture; then top with cheese sauce.
Makes 4 servings.

*Per serving: 439 calories, 20 g protein, 25 g fat, 38 g carbohydrate, 67 mg cholesterol, 527 mg sodium.*

## CRISPY CARROT-AND-CUCUMBER SALAD

2 tablespoons olive oil
1 tablespoon cider vinegar
1 tablespoon Dijon mustard
3 large carrots, julienned
2 medium cucumbers, julienned

In medium salad bowl, whisk first 3 ingredients. Add carrots and cucumbers; gently toss with dressing.
Makes 4 servings.

*Per serving: 112 calories, 1 g protein, 7 g fat, 12 g carbohydrate, 0 mg cholesterol, 141 mg sodium.*

# MENU

*New Orleans-Style Sausage Ragout*

*Parsley Rice*

**Tossed green salad**

*This robust dish is ready in less than 29 minutes! First, put the rice on to cook and cut up onion and green pepper for the ragout. Brown the sausage, pepper and onion together in a saucepan; then add tomatoes, okra and spices. While the ragout simmers, make a green salad. Finishing touches take minutes—serve ragout over the rice to soak up the luscious sauce.*

## NEW ORLEANS-STYLE SAUSAGE RAGOUT

½ pound ready-cooked kielbasa or other smoked sausage, cut into ½-inch-thick slices
1 medium green pepper, chopped
1 medium onion, chopped
2 cans (14½-ounce size) no-salt-added stewed tomatoes
1 package (10 ounces) frozen cut okra
2 tablespoons chopped parsley
½ teaspoon dried thyme
¼ to ½ teaspoon cayenne pepper
1 can (16 ounces) black beans, rinsed and drained

1. In large saucepan over medium-high heat, cook sausage, green pepper and onion for 3 to 4 minutes, or until lightly browned; stir occasionally. Drain and discard excess fat.
2. Add tomatoes, breaking them up with a spoon; then add okra, parsley, thyme, cayenne and 1 cup water. Bring to a boil. Reduce heat to low; cover and simmer for 10 minutes, stirring occasionally. Add beans; heat through.
Makes 4 servings.

*Per serving: 376 calories, 18 g protein, 16 g fat, 42 g carbohydrate, 38 mg cholesterol, 1,131 mg sodium.*

## PARSLEY RICE

1 cup uncooked long-grain rice
3 tablespoons chopped fresh parsley

Cook rice according to package directions. Stir in parsley.
Makes 4 servings.

*Per serving: 113 calories, 2 g protein, 9 g fat, 25 g carbohydrate, 0 mg cholesterol, 1 mg sodium.*

# Chicken Menus

## MENU
### Chicken Kabobs with Peach Sauce
~~~~
### Two-Vegetable Couscous
~~~~
### Sparkling water

*Seasoned with rosemary and served with a tangy peach sauce, these kabobs are a snap to make. First, prepare the one-step peach sauce. Next, preheat the broiler and thread rosemary-scented chicken and lemon wedges on skewers. (If you're lucky enough to have fresh rosemary in your garden, use larger branches as skewers.) While the chicken cooks, make the colorful couscous.*

### CHICKEN KABOBS WITH PEACH SAUCE

1 can (16 ounces) sliced peaches in light syrup, drained
2 tablespoons peach preserves
1 tablespoon spicy brown mustard
1 tablespoon cider vinegar
2 tablespoons olive oil
1 teaspoon dried rosemary, crushed
½ teaspoon salt
½ teaspoon cracked black pepper
1 pound boneless, skinless chicken-breast halves, cut into 1-inch chunks
1 to 2 lemons, cut into thin wedges
Fresh rosemary (optional garnish)

1. For peach sauce: In blender or food processor fitted with steel blade, puree peaches, peach preserves, mustard and vinegar; set sauce aside.

2. Preheat broiler. In shallow bowl, mix oil, dried rosemary, salt and pepper; add chicken, stirring to coat.

3. Alternate chicken and lemon wedges on skewers; place on broiling rack about 4 inches from heat source. Broil for 8 to 10 minutes, or until chicken is cooked through, turning once. Serve kabobs with peach sauce; squeeze juice from lemons on chicken. Garnish with rosemary.

Makes 4 servings.

*Per serving: 284 calories, 27 g protein, 9 g fat, 27 g carbohydrate, 66 mg cholesterol, 393 mg sodium.*

*Note:* These kabobs may be grilled instead of broiled.

### TWO-VEGETABLE COUSCOUS

1½  cups chicken broth or water
1  cup quick-cooking couscous
1  cup frozen green peas
1  jar (7 ounces) roasted red peppers, drained and chopped

In medium saucepan over high heat, bring chicken broth to a boil. Stir in couscous and peas. Remove from heat; cover and let stand for 5 minutes. Add peppers; fluff with a fork to separate grains of couscous.

Makes 4 servings.

*Per serving: 164 calories, 7 g protein, 1 g fat, 33 g carbohydrate, 0 mg cholesterol, 416 mg sodium.*

*Left: Chicken Kabobs with Peach Sauce menu.*

## MENU
### Moroccan Chicken with Vegetables
~~~~
### Toasted Couscous
~~~~
### Orange or kiwi wedges

*There's so much flavor, but only 284 calories per serving in this chicken dish. For a taste of India, eliminate the cinnamon and substitute ½ teaspoon curry powder. First, brown the chicken on both sides. Remove to a platter and sauté carrots, onion and garlic in pan drippings. Return chicken to skillet with remaining ingredients and simmer until chicken is done. Meanwhile, toast the couscous; then cook in chicken broth or water for a few minutes. Kiwi or orange wedges are a lovely dessert.*

### MOROCCAN CHICKEN WITH VEGETABLES

4  boneless, skinless chicken-breast halves
½  teaspoon salt, or to taste
2  tablespoons salad oil
3  medium carrots, thinly sliced
1  small onion, thinly sliced
1  small clove garlic, minced
1  can (8 ounces) whole tomatoes
1  cup frozen green peas
¼  cup raisins
¼  teaspoon ground cinnamon
⅛  teaspoon black pepper

1. Sprinkle chicken with salt. Heat oil in large skillet over medium-high heat. Add chicken; cook for 5 minutes, or until lightly browned on both sides. Remove chicken to a platter.

2. To drippings in skillet, add carrots, onion and garlic; sauté for 5 minutes, stirring occasionally. Stir in remaining ingredients (include tomato juice), breaking up tomatoes with a spoon. Bring to a boil; taste sauce and add more salt if necessary.

3. Return chicken to skillet, topping with sauce. Reduce heat to low; cover and simmer for 10 minutes, or until chicken is cooked through.
Makes 4 servings.
*Per serving: 284 calories, 31 g protein, 9 g fat, 21 g carbohydrate, 68 mg cholesterol, 503 mg sodium.*

### TOASTED COUSCOUS

2  tablespoons butter or margarine
1  cup quick-cooking couscous
1½  cups chicken broth or water
½  teaspoon salt (if using water)

Melt butter in medium skillet over medium heat. Add couscous; cook until lightly browned, stirring frequently. Add broth; bring to a boil. Remove from heat. Cover and let stand for 5 minutes; fluff with a fork to separate grains of couscous.
Makes 4 servings.
*Per serving: 171 calories, 4 g protein, 6 g fat, 26 g carbohydrate, 16 mg cholesterol, 337 mg sodium.*

*Right: Orange-Glazed Curry Chicken menu.*

## MENU
*Orange-Glazed Curry Chicken*

~~~~~

*Creamy Cucumber-and-Lettuce Salad*

~~~~~

*Mint tea*

*This meal of tender chicken with couscous or rice is simple to make—and touched with honey so kids will love it. First, prepare dressing for the salad and clean the lettuce. Then start the couscous or rice and sauté the chicken. Make the curry-orange sauce and return chicken to the skillet to heat through. For a soothing beverage, serve hot mint tea.*

## ORANGE-GLAZED CURRY CHICKEN

1  cup couscous or rice
2  tablespoons salad oil
1  pound chicken cutlets, cut into 2-inch chunks
1  small onion, chopped
1  medium clove garlic, minced
1  teaspoon curry powder
¼  teaspoon salt
½  cup orange juice
1  tablespoon honey
2  teaspoons minced fresh cilantro or parsley
Orange wedges and fresh cilantro (optional garnish)

1.  Cook couscous according to package directions.

2.  Meanwhile, heat oil in large skillet over medium-high heat. Add chicken; sauté for 3 to 4 minutes, or until lightly browned but not cooked through. With slotted spoon, remove chicken to a bowl. Reduce heat to medium. To drippings in skillet, add onion, garlic, curry powder and salt; cook for 2 to 3 minutes, stirring constantly. Add orange juice and honey; bring to a boil and cook for 3 to 4 minutes, or until sauce is slightly reduced.

3.  Return chicken to skillet and stir to coat with sauce. Cook for 3 to 4 minutes, or until chicken is cooked through. Spoon chicken over couscous; sprinkle with minced cilantro. Garnish with orange wedges and cilantro.

Makes 4 servings.

*Per serving: 341 calories, 31 g protein, 8 g fat, 35 g carbohydrate, 66 mg cholesterol, 215 mg sodium.*

## CREAMY CUCUMBER-AND-LETTUCE SALAD

1   small clove garlic, minced
½   cup plain yogurt
2   tablespoons mayonnaise or salad
    dressing
½   teaspoon dried dillweed
1   medium head green leaf lettuce, leaves
    torn
1   large cucumber, thinly sliced

In small bowl, mix first 4 ingredients. Place lettuce in a large salad bowl; top with cucumber slices. Drizzle dressing over salad.
Makes 4 servings.

*Per serving: 98 calories, 4 g protein, 6 g fat, 7 g carbohydrate, 6 mg cholesterol, 72 mg sodium.*

# MENU
*Shanghai Chicken Wings*
~~~~
*Sesame Cabbage*
~~~~
*Chinese noodles*
~~~~
*Orange wedges*

*These no-fuss favorites make great party appetizers, too. Here's the plan: Start the water for Chinese noodles (look for them in the oriental section of your supermarket—or simply substitute vermicelli or angel's-hair pasta). Next, preheat the broiler and mix together ketchup-soy-ginger sauce for wings. Broil wings for several minutes, and then coat with some sauce. While wings finish cooking, cut up the cabbage and quickly sauté in a little oriental sesame oil.*

## SHANGHAI CHICKEN WINGS

2   tablespoons ketchup
2   tablespoons reduced-sodium soy sauce
1   tablespoon minced fresh ginger or ¾
    teaspoon ground ginger
1   large clove garlic, minced
12  chicken wings

1.  Preheat broiler. In small bowl, mix ketchup, soy sauce, ginger, garlic and 2 tablespoons water until well combined.
2.  Place chicken wings, meaty side down, on broiling rack about 4 inches from heat source. Broil for 7 minutes. Brush chicken with half the ketchup mixture; broil for 1 minute. Turn chicken; broil for 5 minutes, or until cooked through. Brush with remaining ketchup mixture; broil for 1 minute.
Makes 4 servings.

*Per serving: 312 calories, 28 g protein, 20 g fat, 3 g carbohydrate, 86 mg cholesterol, 473 mg sodium.*

## SESAME CABBAGE

2   tablespoons sesame seeds
1   tablespoon salad oil
2   teaspoons oriental sesame oil
2   pounds Chinese or savoy cabbage, thinly
    sliced
¼   teaspoon salt

In large saucepan over medium heat, toast sesame seeds in salad and sesame oils for 2 minutes, stirring constantly. Add cabbage and salt; cook for 5 minutes, or until cabbage wilts, stirring frequently.
Makes 4 servings.

*Per serving: 112 calories, 4 g protein, 8 g fat, 8 g carbohydrate, 0 mg cholesterol, 156 mg sodium.*

## MENU
### Chili-Rubbed Chicken
~~~~
### Tangy Fruit Salsa
~~~~
### Corn niblets
~~~~
### Tortilla chips

*This wonderful Southwestern recipe calls for boneless chicken thighs, but if your family prefers white meat, substitute chicken breasts—just cook a few minutes less. Here's the plan: Preheat the broiler; make the chili butter and spread some on chicken. While chicken broils, make the fruit salsa and boil some corn.*

*Above: Chili-Rubbed Chicken menu.*

### CHILI-RUBBED CHICKEN

8  boneless chicken thighs, with skin
3  tablespoons butter or margarine, softened
1  large clove garlic, minced
1  tablespoon chili powder
¼  teaspoon black pepper
½  teaspoon salt
Fresh cilantro (optional garnish)

1. Preheat broiler. Partially loosen skin on each chicken thigh by working your hand between meat and skin.

2. In small bowl, mix butter, garlic, chili powder and pepper until well combined. Spread half of chili butter evenly under skin of chicken. Sprinkle chicken with salt.

3. Place chicken, skin side down, on broiling rack about 4 inches from heat source. Broil for 15 to 18 minutes, or until cooked through, brushing chicken occasionally with remaining chili butter and turning once. Garnish with cilantro.

Makes 4 servings.

*Per serving: 480 calories, 33 g protein, 38 g fat, 1 g carbohydrate, 181 mg cholesterol, 523 mg sodium.*

### TANGY FRUIT SALSA

1  small red pepper, finely chopped
½  pear, cored and finely chopped
½  can (8-ounce size) crushed pineapple in juice
1  tablespoon minced onion
1  tablespoon chopped fresh cilantro
1  tablespoon cider vinegar
⅛  teaspoon salt
⅛  teaspoon cayenne pepper

In small bowl, combine all ingredients, stirring well. Refrigerate any leftovers.

Makes 4 servings.

*Per serving: 34 calories, trace protein, trace fat, 9 g carbohydrate, 0 mg cholesterol, 70 mg sodium.*

# Turkey Menus

*Above: Turkey Cutlets Caponata menu.*

## MENU

### *Turkey Cutlets Caponata*

~~~~~

### *Yellow-Pepper Salad*

~~~~~

### *Pasta with parsley butter*

*Caponata, the Italian version of ratatouille, is a zesty complement to lean turkey cutlets. First, put water on to boil for pasta; then prep vegetables for caponata and salad. Next, sauté the turkey cutlets, remove to a serving platter and cook caponata in the same pan. Toss the cooked pasta with some butter, chopped parsley and the salad with basil vinaigrette. Spoon caponata on top of cutlets— you're ready to serve!*

## TURKEY CUTLETS CAPONATA

3  tablespoons olive oil
1  pound turkey cutlets
¼  pound baby eggplant (or ½ medium eggplant), cut into thin strips
1  small onion, thinly sliced
2  large tomatoes, diced
1  tablespoon capers
1  teaspoon red-wine vinegar
½  teaspoon salt
½  teaspoon sugar
½  teaspoon dried oregano
⅛  teaspoon black pepper
2  tablespoons chopped ripe olives
**Fresh oregano (optional garnish)**

1. Heat oil in large skillet over medium-high heat. Add turkey; sauté for 3 minutes, or until just cooked through. Remove to a platter; cover and keep warm.

2. To drippings in skillet, add eggplant and onion; cook for 2 minutes, or until lightly browned, stirring frequently. Add next 7 ingredients; reduce heat to low. Cover and simmer for 3 minutes, just until tomatoes are soft. Stir in olives. Spoon eggplant mixture (called caponata) over turkey. Garnish with oregano.

Makes 4 servings.

*Per serving: 255 calories, 28 g protein, 13 g fat, 7 g carbohydrate, 70 mg cholesterol, 443 mg sodium.*

## YELLOW-PEPPER SALAD

2  tablespoons olive oil
4  teaspoons balsamic or red-wine vinegar
¼  teaspoon salt
¼  teaspoon dried basil
2  yellow peppers, thinly sliced
1  bunch watercress, stemmed

In large salad bowl, whisk first 4 ingredients. Add peppers and watercress; gently toss with dressing.

Makes 4 servings.

*Per serving: 74 calories, 1 g protein, 7 g fat, 3 g carbohydrate, 0 mg cholesterol, 154 mg sodium.*

*Above: Turkey Cutlets with Peanut Sauce menu.*

## MENU

*Turkey Cutlets with Peanut Sauce*

～～～～

*Gingered Vegetables*

～～～～

*Spring berries*

*First, start cooking the pasta and prepping the gingered vegetables. Next, cook cutlets. Make the peanut sauce; while it is cooking, stir-fry the vegetables. Toss the pasta and vegetables; cut turkey into thin strips and place on pasta; drizzle with sauce.*

### TURKEY CUTLETS WITH PEANUT SAUCE

8 ounces spaghetti or linguine
1 egg
⅓ cup plain dried bread crumbs
¼ cup sesame seeds
1 pound turkey cutlets
3 tablespoons salad oil
2 scallions, thinly sliced
2 packages or cubes low-sodium chicken-flavor instant bouillon
¼ cup smooth peanut butter
1 tablespoon reduced-sodium soy sauce

1. Cook spaghetti according to package directions.

2. Meanwhile, in pie plate, beat egg and 1 tablespoon water. On wax paper, combine bread crumbs and sesame seeds. Dip turkey cutlets into egg mixture, and then into bread-crumb mixture to coat.

3. Heat oil in large skillet over medium-high heat. Add turkey cutlets a few at a time; sauté for 3 to 4 minutes, or until browned and just cooked through, adding more oil if needed. Remove to a platter.

4. Reduce heat to medium. To drippings in skillet, add scallions; cook for 2 minutes, stirring frequently. Stir in remaining ingredients and 2 cups water. Over high heat, bring mixture to a boil. Cook for 5 minutes, or until sauce is slightly thickened, stirring occasionally. (You should have about 1¼ to 1½ cups peanut sauce.)

5. To serve, toss pasta with Gingered Vegetables (recipe follows). Cut turkey into thin strips and arrange on top of pasta. Spoon some peanut sauce over turkey and pasta.

Makes 4 servings.

*Per serving: 638 calories, 43 g protein, 27 g fat, 55 g carbohydrate, 139 mg cholesterol, 385 mg sodium.*

## GINGERED VEGETABLES

2  tablespoons salad oil
1  large carrot, thinly sliced
1  pound asparagus, trimmed and cut
   diagonally into 2-inch pieces
1  teaspoon ground ginger

Heat oil until very hot in medium skillet over medium-high heat. Add carrot, asparagus and ginger; stir-fry for 5 to 7 minutes, or until tender-crisp.
Makes 4 servings.
*Per serving: 86 calories, 2 g protein, 7 g fat, 5 g carbohydrate, 0 mg cholesterol, 10 mg sodium.*

---

# MENU
### Turkey Sandwiches with Honey-Mustard Mayonnaise
~~~~~~
### Spicy Tomato-Corn Soup
~~~~~~
### Sparkling water

---

*The light and tangy soup may be served warm or refreshingly chilled. Here's the plan: First cook bacon for the soup; then sauté chopped dill, corn and onion in the same pan. Stir in the vegetable juice and top with a dollop of sour cream and some crumbled bacon. The sandwiches take just minutes to make: layer watercress, pepper strips and turkey on hearty rolls, and then top with the honey-mustard-and-mayonnaise mixture.*

## TURKEY SANDWICHES WITH HONEY-MUSTARD MAYONNAISE

⅓  cup mayonnaise
2  tablespoons Dijon mustard
1  tablespoon honey
¼  teaspoon black pepper
1  bunch watercress, stemmed
1  medium red pepper, cut into ¼-inch
   strips
¾  pound sliced plain or smoked turkey
4  kaiser rolls, split

In small bowl, combine mayonnaise, mustard, honey and pepper. Layer watercress, pepper strips and turkey on bottom halves of rolls. Spread with honey-mustard mayonnaise; then sandwich with top halves of rolls. Serve with olives and pickles, if you like.
Makes 4 servings.
*Per serving: 464 calories, 31 g protein, 21 g fat, 37 g carbohydrate, 78 mg cholesterol, 722 mg sodium.*

## SPICY TOMATO-CORN SOUP

2  strips lean bacon, cut into 1-inch pieces
3  tablespoons minced fresh dill, or 1
   tablespoon dried dillweed
1  package (10 ounces) frozen corn,
   thawed, or about 2 cups fresh corn
   kernels
1  small onion, minced
3  cups no-salt-added vegetable or tomato
   juice
¼  to ½ teaspoon hot-pepper sauce
¼  teaspoon black pepper
¼  cup light sour cream
**Fresh dill sprigs (optional garnish)**

1.  In large saucepan over medium-high heat, cook bacon until crisp. Remove to paper

*Above: Turkey Sandwiches with Honey-Mustard Mayonnaise menu.*

towels to drain; set aside. Discard all but 1 tablespoon drippings from saucepan. Cook minced dill, corn and onion in drippings until tender, stirring occasionally. Remove and set aside 2 tablespoons dill-corn mixture for garnish.

2. Add vegetable juice, hot-pepper sauce and pepper to remaining dill-corn mixture; over high heat, bring to a boil. Ladle into serving bowls. Top soup with sour cream and

bacon; garnish with dill-corn mixture and dill sprigs. (To serve chilled: Omit bacon; cook dill, corn and onion in 1 tablespoon salad oil. Add vegetable juice, hot-pepper sauce and pepper; don't heat through. Chill before serving.)

Makes 4 servings.

*Per serving: 167 calories, 5 g protein, 6 g fat, 26 g carbohydrate, 9 mg cholesterol, 141 mg sodium.*

## MENU
### Turkey Tacos with Black Beans
*~~~*
### Best-Ever Guacamole
*~~~*
### Orange-jicama salad

*Quickly cooked turkey and black beans make the protein-packed filling for this Mexican favorite. Prepare guacamole first; then toss orange slices and jicama with bottled vinai-grette. (Jicama is a crunchy, slightly sweet root vegetable—you can substitute celery.) Briefly heat taco shells in the oven while you sauté the turkey mixture. For fun and serving ease, let each person stuff his or her own taco—just set out bowls of turkey-and-black-bean filling, lettuce, cheese and guacamole.*

## TURKEY TACOS WITH BLACK BEANS

2   tablespoons salad oil
¾   pound turkey cutlets, cut into
     ½-inch-wide strips
3   scallions, chopped
2   teaspoons ground cumin
½   teaspoon salt
1   can (15 to 16 ounces) black beans, rinsed
     and drained
8   taco shells, warmed in oven
1½  cups shredded romaine lettuce
½   cup (2 ounces) shredded Monterey Jack
     cheese

1. Heat oil in large skillet over high heat. Add turkey, scallions, cumin and salt; sauté for 1 to 2 minutes, or until turkey is just cooked through, stirring frequently. Stir in black beans; heat through.

2. Fill each taco shell with some lettuce, turkey mixture and cheese; then top with Best-Ever Guacamole (recipe follows).
Makes 4 servings.
*Per serving (taco shells and filling only; without guacamole topping): 420 calories, 31 g protein, 17 g fat, 36 g carbohydrate, 65 mg cholesterol, 842 mg sodium.*

## BEST-EVER GUACAMOLE

1   large avocado, peeled and pitted
1   small tomato, diced
1   tablespoon minced red onion
1   tablespoon chopped fresh cilantro
1   teaspoon grated lime peel
1   teaspoon lime juice
½   teaspoon salt
¼   teaspoon hot-pepper sauce

In small bowl, mash avocado with a fork. Stir in remaining ingredients until mixture is well combined.
Makes 4 servings.
*Per serving: 107 calories, 1 g protein, 10 g fat, 6 g carbohydrate, 0 mg cholesterol, 290 mg sodium.*

### TURKEY HOTLINE
Q: How long can a turkey be safely stored in the freezer?

A: A turkey can be stored for at least a year. After that, the quality may begin to deteriorate but the turkey will still be safe to eat.

Q: How far in advance is it safe to buy a fresh turkey?

A: It's wise to buy a fresh turkey no more than one to two days in advance because store refrigerators keep the birds colder—and fresher—than you can in a home refrigerator.

# Fish Menus

## MENU
### Boston Fish Cakes with Creamy Cucumber Sauce
~~~~~
### New potatoes with chives
~~~~~
### Deli vegetable salad
~~~~~
### Iced tea

*You'll be surprised at how much these fish cakes taste like crab cakes—at a fraction of the cost. Start cooking some potatoes first, and then prepare the fish cakes. While fish cakes brown in a skillet, make the cucumber sauce. The perfect accompaniments—vegetable salad or coleslaw from your deli and a big glass of iced tea.*

*Above: Boston Fish Cakes with Creamy Cucumber Sauce menu.*

### BOSTON FISH CAKES

1 pound cod or haddock fillets, cut into
   1-inch pieces
1 cup fresh bread crumbs
2 eggs
½ small onion, finely chopped
2 teaspoons spicy brown mustard
2 teaspoons Worcestershire sauce
1 teaspoon Old Bay Seasoning
1 teaspoon grated lemon peel
2 tablespoons salad oil

1. In large skillet over medium-high heat, bring 2 inches of water to a boil. Add cod; return to a boil. Reduce heat to low and simmer for 5 minutes. With slotted spoon, remove cod to paper towels to drain. Finely chop cod, removing any bones.

2. In large bowl, mix cod with remaining ingredients except oil, until combined. Shape into 8 small fish cakes.

3. Heat oil in large skillet over medium-high heat. Add fish cakes; sauté for 6 minutes, or until browned and cooked through, turning once.

Makes 4 servings.

*Per serving (without Old Bay Seasoning; data unavailable): 228 calories, 25 g protein, 11 g fat, 7 g carbohydrate, 155 mg cholesterol, 211 mg sodium.*

## CREAMY CUCUMBER SAUCE

1  scallion, chopped
½  small cucumber, finely chopped
⅓  cup plain nonfat yogurt
3  tablespoons mayonnaise
1  teaspoon spicy brown mustard
Lettuce leaves (optional)

In small bowl, combine first 5 ingredients, stirring well. Serve in lettuce leaves (if using).
Makes 4 servings.

*Per serving: 89 calories, 1 g protein, 8 g fat, 3 g carbohydrate, 6 mg cholesterol, 86 mg sodium.*

## MENU
*Sesame Red Snapper*

*Ginger Stir-Fried Vegetables with Rice*

*Fresh fruit and cookies*

*Watching your fat intake? This menu has only 7 grams of fat per serving! First, preheat the broiler for the fish and put the rice on to cook. Next, prepare the stir-fried vegetables and keep them warm while you broil the fish.*

## SESAME RED SNAPPER

1½  pounds red-snapper fillets
1  large clove garlic, halved
3  tablespoons dry sherry
1  tablespoon lemon juice
1  tablespoon soy sauce
1½  teaspoons sesame seeds, toasted
1  scallion, chopped

1. Preheat broiler.
2. Grease bottom of a broiling pan (do not use rack). Cut fish fillets into serving-size portions. Rub both sides of fish with garlic; discard garlic. Place fish, skin side down, in pan. Pour next 3 ingredients over fish. Broil for 8 to 10 minutes, or until fish flakes, basting occasionally with liquid in pan (no need to turn).
3. Place fish and pan juices on a platter; sprinkle with sesame seeds and scallion.
Makes 4 servings.

*Per serving: 187 calories, 35 g protein, 3 g fat, 3 g carbohydrate, 63 mg cholesterol, 368 mg sodium.*

## GINGER STIR-FRIED VEGETABLES WITH RICE

1  cup uncooked long-grain rice
1  tablespoon salad oil
¾  pound green beans, trimmed
1  large red pepper, cut into thin strips
1  small onion, thinly sliced
2  teaspoons minced fresh ginger
1  teaspoon white-wine vinegar
1  teaspoon oriental sesame oil (optional)

1. Cook long-grain rice according to package directions.
2. Meanwhile, heat oil in large skillet over high heat. Add beans, pepper and onion; stir-fry for 3 minutes. Add ginger, vinegar and sesame oil (if using); cook for 3 to 5 minutes, or until vegetables are tender-crisp, stirring frequently. Serve vegetables on top of rice.
Makes 4 servings.

*Per serving: 232 calories, 5 g protein, 4 g fat, 45 g carbohydrate, 0 mg cholesterol, 8 mg sodium.*

*Above: Sesame Red Snapper menu.*

*For a new twist on fish 'n' chips, try these crunchy fish nuggets with vitamin A-rich sweet potatoes. Here's the plan: Preheat the oven and put the potato slices in to bake. While they're roasting, make the zesty tartar sauce; then dip fish in cornmeal coating and quickly fry in a skillet. Coleslaw from the deli completes the meal.*

## GOLDEN FISH NUGGETS WITH HORSERADISH TARTAR SAUCE

⅓ cup mayonnaise
¼ cup plain nonfat yogurt
2 tablespoons chopped parsley
1 to 2 tablespoons prepared horseradish
1 teaspoon lemon juice
¼ cup milk
⅓ cup all-purpose flour
⅓ cup yellow cornmeal
½ teaspoon cayenne pepper
½ teaspoon salt
1 pound flounder fillets, cut into large chunks
3 tablespoons salad oil
Lemon wedges

*Left: Golden Fish Nuggets with Horseradish Tartar Sauce menu.*

1. For tartar sauce: In small bowl, mix first 5 ingredients. Add salt, if you like.

2. Prepare fish nuggets: Place milk in a shallow dish. In another shallow dish, mix flour, cornmeal, cayenne and ½ teaspoon salt. Dip fish into milk and then into cornmeal mixture to coat well.

3. Heat oil in large skillet over medium-high heat. Add fish in batches; sauté until fish is browned and flakes easily, about 5 minutes. Drain on paper towels. Serve with tartar sauce and lemon wedges.

Makes 4 servings.

*Per serving: 393 calories, 25 g protein, 23 g fat, 20 g carbohydrate, 68 mg cholesterol, 767 mg sodium.*

## OVEN-FRIED SWEET POTATOES

2 large unpeeled sweet potatoes, cut into thin wedges
1 tablespoon salad oil
½ teaspoon salt

Preheat oven to 350°F. In medium bowl, toss potato wedges with oil and salt. Place wedges in a single layer on baking sheet; bake for 20 to 25 minutes, or until tender.

Makes 4 servings.

*Per serving: 115 calories, 1 g protein, 4 g fat, 20 g carbohydrate, 0 mg cholesterol, 284 mg sodium.*

◗ Smart cooks know that using prepared horseradish makes quick work of preparing tartar sauce for seafood dinners. But this pungent condiment can also add zest to sauces, sandwiches and ground-beef dishes.

> # MENU
> *Chinese Baked Fish in Foil*
>
> ~~~~~
>
> *Stir-Fried Cabbage and*
> *Snow Peas*
>
> ~~~~~
>
> *White or brown rice*

*Accented with fresh ginger and soy sauce, this super-simple fish dish has only 150 calories per serving! First, preheat the oven and put some rice on to cook. Then cut up all the vegetables for the fish and the side-dish accompaniment. Prepare fish packets, using aluminum foil, and put them in the oven to bake for 10 minutes. Meanwhile, stir-fry cabbage and snow peas. Put vegetables in a serving bowl, open fish packets at the table and you're ready to eat!*

### CHINESE BAKED FISH IN FOIL

1  tablespoon soy sauce
1  teaspoon oriental sesame oil
4  catfish, flounder or perch fillets (about 4 ounces each)
1  scallion, thinly sliced
½  cup diced red pepper
¼  cup seeded, diced cucumber
1  tablespoon minced fresh ginger

1.  Preheat oven to 450°F. In a cup, mix soy sauce and sesame oil until well combined and set mixture aside.

2.  Tear off four 12-inch squares of aluminum foil; place 1 fish fillet on one side of each square. Sprinkle each fillet evenly with some sliced scallion, diced red pepper, diced cucumber and minced ginger; then drizzle each fillet with 1 teaspoon soy-sauce mixture. Fold foil over fillets to make packets and seal edges tightly.

3.  Place fish packets on baking sheet; bake for 10 minutes. Open packets at table, being careful of steam.
Makes 4 servings.
*Per serving: 150 calories, 21 g protein, 6 g fat, 2 g carbohydrate, 66 mg cholesterol, 330 mg sodium.*

### STIR-FRIED CABBAGE AND SNOW PEAS

1  tablespoon sesame seeds
2  tablespoons peanut oil
1  large clove garlic, thinly sliced
4  cups Chinese (Napa) cabbage, thickly sliced
8  ounces snow peas, trimmed
½  teaspoon salt

In large skillet over medium heat, toast sesame seeds for 3 minutes, stirring frequently; remove seeds from skillet. In same skillet, in peanut oil, stir-fry garlic for 3 minutes. Add cabbage, snow peas and salt to skillet. Over high heat, stir-fry vegetables for 3 minutes, or until tender-crisp. Stir in sesame seeds.
Makes 4 servings.
*Per serving: 110 calories, 3 g protein, 8 g fat, 8 g carbohydrate, 0 mg cholesterol, 283 mg sodium.*

# Pastas & More

## MENU
### Roman Sandwiches
~~~~~
### Skillet Peppers with Rosemary
~~~~~
### Green or red grapes

*Get the kids involved in making this savory pizza-style French toast. Here's the plan: Make the pepper side dish first—it's fine served at room temperature. Next, prepare the sandwiches: Spread slices of Italian bread with pizza sauce and sandwich together with thinly sliced mozzarella and ham. Dip in egg batter and sauté until golden brown. Fresh fruit is a refreshing finish for this light yet satisfying dinner.*

*Above: Roman Sandwiches menu.*

### ROMAN SANDWICHES

¼  cup prepared pizza sauce
8  slices (cut diagonally ¾ inch thick) Italian bread
½  pound thinly sliced part-skim mozzarella cheese
¼  pound thinly sliced baked ham (optional)
1  egg
2  tablespoons (¼ stick) butter or margarine

1.  Spread 1 tablespoon pizza sauce on each of 4 bread slices; layer with cheese. Place ham (if using) between cheese slices. Top with remaining bread slices; press together.

2.  In shallow bowl, beat egg with 1 tablespoon water. Dip both sides of sandwiches in egg mixture to coat.

3.  Melt butter in large skillet over medium heat. Carefully place sandwiches in skillet and cook for 5 minutes, or until lightly browned, turning once.

Makes 4 servings.

*Per serving: 378 calories, 21 g protein, 17 g fat, 35 g carbohydrate, 102 mg cholesterol, 734 mg sodium.*

## SKILLET PEPPERS WITH ROSEMARY

1 tablespoon olive oil
1 medium red pepper, thinly sliced
1 medium green pepper, thinly sliced
1 medium yellow pepper, thinly sliced
1 large clove garlic, minced
½ teaspoon dried rosemary, crushed
¼ teaspoon salt
1 tablespoon balsamic or red-wine vinegar

Heat oil in medium skillet over medium heat. Add next 6 ingredients; sauté for 5 minutes, or until peppers are tender-crisp, stirring occasionally. Stir in vinegar.

Makes 4 servings.

*Per serving: 46 calories, 1 g protein, 4 g fat, 3 g carbohydrate, 0 mg cholesterol, 137 mg sodium.*

---

# MENU

*Sweet-Onion Pizza*

~~~~~

*Cherry Tomato and Arugula Salad*

~~~~~

*Red wine*

---

*This pizza is faster than delivery and easier than eating out! Preheat the oven and cook onions for the topping until brown and caramelized. Meanwhile, pat prepared dough out on a baking sheet, and then top with cheeses. Put pizza in the oven; while it bakes, make the salad. Top pizza with caramelized onions, zippy sun-dried tomatoes and parsley. A glass of dry red wine complements the richness of the pizza.*

## SWEET-ONION PIZZA

1 tablespoon butter or margarine
1 tablespoon olive or salad oil
2 large Spanish or Vidalia onions, thinly sliced
1 tablespoon sugar
1 package (10 ounces) all-ready pizza crust
1 container (15 ounces) part-skim ricotta cheese
⅓ cup grated Parmesan cheese
½ cup (2 ounces) shredded part-skim mozzarella cheese
1 ounce oil-packed sun-dried tomatoes, drained and thinly sliced (optional)
¼ cup parsley leaves

1. Preheat oven to 450°F. Grease a baking sheet. Heat butter and oil in large skillet over medium-high heat. Add onions and sugar; sauté for 15 minutes, or until onions are caramelized, stirring frequently.

2. Meanwhile, unroll pizza crust on prepared baking sheet. Press dough into a 15-by-10-inch rectangle. In medium bowl, combine ricotta and Parmesan. Sprinkle mozzarella over dough; cover with ricotta mixture. Bake on bottom rack of oven for 15 to 20 minutes, or until crust is browned. Top with caramelized onions, sun-dried tomatoes (if using) and parsley.

Makes 6 servings.

*Per serving: 333 calories, 17 g protein, 14 g fat, 33 g carbohydrate, 36 mg cholesterol, 463 mg sodium.*

*Right: Sweet-Onion Pizza menu.*

## CHERRY TOMATO AND ARUGULA SALAD

3  tablespoons olive or salad oil
2  teaspoons cider vinegar
1½  teaspoons grainy Dijon mustard
1  pint cherry tomatoes
1  large bunch arugula

In large bowl, whisk first 3 ingredients. Add cherry tomatoes and arugula; gently toss with dressing.

Makes 6 servings.

*Per serving: 71 calories, 1 g protein, 7 g fat, 2 g carbohydrate, 0 mg cholesterol, 52 mg sodium.*

# MENU
## *Chili Lasagna Roll-Ups*
~~~~
## *Citrus-Avocado Salad*
~~~~
## *Garlic bread*

*Combine two favorite dishes in one—it's possible in 29 minutes! Here's how: Cook the pasta first, and then make the chili-spiced ground beef filling. While chili mixture cooks, toss oranges and avocado with the honey dressing. Preheat the broiler, assemble the lasagna rolls and top with shredded cheddar cheese. Toast some garlic bread and broil lasagna to melt the cheese.*

## CHILI LASAGNA ROLL-UPS

8  lasagna noodles
¾  pound lean ground beef
1  medium green pepper, chopped
1  small onion, chopped
1  medium clove garlic, minced
2½  teaspoons chili powder
1  can (14½ to 16 ounces) tomatoes in tomato puree
½  teaspoon salt
⅛  to ¼ teaspoon cayenne pepper
1  can (15¼ ounces) red kidney beans, drained
½  cup (2 ounces) shredded cheddar cheese
**Italian parsley (optional garnish)**

1. Cook lasagna noodles according to package directions.

2. Meanwhile, in large skillet over high heat, brown beef with green pepper, onion and garlic, stirring frequently. Add chili powder; cook for 1 minute, stirring constantly. Add tomatoes, breaking them up with a spoon; add salt, cayenne and ½ cup water. Reduce heat to low; cook for 10 minutes. Add drained beans; heat through.

3. Preheat broiler. Spoon half the chili into 9-inch baking dish. Drain lasagna; loosely roll up each noodle. Place seam side down on top of chili. Top with remaining chili, then with cheese. Broil for 1 minute, or until cheese melts. Garnish with parsley.

Makes 4 servings.

*Per serving: 568 calories, 28 g protein, 24 g fat, 59 g carbohydrate, 79 mg cholesterol, 797 mg sodium.*

*Right: Chili-Lasagna Roll-Ups menu.*

## CITRUS-AVOCADO SALAD

1 can (11 ounces) mandarin oranges
2 tablespoons salad oil
2 teaspoons cider vinegar
2 teaspoons honey
½ teaspoon salt
⅛ teaspoon cayenne pepper
2 medium avocados, peeled, pitted and
  sliced
1 head Belgian endive, leaves separated

Drain mandarin oranges, reserving 3 tablespoons syrup. In medium bowl, whisk syrup, salad oil, vinegar, honey, salt and cayenne. Add oranges and avocado slices; gently toss to coat with dressing. Serve on top of Belgian endive.

Makes 4 servings.

*Per serving: 283 calories, 2 g protein, 22 g fat, 24 g carbohydrate, 0 mg cholesterol, 289 mg sodium.*

## MENU
*Pasta with Sage Chicken*

~~~~~

*Carrot-and-Watercress Salad*

~~~~~

*French bread*

~~~~~

*Sparkling water*

*This hearty pasta dish is almost a meal in itself! Here's the plan: Start boiling the pasta water; then make the vinaigrette and prep vegetables for the pasta and the salad (clean spinach for pasta or use prewashed spinach from a grocery-store salad bar). Meanwhile, fry bacon until crisp. Next, sauté chicken in the same skillet. Toss chicken and bacon with cooked pasta and Parmesan. Stir spinach in skillet until just wilted, and then place on plates to make "beds" for chicken. Toss salad with vinaigrette, slice the French bread, and dinner's ready!*

1. Cook bow-tie pasta according to package directions.
2. Meanwhile, in skillet over medium-high heat, cook bacon until crisp. With slotted spoon, remove bacon; crumble into large bowl. Discard all but 2 tablespoons drippings in skillet.
3. To drippings in skillet, add chicken, dried sage and pepper; sauté for 3 to 4 minutes, or until cooked through, stirring frequently. With slotted spoon, remove chicken to bowl with bacon. Reserve skillet with drippings. Drain pasta and add to chicken-bacon mixture along with cheese; toss until well combined.
4. To drippings in skillet, add spinach; cook for 2 minutes, or until just wilted, stirring constantly. Divide spinach among plates; spoon some chicken-pasta mixture over each. Garnish with sage.
Makes 4 servings.
*Per serving: 418 calories, 38 g protein, 13 g fat, 34 g carbohydrate, 82 mg cholesterol, 392 mg sodium.*

### PASTA WITH SAGE CHICKEN

6   ounces bow-tie, penne or rotelle pasta
6   strips lean bacon
4   boneless, skinless chicken-breast halves, cut crosswise into ½-inch-wide strips
1   teaspoon dried sage
½   teaspoon black pepper
¼   cup grated Parmesan cheese
1   package (10 ounces) fresh spinach, trimmed
Fresh sage (optional garnish)

*Left: Pasta with Sage Chicken menu.*

### CARROT-AND-WATERCRESS SALAD

2   tablespoons olive oil
1   tablespoon red-wine vinegar
2   teaspoons Dijon mustard
¼   teaspoon dried oregano
¼   teaspoon black pepper
4   small carrots, coarsely shredded
1   bunch watercress, stemmed

In large salad bowl, whisk first 5 ingredients. Add carrots and watercress; gently toss with dressing.
Makes 4 servings.
*Per serving: 99 calories, 2 g protein, 7 g fat, 8 g carbohydrate, 0 mg cholesterol, 118 mg sodium.*

## MENU
### Pasta with Chicken and Creamy Tomato Sauce
~~~~~
### Salad Greens with Citrus Vinaigrette
~~~~~
### Flat breads

*There's very little cream, but lots of flavor in this pasta dish! Put the water on to boil first; then sauté the chicken strips with carrot, onion and garlic. Add tomatoes and seasonings; cover and simmer. While pasta sauce cooks, prepare the salad and citrus vinaigrette. Toss pasta with watercress, and then top with some of the tomato sauce. Serve with crunchy flat bread or bread sticks.*

## PASTA WITH CHICKEN AND CREAMY TOMATO SAUCE

12  ounces ziti rigati or penne pasta
2  tablespoons olive oil
1½  pounds boneless, skinless chicken-breast halves, cut into ½-inch-wide strips
1  large carrot, diced
1  large onion, diced
1  large clove garlic, minced
1  can (28 ounces) crushed tomatoes
1  teaspoon salt
1  teaspoon black pepper
½  cup whipping cream
1  bunch watercress, stemmed
Fresh tomato, diced (optional garnish)

1. Cook pasta according to package directions while preparing sauce.
2. Heat oil in large skillet over high heat. Add next 4 ingredients; sauté for 3 minutes, stirring frequently. Add tomatoes, salt and pepper; bring to a boil. Reduce heat to low; cover and simmer for 10 minutes. Gradually stir in cream; heat through (do not boil).
3. Drain pasta; return to cooking pot. Toss pasta with watercress; divide among plates. Top with some chicken-tomato sauce and garnish with diced tomato. (Recipe makes extra sauce; freeze leftovers.)
Makes 4 servings.
*Per serving (with half the chicken and creamy tomato sauce): 516 calories, 32 g protein, 11 g fat, 71 g carbohydrate, 66 mg cholesterol, 506 mg sodium.*

## SALAD GREENS WITH CITRUS VINAIGRETTE

3  tablespoons olive oil
2  tablespoons orange juice
1  tablespoon balsamic or red-wine vinegar
¼  teaspoon salt
¼  teaspoon black pepper
6  cups mixed salad greens

In large bowl, whisk oil, orange juice, vinegar, salt and pepper. Add salad greens; gently toss with dressing.
Makes 4 servings.
*Per serving: 108 calories, 1 g protein, 10 g fat, 3 g carbohydrate, 0 mg cholesterol, 142 mg sodium.*

*Left: Pasta with Chicken and Creamy Tomato Sauce menu.*

*Above: Pasta with Chunky Peppers menu.*

## MENU

*Pasta with Chunky Peppers*

~~~

*Fennel and Lettuce Salad*

~~~

*Sesame bread sticks*

*The colorful pepper sauce in this menu could be served with any pasta, but it's especially good with cheese- or meat-filled tortellini. First, put pasta water on to boil; then prep vegetables for the sauce and the salad. Sauté peppers with garlic, herbs and a little wine. Meanwhile, cook pasta and toss salad with a lemon-chive vinaigrette. Serve with crunchy sesame bread sticks.*

### PASTA WITH CHUNKY PEPPERS

1   package (9 ounces) fresh cheese-or meat-filled tortellini
3   tablespoons olive oil
4   medium red and/or yellow peppers, cut into ¾-inch chunks
1   small onion, chopped
1   large clove garlic, minced
1   teaspoon dried basil
½   teaspoon salt
½   teaspoon black pepper
¼   cup dry white wine or chicken broth
¼   cup grated Parmesan cheese
Fresh basil (optional garnish)

1.  Cook tortellini according to package directions.
2.  Meanwhile, heat oil in large saucepan over medium-high heat. Add pepper chunks, onion, garlic, basil, salt and pepper; sauté for 5 minutes, stirring occasionally. Add wine; reduce heat to low. Cover vegetable mixture and simmer for 10 minutes, or until peppers are very soft.
3.  Drain tortellini; toss with pepper sauce. Sprinkle with cheese. Garnish with basil.
Makes 4 servings.
*Per serving: 327 calories, 13 g protein, 17 g fat, 31 g carbohydrate, 4 mg cholesterol, 592 mg sodium.*

### FENNEL AND LETTUCE SALAD

2   tablespoons olive oil
1   tablespoon lemon juice
2   teaspoons snipped fresh chives
½   teaspoon coarsely grated lemon peel
¼   teaspoon black pepper
⅛   teaspoon salt
1   medium bulb fennel, sliced, or 2 small stalks celery, sliced
1   head Boston lettuce, leaves separated
Fresh chives (optional garnish)

In bowl, whisk first 6 ingredients. Toss with fennel and lettuce. Garnish with chives.
Makes 4 servings.
*Per serving: 80 calories, 1 g protein, 7 g fat, 4 g carbohydrate, 0 mg cholesterol, 126 mg sodium.*

# MENU
### Pasta with Sausage and Vegetables
~~~
### Tomato Tapenade Toasts
~~~
### Red wine

*This is a good-for-you pasta dish with lots of colorful vegetables and very little added oil. To make: Put pasta water on to boil; then make tapenade for the toasts. Prep the pasta vegetables—cut vegetables into same-size pieces for even cooking. Brown sausage and vegetables; then toss with the pasta. Finally, broil bread for toasts and top with tapenade.*

## PASTA WITH SAUSAGE AND VEGETABLES

8 ounces radiatore or medium-shell pasta
½ pound hot or sweet turkey sausage or Italian sausage, cut into 1-inch pieces
3 cups broccoli florets
1 large red pepper, cut into small chunks
1 large clove garlic, minced
1 medium zucchini, cut into small chunks
1 tablespoon olive oil
1 package or cube chicken-flavor instant bouillon
¾ teaspoon fennel seeds, crushed
½ teaspoon salt
¼ teaspoon cracked black pepper
Parmesan cheese, coarsely grated (optional)

1. Cook pasta according to package directions while preparing sauce.

2. In large skillet over medium heat, brown sausage for 8 minutes, stirring frequently. Add next 9 ingredients; cook for 5 minutes, stirring frequently. Add 1 cup water; over high heat, bring mixture to a boil. Reduce heat to low; cover and simmer for 5 minutes, or until vegetables are tender.

3. Drain pasta; toss with sausage-vegetable mixture. Divide among plates; sprinkle with cheese (if using).

Makes 4 servings.

*Per serving: 383 calories, 21 g protein, 11 g fat, 51 g carbohydrate, 34 mg cholesterol, 972 mg sodium.*

## TOMATO TAPENADE TOASTS

1 large tomato, diced
10 Kalamata or other Mediterranean olives, pitted and chopped
1 tablespoon minced parsley
1 tablespoon olive oil
¼ teaspoon salt
¼ teaspoon cracked black pepper
8 slices (cut diagonally ½ inch thick) Italian bread
1 large clove garlic, halved

Preheat oven to 450°F. For tapenade: In small bowl, combine first 6 ingredients; set aside. Place bread slices on baking sheet; bake for 5 minutes, or until crisp and lightly browned. Rub cut sides of garlic over bread; discard garlic. Top each slice of toast with some tapenade.

Makes 4 servings.

*Per serving: 153 calories, 4 g protein, 5 g fat, 24 g carbohydrate, trace cholesterol, 444 mg sodium.*

*We've taken the oven-baking out of a tuna casserole! This homey pasta dish is perfect for kids—omit the mushrooms if your family doesn't like them. Start by heating the pasta water; then clean the salad greens and make the tomato vinaigrette. Next, make the creamy tuna sauce and toss with pasta—it's best when served immediately.*

### CHEESY PASTA 'N' TUNA TOSS

8   ounces wagon-wheel or medium-shell pasta
3   tablespoons butter or margarine
1   small onion, chopped
½   pound small mushrooms, halved (optional)
3   tablespoons all-purpose flour
1¾  cups milk
1   package (10 ounces) frozen green peas and carrots
¾   teaspoon salt
½   teaspoon black pepper
1   cup (4 ounces) shredded cheddar cheese
1   can (6½ ounces) water-packed tuna, drained and flaked

1.  Cook pasta according to package directions while preparing sauce.

2.  Melt butter in medium saucepan over medium heat. Add onion and mushrooms (if using); sauté for 5 minutes, or until tender, stirring occasionally. Add flour and cook for 1 minute, stirring constantly. Gradually stir in milk. Add peas and carrots, salt and pepper; cook for 8 to 10 minutes, or until mixture thickens and comes to a boil, stirring constantly. Remove from heat; stir in cheese until melted, then tuna. Return saucepan to low heat and warm through.

3.  Drain pasta and place in serving bowl; toss with sauce. Serve immediately.

Makes 4 servings.

*Per serving: 582 calories, 33 g protein, 23 g fat, 61 g carbohydrate, 85 mg cholesterol, 932 mg sodium.*

### ROMAINE WITH TOMATO VINAIGRETTE

1   medium tomato, finely chopped
⅓   cup olive oil
2   tablespoons cider vinegar
¼   teaspoon salt
⅛   teaspoon black pepper
Pinch of ground cinnamon
1   head romaine lettuce, leaves torn

In large bowl, whisk first 6 ingredients. Add lettuce; gently toss with dressing.

Makes 4 servings.

*Per serving: 187 calories, 3 g protein, 18 g fat, 5 g carbohydrate, 0 mg cholesterol, 149 mg sodium.*

## MENU
### Ravioli with Tomato-Cream Sauce
~~~~
### Garlic-Sautéed Greens
~~~~
### Crusty rolls

*Though it's ready in 15 minutes, this sauce tastes as if it cooked for hours! Heat water for pasta first, and then make the sauce. While ravioli and sauce cook, clean mustard greens or escarole and quickly sauté in olive oil and garlic. Stir a little cream into sauce and spoon on top of cooked ravioli. Serve with crusty rolls to mop up the yummy sauce.*

### RAVIOLI WITH TOMATO-CREAM SAUCE

2   packages (8-ounce size) fresh or frozen cheese or meat ravioli
1   tablespoon olive oil
1   small onion, finely chopped
1   small red pepper, finely chopped
1   medium clove garlic, minced
1   can (14½ to 16 ounces) tomatoes
1   teaspoon sugar
½   teaspoon dried basil
½   teaspoon salt
¼   teaspoon black pepper
¼   cup whipping cream
2   tablespoons chopped parsley

1.  Cook ravioli according to package directions while preparing sauce.
2.  Heat oil in medium saucepan over medium heat. Add onion, red pepper and garlic; sauté for 4 minutes, or until tender, stirring occasionally. Add tomatoes, breaking them up with a spoon; add sugar, basil, salt

and pepper. Bring to a boil. Reduce heat to low and simmer for 10 minutes, stirring occasionally. Gradually stir in cream; heat through (do not boil).

3.  Drain ravioli; place in large serving bowl. Spoon sauce over ravioli and sprinkle with parsley.
Makes 4 servings.
*Per serving: 445 calories, 18 g protein, 23 g fat, 42 g carbohydrate, 105 mg cholesterol, 928 mg sodium.*

### GARLIC-SAUTEED GREENS

1   tablespoon olive oil
1   pound mustard greens or escarole, trimmed
1   large clove garlic, minced
½   teaspoon salt

Heat oil in large saucepan over high heat. Add greens, garlic and salt; sauté for 3 minutes, or until greens wilt, stirring constantly.
Makes 4 servings.
*Per serving: 58 calories, 3 g protein, 4 g fat, 5 g carbohydrate, 0 mg cholesterol, 300 mg sodium.*

### QUICK FLAVOR FOR PASTA
● Bottled pesto sauce tossed with rice or pasta makes a simple yet impressive side dish.
● Anchovy paste—just a teaspoon or two—can be mixed with chopped tomatoes, olive oil, capers and garlic for a quick-fix pasta sauce. (Used in tiny amounts, anchovy paste will pep up salad dressings.)
● Olives complement the flavor of pasta and pizza. Try them sliced and mixed into hot and cold pasta dishes or scattered over a pizza. (Olives make a great instant hors d'oeuvre—serve a variety of your favorites.)

## MENU
### Dilled Seafood-Pasta Salad
~~~~~
### Warm Broccoli Vinaigrette
~~~~~
### Bread sticks
~~~~~
### Iced tea

*For those days when you don't feel like eating a heavy meal, this family-pleasing salad supper is the perfect menu. It couldn't be easier to make: First, start the pasta. While it cooks, mix the dill-mayonnaise dressing and prep the scallions and celery. Toss all the pasta salad ingredients together; then set aside while you prepare the crunchy, colorful broccoli side dish—dinner's ready!*

### DILLED SEAFOOD-PASTA SALAD

¼  pound medium-shell pasta
½  cup cholesterol-free, reduced-calorie mayonnaise
½  cup light sour cream
¼  cup milk
¼  cup chopped fresh dill
2  tablespoons tarragon or white-wine vinegar
½  teaspoon salt
¼  teaspoon black pepper
¾  pound Surimi Seafood (imitation crabmeat) or lump crabmeat
3  scallions, thinly sliced
2  medium stalks celery, thinly sliced
¾  cup frozen green peas, thawed (see Note)

1.  Cook medium-shell pasta according to package directions.

2.  Meanwhile, in large bowl, mix mayonnaise, sour cream, milk, dill, vinegar, salt and pepper.

3.  Drain pasta, rinse under cold water and drain again. Add pasta, Surimi, scallions, celery and peas to mayonnaise mixture; toss gently until combined.

Makes 4 servings.

*Per serving: 379 calories, 21 g protein, 16 g fat, 38 g carbohydrate, 38 mg cholesterol, 606 mg sodium.*

*Note*: It's not necessary to cook the peas before adding to salad.

### WARM BROCCOLI VINAIGRETTE

1  large head broccoli
2  tablespoons olive oil
1  tablespoon balsamic or red-wine vinegar
1  teaspoon grainy Dijon mustard
¼  teaspoon salt
¼  teaspoon black pepper
10  cherry tomatoes, halved

Cut broccoli into florets. In deep skillet of boiling water, cook broccoli for 4 minutes, or until tender-crisp; drain. Meanwhile, mix olive oil, vinegar, mustard, salt and pepper until well combined. Toss broccoli and tomatoes with vinaigrette.

Makes 4 servings.

*Per serving: 83 calories, 2 g protein, 7 g fat, 4 g carbohydrate, 0 mg cholesterol, 187 mg sodium.*

◆ Surimi Seafood—imitation crabmeat—is made from Alaska pollock, a mild, white-fleshed fish. Surimi is an inexpensive substitute for crabmeat in this hearty main-dish salad.

## MENU
### Frittata-Stuffed Pitas

*～～～*

### Romaine-and-Avocado Salad with Lime Dressing

*～～～*

### Fruit with yogurt

*Fast to fix, hearty and delicious—this easy frittata-sandwich supper is a satisfying way to feed the family without a lot of fuss. First, make the frittata; while it's cooking, prepare romaine lettuce and avocado and toss with the lime dressing. Then stuff pitas with lettuce and wedges of warm frittata. For a perfect finish, serve fruit with your favorite yogurt.*

### FRITTATA-STUFFED PITAS

8 eggs
¼ cup grated Parmesan cheese
¾ teaspoon dried oregano
½ teaspoon salt
2 tablespoons (¼ stick) butter or
   margarine
1 small onion, chopped
1 can (14 ounces) artichoke hearts
   (do not use marinated), drained and
   quartered
2 plum tomatoes, thinly sliced
4 whole-wheat pitas
4 romaine leaves from 1 head romaine
   lettuce (use remaining lettuce in
   romaine salad)

1. In large bowl, beat eggs, cheese, oregano, salt and 2 tablespoons water.

2. Melt butter in 10-inch ovenproof skillet over medium-high heat. Add onion; sauté for 3 minutes, or until tender. Add artichoke hearts; sauté for 1 minute. Pour egg mixture over vegetables. Reduce heat to low; cover and cook for 10 to 15 minutes, or until bottom is lightly browned but top of frittata is still slightly runny.

3. Preheat broiler. Arrange tomatoes on top of frittata. Broil for 2 to 3 minutes, or until frittata is just set; cut into 4 wedges. Stuff pitas with frittata wedges and lettuce leaves.

Makes 4 servings.

*Per serving: 427 calories, 23 g protein, 18 g fat, 44 g carbohydrate, 444 mg cholesterol, 951 mg sodium.*

### ROMAINE-AND-AVOCADO SALAD WITH LIME DRESSING

3 tablespoons olive oil
2 tablespoons lime juice
½ teaspoon cracked black pepper
Dash of salt
Romaine lettuce
1 small avocado, peeled, pitted and sliced

In small bowl, whisk first 4 ingredients. Arrange lettuce leaves and avocado on salad plates; drizzle with dressing.

Makes 4 servings.

*Per serving: 173 calories, 3 g protein, 16 g fat, 7 g carbohydrate, 0 mg cholesterol, 48 mg sodium.*

● An ovenproof skillet is handy for making frittatas and other stovetop-to-oven dishes. If you don't own an ovenproof skillet, wrap the handle of a regular skillet in aluminum foil.

## MENU
*Roman Pasta Frittata*

~~~~~

*Zucchini and Roasted-Pepper Salad*

~~~~~

*Green grapes*

*Turn leftover pasta into a scrumptious frittata. We suggest ziti or penne, but you can use the same amount of almost any pasta. Since the frittata is best served piping hot, make the salad first—zucchini doesn't wilt the way lettuce does, and the salad will taste even better after sitting a few minutes. Next, preheat the broiler, beat the frittata ingredients and cook on top of the stove before finishing off in the broiler. Sweet green grapes for dessert complete the meal.*

### ROMAN PASTA FRITTATA

5  eggs
⅓  cup grated Parmesan cheese
½  teaspoon white pepper
3  cups cooked ziti or penne pasta
¼  cup chopped oil-packed sun-dried
   tomatoes (optional)
2  tablespoons (¼ stick) butter or
   margarine
½  cup (2 ounces) shredded smoked
   mozzarella or Fontina cheese
1  tablespoon chopped parsley

1. Preheat broiler. In large bowl, beat eggs, Parmesan, pepper and 2 tablespoons water; stir in cooked pasta and tomatoes (if using).

2. Melt butter in 10-inch nonstick skillet over medium heat. Add egg mixture; cook (do not stir) for 5 minutes, or until bottom is browned.

3. Wrap handle of skillet with aluminum foil. Place skillet under broiler about 3 inches from heat source; broil for 2 to 3 minutes, or until frittata is just set. Sprinkle with mozzarella; broil for 30 seconds. Remove from oven; sprinkle with parsley.

Makes 4 servings.

*Per serving: 440 calories, 21 g protein, 19 g fat, 44 g carbohydrate, 303 mg cholesterol, 262 mg sodium.*

### ZUCCHINI AND ROASTED-PEPPER SALAD

1  large zucchini, thinly sliced
1  jar (7 ounces) roasted red peppers,
   drained and sliced
1  tablespoon olive oil
1  small clove garlic, minced
¼  teaspoon dried oregano
Chicory or other lettuce leaves (optional)
2  tablespoons coarsely grated Parmesan
   cheese

In medium salad bowl, toss first 5 ingredients until well combined. Serve on lettuce (if using); top with cheese.

Makes 4 servings.

*Per serving: 55 calories, 2 g protein, 4 g fat, 3 g carbohydrate, 2 mg cholesterol, 49 mg sodium.*

*Left: Roman Pasta Frittata menu.*

# Relax While It Cooks

*When you're bushed after a busy day, cut short your kitchen duty with a no-fuss menu. Here are ten delicious dinners you can start in 20 minutes or less, and forget for 40 minutes to one hour while you enjoy some quiet time or unwind with your family. Final touches take 20 minutes or less. It all adds up to a relaxing meal. (Pictured, Tex-Mex Lasagna menu, page 71.)*

## Menu Plans:
## Beef
## Pork
## Chicken
## Meatless

# Beef Menus

## MENU

*Pepper-Parmesan Stuffed Steak*

~~~~

*Easy Orzo Primavera*

~~~~

*Italian green beans*

## PEPPER-PARMESAN STUFFED STEAK

1½  pounds beef flank steak, trimmed
2  tablespoons grated Parmesan cheese
½  teaspoon black pepper
1  small bunch arugula or watercress, stemmed
1  jar (7 ounces) roasted red peppers or pimientos, drained and cut into thin strips
2  tablespoons olive oil
1  can (14½ ounces) stewed tomatoes
1  large clove garlic, minced

1. Preheat oven to 350°F. Pound steak to a little less than ½-inch thickness. Sprinkle steak with cheese and black pepper; top with arugula and red-pepper strips. Starting from long side, tightly roll steak; tie every 2 inches with kitchen string.

2. Heat olive oil in 5-quart Dutch oven over medium-high heat. Add steak roll; brown on all sides. Add tomatoes and garlic; place Dutch oven, uncovered, in oven. Relax for 45 minutes while steak cooks.

3. Return to kitchen. Start orzo side dish. Check steak; it should be fork-tender. Place steak on cutting board and let stand while finishing orzo.

4. Remove string from steak; cut crosswise into ½-inch-thick slices. Spoon tomato sauce in Dutch oven on serving platter; arrange steak slices on top.
Makes 4 servings.
*Per serving: 450 calories, 36 g protein, 29 g fat, 10 g carbohydrate, 91 mg cholesterol, 453 mg sodium.*

## EASY ORZO PRIMAVERA

1  cup orzo or other small pasta
2  tablespoons olive oil
1  medium carrot, diced
1  small onion, diced
1  small zucchini, diced
¼  teaspoon salt
¼  teaspoon dried oregano
2  tablespoons grated Parmesan cheese
2  tablespoons pine nuts, toasted (optional)

Prepare orzo according to package directions. Meanwhile, heat oil in medium saucepan over medium-high heat. Add carrot, onion, zucchini, salt and oregano; sauté for 3 to 5 minutes, or until vegetables are tender-crisp, stirring occasionally. Drain orzo; stir orzo and cheese into vegetables. Spoon mixture into serving bowl; sprinkle with pine nuts (if using).
Makes 4 servings.
*Per serving: 271 calories, 8 g protein, 8 g fat, 41 g carbohydrate, 2 mg cholesterol, 190 mg sodium.*

*Right: Pepper-Parmesan Stuffed Steak menu.*

## MENU
*Rosemary Steak Dijon*

~~~

*Oven-Roasted Peppers and Potatoes*

~~~

*Mixed green salad*

~~~

*Crusty rolls*

## ROSEMARY STEAK DIJON

3 tablespoons dry red wine
2 tablespoons olive oil
2 tablespoons grainy Dijon mustard
1¼ teaspoons dried rosemary, crushed
1 pound beef top round or sirloin steak, trimmed, 1 inch thick
Fresh rosemary (optional garnish)

1. In a large glass casserole dish, mix first 4 ingredients until well combined. With sharp knife, lightly score both sides of steak. Add steak to wine mixture; turn once. Prepare roasted vegetables. Cover steak and let stand at room temperature. Relax for 45 minutes while steak marinates and vegetables roast.

2. Return to kitchen. Place vegetables in roasting pan on bottom rack of oven. Turn oven control to broil. Place steak on broiling rack about 4 inches from heat source. Broil for 7 to 8 minutes for rare, or until of desired doneness, turning once. Let stand for a few minutes before thinly slicing on diagonal, across the grain. Garnish with fresh rosemary.

Makes 4 servings.

*Per serving: 189 calories, 27 g protein, 8 g fat, 1 g carbohydrate, 72 mg cholesterol, 165 mg sodium.*

## OVEN-ROASTED PEPPERS AND POTATOES

1 pound medium red-skinned potatoes
4 scallions
1 large red or green pepper
1 tablespoon olive oil
½ teaspoon salt
¼ teaspoon cracked black pepper

Preheat oven to 425°F. Cut potatoes into ¾-inch-thick wedges. Cut scallions diagonally into 1-inch pieces. Cut red or green pepper into 1-inch pieces. In large, shallow roasting pan, mix vegetables with remaining ingredients until well combined. Bake for 45 minutes, or until vegetables are tender, stirring occasionally.

Makes 4 servings.

*Per serving: 132 calories, 3 g protein, 4 g fat, 23 g carbohydrate, 0 mg cholesterol, 284 mg sodium.*

### A KITCHEN FULL OF FLAVOR

Sometimes a dish just needs that certain something to help bring out its best taste. Here, a variety of simple flavor enhancers to stock in fridge or cupboard with suggestions on how to use them.

● Dijon mustard lends a robust tang to mayonnaise, sauces or vinaigrettes.

● Maple syrup adds a hint of sweetness when brushed on ham or chicken before roasting.

● Sesame oil should be used in small quantities to give a nutty taste to salads and stir-fries. Heating lessens its flavor impact, so add just at the end of cooking.

## MENU
*Tex-Mex Lasagna*

~~~~~

*Tomato-Avocado Salad*

~~~~~

*Limeade*

### TEX-MEX LASAGNA

(Menu pictured, pages 66 and 67.)

1 pound lean ground beef
3 scallions, thinly sliced
1½ tablespoons chili powder
2 teaspoons ground cumin
2 cups frozen corn, thawed
1 can (28 ounces) tomatoes, drained and chopped
1 can (15 to 16 ounces) black beans, drained and rinsed
1 container (15 to 16 ounces) part-skim ricotta cheese
2 eggs
2 cups (8 ounces) shredded Monterey Jack cheese
12 (6-inch) corn tortillas
Sliced scallions (optional garnish)

1. Preheat oven to 375°F. Grease a 3-quart casserole. In large skillet over high heat, brown beef with scallions. Drain off fat. Add chili powder and cumin; cook for 1 minute, stirring constantly. Remove from heat; stir in vegetables. In bowl, mix ricotta, eggs and 1 cup of the Monterey Jack.

2. Line bottom and sides of prepared casserole with 8 of the tortillas; top with two-thirds of the beef mixture. Cover with ricotta mixture, remaining tortillas, and remaining beef mixture. Place in oven. Relax for 40 minutes while lasagna bakes.

3. Return to kitchen. Sprinkle lasagna with remaining Monterey Jack; bake for 5 minutes. Garnish with scallions. Let lasagna stand while preparing salad.
Makes 6 to 8 servings.
*Per serving: 600 calories, 38 g protein, 28 g fat, 52 g carbohydrate, 148 mg cholesterol, 834 mg sodium.*

### TOMATO-AVOCADO SALAD

1 pint cherry tomatoes, halved
1 medium avocado, peeled, pitted and cut into chunks
1 medium jicama (about 2 pounds), peeled and julienned, or 3 medium stalks celery, julienned
¼ cup salad oil
3 tablespoons chopped fresh cilantro
2 tablespoons lime juice
½ teaspoon sugar
¼ teaspoon salt

On a platter, arrange tomatoes, avocado and jicama. In a cup, whisk remaining ingredients; drizzle over salad.
Makes 6 to 8 servings.
*Per serving: 172 calories, 3 g protein, 12 g fat, 14 g carbohydrate, 0 mg cholesterol, 90 mg sodium.*

◆ Here's a sassy spritzer with a delightfully different fizz! In large pitcher, combine 1 cup lime juice (6 to 8 limes), 1 cup lemon juice (5 to 7 lemons) and 1 cup superfine granulated sugar; stir until sugar dissolves. Add 2 limes, very thinly sliced, 1 bottle (1 liter) chilled club soda or seltzer and lots of ice cubes. If you can't find superfine sugar, whirl regular granulated in a food processor fitted with steel blade for about 15 seconds.

# Pork Menus

## MENU

*Cheesy Italian Pork Chops*

⌇⌇⌇⌇

*Parmesan Pasta-and-Peas*

⌇⌇⌇⌇

*Crusty Italian bread*

⌇⌇⌇⌇

*Fresh fruit*

⌇⌇⌇⌇

*Red wine*

### CHEESY ITALIAN PORK CHOPS

4 pork-loin rib chops, trimmed, 1 inch thick
½ teaspoon salt
1 tablespoon olive oil
1 bay leaf
¾ teaspoon chicken-flavor instant bouillon
4 ounces mushrooms, halved or quartered
½ pint cherry tomatoes, halved
¼ pound Fontina or Muenster cheese, cut into 4 slices
½ teaspoon cracked black pepper

1. Sprinkle chops with salt. Heat oil in large skillet over medium-high heat. Add chops in batches; cook for 3 minutes, or until browned on both sides. Remove chops to a platter as they brown. Skim excess fat from drippings in skillet; discard.

2. Return chops and any meat juices on platter to skillet. Add bay leaf, bouillon and ½ cup water; bring to a boil. Reduce heat to low; cover tightly and simmer. Relax for 40 minutes while chops cook.

3. Return to kitchen; start heating large pot of water for pasta. Add mushrooms and cherry tomatoes to chops in skillet. Place 1 slice of cheese on each chop and sprinkle with pepper. Cover and cook for 5 minutes, or until cheese melts and mushrooms are tender. Meanwhile, prepare pasta.

Makes 4 servings.

*Per serving: 352 calories, 32 g protein, 22 g fat, 5 g carbohydrate, 121 mg cholesterol, 517 mg sodium.*

### PARMESAN PASTA-AND-PEAS

6 ounces ditalini or other small pasta
1 package (10 ounces) frozen baby green peas
¼ cup grated Parmesan cheese
2 tablespoons (¼ stick) butter or margarine
½ teaspoon salt
½ teaspoon cracked black pepper
Kale leaves (optional garnish)

In large pot of lightly salted boiling water, cook pasta for 8 minutes, or until almost tender. Add peas and continue to cook for 2 minutes. Drain pasta and peas; return to pot. Stir in cheese, butter, salt and pepper until well combined. Serve pasta on top of kale.

Makes 4 servings.

*Per serving: 285 calories, 11 g protein, 5 g fat, 42 g carbohydrate, 20 mg cholesterol, 490 mg sodium.*

*Left: Cheesy Italian Pork Chops menu.*

## MENU
### Cider-Braised
### Pork Chops
~~~~
### Sautéed Savoy Cabbage
~~~~
### Baked sweet potatoes

### CIDER-BRAISED PORK CHOPS

1 tablespoon salad oil
4 pork rib chops, trimmed, 1 inch thick
1 medium Spanish onion, thickly sliced
1 cup apple cider or juice
½ teaspoon salt
¼ teaspoon dried thyme
1 Rome Beauty apple, cored and sliced
¼ cup currants or raisins
4 teaspoons cider vinegar
Black pepper to taste

1. Heat oil in large skillet over medium-high heat. Add chops in batches; cook for 3 minutes, or until browned on both sides. Remove pork chops to a platter. Discard all but 1 tablespoon drippings in skillet. To drippings, add onion slices; sauté for 5 minutes, or until lightly browned, stirring occasionally. Return pork chops to skillet; add apple cider, salt and thyme. Bring mixture to a boil; reduce heat to low. Cover and simmer. Relax for 45 minutes while chops cook.

2. Return to kitchen. Check pork chops; they should be fork-tender. Remove chops from skillet. Add apple slices, currants, vinegar and pepper to liquid remaining in skillet. Bring to a boil; cook until apples are tender and liquid is reduced to syrupy consistency. Return chops to skillet; cover and keep warm while preparing cabbage.

Makes 4 servings.

*Per serving: 485 calories, 27 g protein, 32 g fat, 23 g carbohydrate, 98 mg cholesterol, 355 mg sodium.*

### SAUTEED SAVOY CABBAGE

1 tablespoon butter or margarine
1 medium clove garlic, minced
½ medium head Savoy cabbage, thinly sliced (about 1½ pounds)
1 small red pepper, coarsely chopped
¼ teaspoon salt
2 teaspoons minced fresh dill, or ½ teaspoon dried dillweed

Melt butter in large pot or skillet over medium-high heat. Add garlic; sauté for 1 to 2 minutes. Add cabbage, red pepper and salt; cook for 8 to 10 minutes, or until cabbage is tender-crisp, stirring frequently. Spoon cabbage mixture into medium serving bowl; sprinkle with dill.

Makes 4 servings.

*Per serving: 42 calories, 1 g protein, 3 g fat, 4 g carbohydrate, 8 mg cholesterol, 177 mg sodium.*

● Turn a weekday meal into a special occasion with an easy, make-ahead dessert. Try this kid-pleasing banana-split pie: Spread fudge sauce in a graham-cracker piecrust; layer with sliced bananas and some softened vanilla ice cream. Freeze until firm. Top frozen pie with drained, crushed pineapple, whipped cream, cherries and chopped nuts.

# Chicken Menus

## MENU

*Poached Chicken and Winter Vegetables*

~~~~~

*Garlic Crisps*

~~~~~

*Cheese, nuts and pears*

## POACHED CHICKEN AND WINTER VEGETABLES

1 can (10¾ ounces) condensed chicken broth, undiluted
2 medium leeks
1 large bulb fennel, or 2 stalks celery
1 pound medium red-skinned potatoes
1 package (10 ounces) baby carrots
1 medium bunch kale (about 1½ pounds)
1 broiler-fryer (about 3 pounds), cut into eighths
1 teaspoon fennel or anise seeds, crushed
½ teaspoon cracked black pepper
¼ teaspoon salt

1. In 8-quart Dutch oven or large pot over high heat, bring chicken broth and 1 quart water to a boil. While liquid is heating, cut each leek lengthwise in half, and then crosswise into 3-inch pieces. Rinse well to remove all sand. Cut fennel into ½-inch-thick wedges (or cut celery into 3-inch pieces). Cut potatoes in half; trim carrots. Remove tough stems from kale; set kale aside.

2. Add leeks, fennel or celery, potatoes, carrots, chicken, fennel seeds, pepper and salt to liquid in Dutch oven (do not add kale). Bring to a boil. Reduce heat to low; cover and simmer. Relax for 40 minutes while chicken and vegetables cook.

3. Return to kitchen; add reserved kale to chicken mixture. Over high heat, bring to a boil. Reduce heat to low; simmer for 10 to 15 minutes, or until chicken is cooked through and vegetables are tender. Meanwhile, prepare Garlic Crisps (recipe follows).
Makes 4 servings.
*Per serving: 720 calories, 54 g protein, 37 g fat, 43 g carbohydrate, 174 mg cholesterol, 952 mg sodium.*

## GARLIC CRISPS

8 slices (cut ½ inch thick) Italian bread
1 medium clove garlic, halved
4 teaspoons olive oil
1 tablespoon coarsely chopped parsley

Preheat broiler. Place bread slices on baking sheet; broil for 2 to 3 minutes, or until lightly toasted, turning once. Rub cut sides of garlic over bread; discard garlic. In a cup, combine oil and parsley; brush each bread slice on one side with some oil mixture.
Makes 4 servings.
*Per serving: 198 calories, 5 g protein, 5 g fat, 32 g carbohydrate, 1 mg cholesterol, 332 mg sodium.*

## MENU
### Honey-Mustard
### Chicken Teriyaki
~~~~
### Chinese Cabbage Slaw
~~~~
### Take-out sesame noodles

## HONEY-MUSTARD
## CHICKEN TERIYAKI

2   tablespoons honey
1   tablespoon prepared Chinese or other
    hot mustard
4   boneless, skinless chicken-breast
    halves
3   scallions, chopped
1   tablespoon minced fresh ginger
¼   cup dry sherry
3   tablespoons teriyaki sauce

1. In a cup, mix honey and mustard; set
aside. Holding a small, sharp knife parallel to
work surface, cut a lengthwise pocket along
the side of each chicken breast. Fill pockets
with scallions and minced ginger; press to
close pockets. Lightly score tops of chicken
breasts, if you like. Place chicken breasts in
medium glass casserole. Sprinkle chicken with
sherry and teriyaki sauce, turning once to
coat. Cover chicken and refrigerate. Prepare
the slaw and refrigerate. Relax for 1 hour
while chicken marinates and slaw chills in
the refrigerator.

2. Return to kitchen; preheat broiler.
Place chicken on broiling rack; brush with
some honey mustard. Broil (or grill) 4 to 6
inches from heat source for 8 to 10 minutes,
or until chicken is cooked through, brushing
with remaining honey-mustard sauce and
turning once.

Makes 4 servings.

*Per serving: 183 calories, 28 g protein, 2 g
fat, 14 g carbohydrate, 66 mg cholesterol, 631
mg sodium.*

## CHINESE CABBAGE SLAW

½   medium head Chinese (Napa) cabbage,
    thinly sliced (about 1 pound)
2   medium carrots, coarsely shredded
2   tablespoons chopped fresh cilantro
⅓   cup orange juice
2   tablespoons rice-wine vinegar or white-
    wine vinegar
2   tablespoons salad oil
1   teaspoon sugar
½   teaspoon salt
¼   teaspoon crushed red pepper (optional)

In large serving bowl, combine cabbage,
carrots and cilantro. In small saucepan, combine remaining ingredients. Over high heat,
bring mixture to a boil, stirring occasionally. Pour warm dressing over cabbage mixture; toss until well coated. Cover; chill until
ready to serve.

Makes 4 servings.

*Per serving: 108 calories, 2 g protein, 7 g fat,
11 g carbohydrate, 0 mg cholesterol, 297 mg
sodium.*

*Right: Honey-Mustard Chicken Teriyaki menu.*

## MENU
### Lemon-Herb Roast Chicken
*~~~~*
### Couscous with Garden Vegetables
*~~~~*
### Steamed asparagus
*~~~~*
### Rosé wine

meat juices in pan; add broth. Set pan on burner over high heat; bring to a boil, stirring to loosen brown bits. Cook for 3 minutes, or until gravy is slightly reduced, stirring occasionally.

Makes 4 servings.

*Per serving: 511 calories, 54 g protein, 30 g fat, 7 g carbohydrate, 167 mg cholesterol, 682 mg sodium.*

## LEMON-HERB ROAST CHICKEN

1  roasting chicken (3½ to 4 pounds)
1  large clove garlic, halved
½  teaspoon salt
¼  teaspoon black pepper
1  teaspoon dried thyme
2  lemons
1  cup chicken broth

1. Preheat oven to 425°F. Partially loosen skin on chicken breast and legs by working your hand between meat and skin. Rub garlic halves over breast and leg meat; place garlic in cavity of chicken. Sprinkle chicken with salt, pepper and ¼ teaspoon of the thyme.

2. Thinly slice one of the lemons; insert slices between skin and meat of chicken. Cut remaining lemon into wedges; place in cavity of chicken along with remaining ¾ teaspoon thyme. Tie chicken legs together with string. Place chicken on rack in roasting pan. Place in oven. Relax for 55 minutes while chicken roasts.

3. Return to kitchen. Check chicken; leg joint should move easily and chicken should be cooked through. Transfer chicken to serving platter; let stand while preparing couscous and gravy. For gravy, skim fat from

## COUSCOUS WITH GARDEN VEGETABLES

1  tablespoon butter or margarine
1  small onion, chopped
1  medium clove garlic, minced
1  cup frozen green peas
¾  cup chicken broth
¼  teaspoon black pepper
½  cup quick-cooking couscous
12  cherry tomatoes, quartered
2  tablespoons chopped parsley

Melt butter in medium saucepan over medium heat. Add onion and garlic; sauté for 3 minutes, or until tender, stirring occasionally. Add peas, broth and pepper; bring to a boil. Stir in couscous. Remove from heat; cover and let stand for 5 minutes. Stir in tomatoes and parsley; fluff with a fork to separate grains of couscous.

Makes 4 servings.

*Per serving: 155 calories, 6 g protein, 3 g fat, 25 g carbohydrate, 8 mg cholesterol, 260 mg sodium.*

# Meatless Menus

## MENU
*Country-Style Vegetable Strata*

~~~~

*Quick Antipasto Salad*

~~~~

*Fresh fruit*

### COUNTRY-STYLE VEGETABLE STRATA

3 tablespoons butter or margarine
1 medium zucchini, thinly sliced
1 small onion, chopped
1 large clove garlic, minced
1 can (14½ to 16 ounces) tomatoes in puree
½ teaspoon dried thyme
½ teaspoon salt
8 slices white and/or pumpernickel bread, cut diagonally into quarters
1 cup (4 ounces) shredded Swiss cheese
4 eggs
½ cup milk
Fresh thyme (optional garnish)

1. Preheat oven to 325°F. Grease a 9-inch baking dish. Melt 1 tablespoon of the butter in medium saucepan over medium-high heat. Add sliced zucchini; sauté until tender-crisp, stirring occasionally. With slotted spoon, remove zucchini to a medium bowl. Add chopped onion and garlic to saucepan; cook onion mixture until tender. Add tomatoes, breaking them up with a spoon. Add dried thyme, ¼ teaspoon of the salt and ¼ cup

*Above: Country-Style Vegetable Strata menu.*

water; bring mixture to a boil. Reduce heat to low and simmer for 5 minutes.

2. Arrange half of bread in prepared baking dish; layer with cheese, zucchini and half of the tomato sauce. (Reserve remaining sauce to serve with strata.) Overlap remaining slices of bread on top. Beat eggs with milk and remaining ¼ teaspoon salt; pour evenly over bread. Dot with remaining 2 tablespoons butter. Place strata in oven. Relax for 40 minutes while strata bakes.

3. Return to kitchen. Strata should be lightly browned. When ready to serve, heat reserved tomato sauce and garnish strata with fresh thyme. Let strata stand while preparing antipasto salad.

Makes 6 servings.

*Per serving: 301 calories, 14 g protein, 16 g fat, 24 g carbohydrate, 219 mg cholesterol, 629 mg sodium.*

## QUICK ANTIPASTO SALAD

2 jars (6-ounce size) marinated artichoke
  hearts
2 medium stalks celery, thinly sliced
1 bunch radishes, trimmed and halved
½ cup pitted ripe olives
2 tablespoons finely chopped red onion
⅛ teaspoon crushed red pepper
1 medium head Boston lettuce

Drain artichokes; reserve 3 tablespoons of
the marinade. Mix artichokes, next 5 ingredients and reserved marinade. Serve on lettuce.
Makes 6 servings.

*Per serving: 92 calories, 2 g protein, 7 g fat, 7
g carbohydrate, 0 mg cholesterol, 197 mg sodium.*

## MENU
*Spaghetti Squash Primavera*
~~~~
*Endive-and-Watercress Salad*
~~~~
*Whole-grain hard rolls*

## SPAGHETTI SQUASH PRIMAVERA

⅓ cup olive oil
8 ounces mushrooms, halved
2 to 3 medium cloves garlic, minced
2 small zucchini, thinly sliced
2 large tomatoes, coarsely chopped
3 tablespoons coarsely chopped fresh
  basil, or 3 teaspoons dried basil
1 can (16 to 17 ounces) whole-kernel corn,
  drained
½ teaspoon salt
1 large spaghetti squash (3½ to 4 pounds)
¾ cup grated Parmesan cheese

1. Preheat oven to 350°F. Heat oil in large
skillet over medium-high heat. Add mushrooms, garlic and zucchini; cook for 5 to 8
minutes, stirring occasionally. Stir in tomatoes, basil, corn and salt; set aside.

2. Cut spaghetti squash lengthwise in half;
with spoon, scoop out and discard seeds.
Place squash halves, cut side down, on jelly-
roll pan and place in oven. Relax for 45
minutes while squash bakes.

3. Return to kitchen. Remove squash from
oven (flesh should be tender). Set squash
aside to cool slightly while preparing salad.

4. With fork, scrape flesh of squash into
medium serving dish; toss with cheese. Over
medium-high heat, cook mushroom mixture
for 5 minutes, or until heated through.
Spoon sauce over squash.

Makes 4 servings.

*Per serving: 431 calories, 13 g protein, 25 g
fat, 45 g carbohydrate, 12 mg cholesterol, 618
mg sodium.*

## ENDIVE-AND-WATERCRESS SALAD

3 tablespoons olive oil
3 tablespoons balsamic or red-wine
  vinegar
1 teaspoon Dijon mustard
Salt and pepper to taste
2 large heads Belgian endive, leaves
  separated
1 large bunch watercress, stemmed

In medium salad bowl, whisk first 4 ingredients. Add endive and watercress; gently toss
with dressing.

Makes 4 servings.

*Per serving: 104 calories, 2 g protein, 10 g
fat, 2 g carbohydrate, 0 mg cholesterol, 63 mg
sodium.*

*Above: Spaghetti Squash Primavera menu.*

# Easy Entertaining

*Whether you're looking for casual outdoor menus or more elegant fare, you'll find it here. Choose from the seven imaginative menus or design your own by mixing and matching recipes from Grilled Entrées and No-Fuss Entertaining. (Pictured, Backyard Barbecue, page 84.)*

Backyard Barbecue
Grilled Entrées
Picnic Lunch
Savannah-Style Supper
Weekend Brunch
Dazzling Dinner
Holiday Feast
Dessert Buffet
No-Fuss Entertaining
Elegant Desserts

# Backyard Barbecue

## MENU
*Sweet 'n' Sour Cherry Chicken*
~~~~~

*Inside-Out Pizza Burgers*
~~~~~

*Glazed Vidalia-Onion Skewers*
~~~~~

*Grilled Corn with*
*Basil-Parmesan Butter*
~~~~~

*Chocolate-Drizzled Fruit Tarts*
~~~~~

*Lemonade*

## SWEET 'N' SOUR CHERRY CHICKEN

When barbecuing, baste with sweet glazes when food is almost cooked to avoid charring. (Pictured, pages 82 and 83.)

1   tablespoon butter or margarine
1   medium onion, minced
1   medium clove garlic, minced
1   jar (12 ounces) cherry preserves
¼   cup coarsely chopped dried cherries or dried apricots (optional)
¼   cup cider vinegar
3   tablespoons spicy brown mustard
1   teaspoon ground cinnamon
1   broiler-fryer chicken (about 3½ pounds), quartered
¾   teaspoon salt
Fresh cherries and arugula (optional garnish)

1.  Prepare grill (medium heat).

2.  Meanwhile, melt butter in small saucepan over medium heat. Add onion and garlic; sauté for 10 minutes, or until lightly browned, stirring frequently. Stir in preserves, dried cherries (if using), vinegar, mustard and cinnamon; bring to a boil. Reduce heat to low; simmer for 15 minutes, or until glaze is slightly thickened, stirring occasionally. Set glaze aside.

3.  Rub chicken quarters with salt; place skin side down on grill (or oven-broil; see Note). Cook for 30 to 35 minutes, or until cooked through, turning occasionally. If chicken begins to brown too quickly, prop quarters upright, leaning one against the other. During last 5 minutes of cooking, brush chicken frequently with some glaze; reserve leftover glaze.

4.  Cut chicken into smaller serving-size portions, if you like. Garnish with fresh cherries and arugula. Bring reserved glaze to a boil; serve with chicken.

Makes 4 to 6 servings.

*Per serving: 558 calories, 39 g protein, 22 g fat, 51 g carbohydrate, 129 mg cholesterol, 566 mg sodium.*

*Note:* To oven-broil, preheat broiler. Place chicken, skin side down, on broiling rack 8 to 9 inches from heat source. Broil for 10 minutes. Brush with some glaze; broil for 3 minutes. Turn and broil for 10 to 12 minutes. Brush with some glaze; broil for 3 minutes, or until cooked through.

## INSIDE-OUT PIZZA BURGERS

Kids will love the hidden pizza fixings in these burgers. (Pictured, pages 82 and 83.)

¼ cup (1 ounce) shredded part-skim mozzarella cheese
2 tablespoons grated Parmesan cheese
2 tablespoons chopped fresh basil or 1½ teaspoons dried basil
1½ teaspoons chopped fresh oregano, or ½ teaspoon dried oregano
⅓ cup prepared pizza sauce
1½ pounds lean ground beef

1. Prepare grill (medium heat).
2. Meanwhile, in small bowl, mix first 4 ingredients and 2 tablespoons of the pizza sauce until well combined.
3. Divide beef into 6 balls; with a spoon, make an indentation in center of each ball. Spoon ⅙ of mozzarella filling into each indentation; shape beef over filling. Flatten into patties, about 3½ inches in diameter.
4. Place burgers on grill (or oven-broil; see Note). Cook for 10 minutes for medium, or until of desired doneness, turning occasionally. During last 5 minutes of cooking, brush burgers frequently with remaining pizza sauce. Serve with lettuce on hamburger buns or toasted Italian bread, if you like.
Makes 6 servings.
*Per serving: 247 calories, 22 g protein, 16 g fat, 1 g carbohydrate, 74 mg cholesterol, 171 mg sodium.*

*Note:* To oven-broil, preheat broiler. Place burgers on broiling rack 4 to 6 inches from heat source. Broil for 4 minutes. Brush with some pizza sauce; broil for 1 minute. Turn and broil for 5 to 6 minutes for medium, or until of desired doneness, brushing occasionally with remaining pizza sauce.

## GLAZED VIDALIA-ONION SKEWERS

Put these delectable onions on the grill to cook before the rest of the meal; then keep warm in the oven or serve at room temperature. (Pictured, pages 82 and 83.)

3 tablespoons butter or margarine
2 tablespoons molasses or maple syrup
½ teaspoon cracked black pepper
¼ teaspoon salt
3 medium Vidalia or Spanish onions

1. If using wooden skewers, soak in cold water to cover for 30 minutes to prevent them from burning. Prepare grill (medium heat).
2. Meanwhile, melt butter in small saucepan over medium heat. Stir in molasses, pepper and salt until well combined; remove from heat and set aside.
3. Cut each onion through root end into wedges about 1 inch thick. Thread onion wedges on skewers; place skewers on grill (or oven-broil; see Note). Cook for 12 to 15 minutes, or until onions are browned and caramelized, turning occasionally and brushing with molasses glaze.
Makes 6 servings.
*Per serving: 115 calories, 2 g protein, 6 g fat, 15 g carbohydrate, 16 mg cholesterol, 162 mg sodium.*

*Note:* To oven-broil, preheat broiler. Place skewers on broiling rack 5 to 7 inches from heat source. Broil for 12 to 15 minutes, or until onions are browned and caramelized, turning occasionally and brushing with molasses glaze.

## GRILLED CORN WITH
## BASIL-PARMESAN BUTTER

Cooking corn on the grill brings out its wonderful flavor and texture. The butter can be made ahead and refrigerated or frozen. (Pictured, pages 82 and 83.)

⅓ cup butter or margarine, softened
2 tablespoons grated Parmesan cheese
1 tablespoon chopped fresh basil, or
   1 teaspoon dried basil
¼ teaspoon black pepper
6 large ears fresh corn with husks

  1. Prepare grill (medium heat).
  2. Meanwhile, prepare Basil-Parmesan Butter: In small bowl, mix first 4 ingredients until well combined; set aside. (If butter was made in advance, let stand at room temperature until spreadable.)
  3. Pull husks back halfway from each ear of corn; remove silk. Rewrap ears of corn with husks, tying ends with string to secure.
  4. Place corn on grill (or oven-broil; see Note). Cook for 20 to 30 minutes, or until corn is tender, turning occasionally. (The fresher the corn, the shorter the grilling time. The husks will become charred while cooking.) To serve, let each person pull back husks and spread corn with some Basil-Parmesan Butter.
  Makes 6 servings.
*Per serving: 175 calories, 4 g protein, 12 g fat, 17 g carbohydrate, 29 mg cholesterol, 148 mg sodium.*

*Note:* To oven-broil, preheat broiler. Prepare corn as directed in step 3. Place corn on broiling rack 8 to 9 inches from heat source. Broil for 20 to 30 minutes, or until tender, turning occasionally. Husked boiled corn is also delicious with the flavored butter.

## CHOCOLATE-DRIZZLED
## FRUIT TARTS

Here's a stunning dessert that's easy on the hostess. The no-cook lemon-flavored ricotta filling is ready in less than 15 minutes—and has fewer than half the calories of a cream-cheese filling. (Pictured, pages 82 and 83.)

1 container (15 to 16 ounces) part-skim
  ricotta cheese
½ cup confectioners' sugar
1 tablespoon lemon juice
1 teaspoon grated lemon peel
1 package (4 ounces) individual graham-cracker tart shells (6 shells; see Note)
2 cups assorted fresh fruit (kiwi, banana and/or strawberry slices, raspberries, grape halves)
1 ounce semisweet chocolate, melted

  In medium bowl, mix first 4 ingredients until well combined. Spoon ricotta mixture into tart shells; arrange fruit on top. Drizzle with melted chocolate.
  Makes 6 servings.
*Per serving: 279 calories, 10 g protein, 12 g fat, 36 g carbohydrate, 22 mg cholesterol, 203 mg sodium.*

*Note:* Instead of using the individual graham-cracker tart shells, you can use a prepared 9-inch graham-cracker or chocolate-crumb crust to make a fruit pie.

# Grilled Entrées

*Now's the time to get out of the kitchen and into your backyard. Nothing's better than grilling to bring out the flavor of summertime dishes. In addition to the Backyard Barbecue menu, here are seven savory recipes for outdoor cooking.*

## WINE-MARINATED ROSEMARY STEAK WITH ROASTED POTATOES

Marinate the steak in a self-sealing plastic bag so you don't even have to wash a pan. (Pictured, page 90.)

¾ cup dry red wine
3 tablespoons olive oil
2 tablespoons chopped fresh rosemary, or 2 teaspoons dried rosemary, crushed
2 tablespoons lemon juice
2 large cloves garlic, minced
½ teaspoon black pepper
¼ teaspoon salt
¼ teaspoon crushed red pepper
1 trimmed beef flank steak (about 1 pound)
1 pound small red-skinned potatoes
2 tablespoons (¼ stick) butter or margarine
1 tablespoon chopped parsley
Fresh rosemary (optional garnish)

1. In self-sealing plastic storage bag or glass baking dish, mix first 8 ingredients. Add steak; turn to coat with marinade. If using a plastic bag, seal carefully, and then place bag inside another self-sealing plastic storage bag. Place in refrigerator to marinate for 8 to 24 hours, turning bag once or twice.

2. Prepare grill (medium heat). Remove steak from refrigerator and drain marinade into a small saucepan; set aside.

3. Meanwhile, place potatoes in large saucepan; add water to cover. Bring to a boil; reduce heat to medium. Partially cover and simmer for 15 minutes, or until potatoes are tender but slightly resistent when pierced. Drain and cool slightly; then place on 4 metal or wooden skewers. (If using wooden skewers, soak in cold water to cover for 30 minutes to prevent burning.)

4. When coals are white, place potato skewers on grill (or oven-broil; see Note). Cook for 5 to 10 minutes, turning occasionally and brushing with some of the reserved red-wine marinade. Move potato skewers to perimeter of grill and place steak in center; cook for 6 to 8 minutes for medium-rare, or until of desired doneness, turning once. Let steak stand for a few minutes before thinly slicing on diagonal, across the grain.

5. Over high heat, bring remaining marinade to a boil. Reduce heat to low and simmer for 3 minutes. Strain into a serving bowl; stir in butter and parsley. Serve steak slices with red-wine sauce and potatoes. Garnish with rosemary.

Makes 4 servings.

*Per serving: 443 calories, 24 g protein, 29 g fat, 23 g carbohydrate, 74 mg cholesterol, 275 mg sodium.*

*Note:* To oven-broil, preheat broiler. Place skewered potatoes on broiling rack 3 to 5 inches from heat source. Broil for 5 to 10 minutes, turning occasionally and brushing with marinade. Remove potatoes to platter; keep warm. Place steak on broiling rack; broil 8 to 10 minutes for medium-rare, or until of desired doneness, turning once.

## TWO-CHEESE BURGERS WITH TOMATO SALSA

If blue cheese is too strong for the kids, use Monterey Jack. (Pictured, right.)

2  medium tomatoes, chopped
1  small Bermuda onion, chopped
2  tablespoons white-wine vinegar
1  tablespoon olive oil
1  tablespoon chopped parsley
½  teaspoon black pepper
¼  teaspoon salt
1½  pounds lean ground beef
6  tablespoons (about 2 ounces) crumbled blue cheese
6  slices (about 3 ounces) Swiss cheese
6  leaves romaine lettuce
6  hamburger buns, toasted

1.  Prepare grill (medium heat).
2.  Meanwhile, prepare salsa: In medium bowl, mix first 7 ingredients; set aside.
3.  Shape beef into 12 patties, about 5 inches in diameter. Place 1 tablespoon blue cheese on 6 patties. Top with remaining patties, sealing edges so cheese will not leak.
4.  When coals are white, place burgers on grill (or oven-broil; see Note). Cook for 8 to 10 minutes for medium-rare, or until of desired doneness, turning once. Top with Swiss cheese and cook until cheese melts.
5.  Layer lettuce, burgers and then salsa between buns.
Makes 6 servings.
*Per serving: 462 calories, 30 g protein, 26 g fat, 26 g carbohydrate, 93 mg cholesterol, 528 mg sodium.*

*Note:* To oven-broil, preheat broiler. Broil 3 to 5 inches from heat source for 8 to 10 minutes for medium-rare, turning once; top with Swiss cheese during last minute.

## LAMB BURGERS WITH FETA CHEESE AND PITA TOASTS

The pita wedges make terrific appetizers!

⅓  cup (2 ounces) crumbled feta cheese
2  tablespoons thinly sliced ripe olives
2  scallions, thinly sliced
3  tablespoons olive oil
1  medium clove garlic, minced
1¾  teaspoons dried oregano
2  pitas, split and each half cut into quarters (16 triangles)
1¼  pounds ground lamb
½  teaspoon black pepper

1.  Prepare grill (medium heat).
2.  Meanwhile, mix first 3 ingredients; set aside. In a cup, mix oil, garlic and ¾ teaspoon oregano; brush on pita triangles.
3.  Mix lamb, pepper and remaining 1 teaspoon oregano until just combined. Shape into 4 patties, about 6 inches in diameter.
4.  When coals are white, place burgers in center of grill (or oven-broil; see Note). Cook for 10 minutes for medium-rare, or until of desired doneness, turning once. Place pita triangles on perimeter of grill to toast for 2 to 3 minutes. When burgers are done, top with feta mixture; serve with pita toasts.
Makes 4 servings.
*Per serving: 563 calories, 27 g protein, 41 g fat, 20 g carbohydrate, 110 mg cholesterol, 425 mg sodium.*

*Note:* To oven-broil, preheat broiler. Broil 5 to 7 inches from heat source for 8 to 10 minutes for medium-rare, turning once. Broil pita triangles during last 30 seconds.

*Right: Two-Cheese Burgers with Tomato Salsa (this page).*

## BLUE-RIBBON RIBS

Precooking these ribs reduces grilling time. If you'd like to use a sauce with a sweet base like this one on foods that require longer grilling, apply in the last 15 to 20 minutes of cooking to prevent the sugar from caramelizing too much and burning. (Pictured, left.)

3 cans (12-ounce size) beer
2 racks of pork-loin back ribs, trimmed (about 2½ pounds)
1 cup (10-ounce jar) apricot spreadable fruit
3 tablespoons reduced-sodium soy sauce
3 tablespoons cider vinegar
2 teaspoons dry mustard
1 to 1½ teaspoons crushed red pepper
2 large cloves garlic, minced
Kale leaves (optional garnish)

1. Place beer and ribs in large pot; add water to cover. Bring to a boil; reduce heat to low. Cover and simmer for 40 minutes; then drain cooking liquid.

2. Meanwhile, prepare grill (medium heat). Then prepare apricot glaze: In small bowl, mix remaining ingredients except garnish; set aside.

3. When coals are white, brush underside of ribs with half of glaze and place on grill, glazed side down (or oven-broil; see Note). Cook for 7 to 9 minutes, or until well browned. Brush with remaining glaze; turn and cook for 7 to 9 minutes. Cut into serving-size portions; garnish with kale.

Makes 4 to 6 servings.

*Per serving: 608 calories, 33 g protein, 34 g fat, 46 g carbohydrate, 134 mg cholesterol, 555 mg sodium.*

*Note:* To oven-broil, preheat broiler. Place ribs on broiling rack 5 to 7 inches from heat source. Broil for 10 to 15 minutes, brushing with glaze and turning once.

---

### BBQ SAFETY TIPS

**Fire it up!** Lighter fluid is a great convenience but should be used with caution. Follow package directions, and after use, recap bottle and place at a safe distance from the fire—and the kids. Never add lighter fluid to a hot fire. (Self-starting briquettes have lighter fluid in them. Don't add more of them to the grill once food is cooking as they may impart a chemical flavor.)

**Health watch:** The heat of the grill will destroy any bacteria in raw meat and poultry. But never use utensils or dishes that have come in contact with uncooked food without thoroughly washing them.

**Safety first!** Never use an outdoor grill indoors. Fumes can cause serious injury or even death. If it's raining, place your grill in a well-ventilated area, such as under a carport or at the edge of an open garage. Only grills designed for the kitchen are safe to use indoors.

*Left: (Clockwise from top left) Blue-Ribbon Ribs (this page), Wine-Marinated Rosemary Steak with Roasted Potatoes (page 87), and Shrimp-and-Vegetable Kabobs (page 93).*

## SMOKY CHICKEN WITH ORANGE, RED ONION AND MINT SALAD

Plan to put the chicken in the fridge to marinate the night before grilling—or in the morning before you leave for work. (Pictured, above.)

Marinade and chicken:
¼ cup orange juice
3 to 5 medium cloves garlic
2 tablespoons balsamic or red-wine vinegar
2 tablespoons olive oil
1 teaspoon cracked black pepper
6 boneless, skinless chicken-breast halves

Orange salad:
5 large oranges
1 medium red onion, thinly sliced
¼ cup coarsely chopped fresh mint
2 tablespoons olive oil
¾ teaspoon cracked black pepper
½ teaspoon salt
1 small head escarole, leaves torn

*Left: Smoky Chicken with Orange, Red Onion and Mint Salad (this page).*

1.  For marinade: Place first 5 ingredients in blender container; blend for 1 minute on medium speed. Place marinade with chicken in self-sealing plastic storage bag or glass baking dish. If using a plastic bag, seal carefully, and then place bag inside another self-sealing plastic bag. Place in refrigerator to marinate for 8 to 24 hours, turning bag once or twice.

2.  Prepare grill (medium heat). Remove chicken from refrigerator 10 to 15 minutes before grilling.

3.  When coals are white, drain and discard chicken marinade; place chicken on grill (or oven-broil; see Note). Cook for 10 to 12 minutes, or until cooked through, turning chicken once.

4.  Meanwhile, prepare orange salad: Squeeze juice from 1 of the oranges and place in medium bowl. Peel and section remaining oranges; place in bowl with juice. Add onion, mint, oil, pepper and salt; gently toss until well combined.

5.  To serve, divide orange salad and escarole evenly among 6 plates, reserving some of the orange liquid to spoon over chicken. Thinly slice chicken and place on plates with salad; spoon reserved orange liquid over sliced chicken.

Makes 6 servings.

*Per serving: 301 calories, 29 g protein, 11 g fat, 21 g carbohydrate, 73 mg cholesterol, 256 mg sodium.*

*Note:* To oven-broil, preheat broiler. Place chicken on broiling rack 3 to 5 inches from heat source. Broil for 8 to 10 minutes, or until cooked through, turning once.

## SHRIMP-AND-VEGETABLE KABOBS

Shrimp cook very quickly, so don't leave on the grill too long. (Pictured, page 90.)

6 tablespoons butter or margarine
1 tablespoon lime juice
½ teaspoon grated lime peel
½ teaspoon ground cumin
4 medium ears corn, husked and cut crosswise into quarters
2 small zucchini, cut crosswise into 1½-inch sections (about ¾ pound)
16 large shrimp, shelled and deveined (about 1 pound)
1 pint cherry tomatoes

1. Prepare grill (medium heat).
2. Meanwhile, in small saucepan over low heat, melt butter with next 3 ingredients. Alternate corn and zucchini on 4 metal skewers. Alternate shrimp and tomatoes on 4 other metal skewers.
3. When coals are white, place corn skewers on grill (or oven-broil; see Note). Cook for 5 minutes, turning often and brushing with some lime butter. Add shrimp skewers to grill. Cook for 4 to 6 minutes, turning often and brushing with some lime butter, until vegetables are tender-crisp and shrimp are just cooked through. Bring remaining lime butter to a boil; serve with kabobs.
Makes 4 servings.
*Per serving: 347 calories, 23 g protein, 20 g fat, 22 g carbohydrate, 186 mg cholesterol, 332 mg sodium.*

*Note:* To oven-broil, preheat broiler. Place corn-zucchini skewers on broiling rack 3 to 5 inches from heat source; broil 3 to 5 minutes. Add shrimp-tomato skewers; broil about 4 minutes longer, turning and brushing with lime butter as directed.

## GRILLED TROUT PRIMAVERA

Serve this dish with lemon wedges.

2 tablespoons (¼ stick) butter or margarine
2 medium carrots, diced
1 medium leek, thinly sliced and cleaned
¾ pound thin asparagus, trimmed and cut into 1½-inch pieces
1 to 2 tablespoons chopped fresh thyme, or 1 teaspoon dried thyme
1 teaspoon grated lemon peel
½ teaspoon black pepper
¼ teaspoon salt
4 trout fillets (about ½ pound each)
¼ cup dry white wine

1. Prepare grill (medium heat).
2. Melt butter in medium skillet over medium-high heat. Add carrots and leek; sauté for 3 minutes. Add asparagus; sauté for 2 minutes. Stir in next 4 ingredients. Remove from heat.
3. Tear off four 12-inch squares of aluminum foil; place 1 fillet in center of each square. Top with vegetable mixture and sprinkle with wine. Fold edges of foil to make packets; seal tightly.
4. When coals are white, place packets on grill. Cook 12 minutes, or until fish flakes.
Makes 4 servings.
*Per serving: 437 calories, 51 g protein, 21 g fat, 12 g carbohydrate, 147 mg cholesterol, 330 mg sodium.*

*Note:* To oven-broil, preheat broiler. Place foil packets on broiling rack 3 to 5 inches from heat source. Broil for 8 to 10 minutes; open top of packets and broil for 2 minutes, or until fish flakes.

# Picnic Lunch

## MENU

*Zesty Lime Chicken*

~~~~~

*Macaroni-and-Cheese*
*Garden Salad*

~~~~~

*Crunchy raw vegetables*

~~~~~

*Fruit Salad with*
*Vanilla-Bean Syrup*

~~~~~

*Banana Black-Bottom Cupcakes*

~~~~~

*Cold beer and fruit juices*

### ZESTY LIME CHICKEN

This simple dish can be prepared the day before a picnic. (Pictured, left.)

⅓ cup lime juice
⅓ cup chopped fresh cilantro or parsley
¼ cup olive oil
2 large cloves garlic, minced
2 tablespoons drained chopped pimiento
2 teaspoons coarsely grated lime peel
1½ teaspoons hot-pepper sauce
1½ teaspoons chopped fresh oregano, or
    ½ teaspoon dried oregano
¾ teaspoon salt
¼ teaspoon black pepper
6 chicken-breast halves

1. In large, shallow glass baking dish, mix all ingredients except chicken until well combined. Add chicken to marinade; turn to coat with marinade. Cover and let stand for at least 30 minutes, or place in refrigerator to marinate for up to 8 hours, turning chicken occasionally.

2. Preheat broiler. Place chicken, skin side down, in broiling pan without rack 7 to 9 inches from heat source (or barbecue; see Note). Reserve marinade. Broil for 20 to 25 minutes, or until cooked through, brushing frequently with marinade and turning once. (Cook chicken for at least 5 minutes after final brushing with marinade.)

3. Place chicken and pan drippings in serving container. If not eating chicken right away, cover container and refrigerate until ready to serve.

Makes 6 servings.

*Per serving: 400 calories, 38 g protein, 26 g fat, 2 g carbohydrate, 116 mg cholesterol, 423 mg sodium.*

*Note:* To barbecue, prepare grill (medium heat). Place chicken skin side down on grill. Cook for 30 to 35 minutes, or until cooked through, turning occasionally and brushing with marinade.

*Left: Picnic Lunch menu.*

## MACARONI-AND-CHEESE
## GARDEN SALAD

Use the cheeses listed below—or any combination you choose. (Pictured, page 94.)

8  ounces elbow macaroni or bow-tie pasta
1  tablespoon salad oil
1  medium onion, finely chopped
1  teaspoon dry mustard
12  cherry and/or yellow pear tomatoes,
   halved
6  ounces cheese: smoked mozzarella,
   cheddar and/or Fontina, cut into thin
   strips (about 1½ cups)
¼  cup coarsely chopped parsley
½  cup cholesterol-free, reduced-calorie
   mayonnaise
2  tablespoons milk
1  teaspoon salt
⅛  teaspoon black pepper

1. Cook macaroni according to package directions.

2. Meanwhile, heat oil in small skillet over medium heat. Add onion; sauté for 5 minutes, or until golden brown, stirring frequently. Add mustard; cook, for 1 minute, stirring constantly. Remove onion mixture to a large serving container.

3. Drain macaroni; rinse with cold water and drain again. Add to onion mixture with tomatoes, cheeses and parsley.

4. Mix mayonnaise, milk, salt and pepper. Pour over macaroni mixture; toss until well coated. Cover and refrigerate. (Salad will absorb dressing; if necessary, stir in a little milk before serving.)

Makes 6 servings.

*Per serving: 342 calories, 12 g protein, 18 g fat, 32 g carbohydrate, 29 mg cholesterol, 651 mg sodium.*

## FRUIT SALAD
## WITH VANILLA-BEAN SYRUP

If you like, save the vanilla bean when Vanilla-Bean Syrup is done. Dry bean thoroughly and use to flavor a canister of sugar—use when baking desserts or in tea or coffee. (Pictured, page 94.)

1  vanilla bean, or 2 teaspoons vanilla
   extract
6  tablespoons sugar
½  cup orange juice
1  teaspoon grated orange peel
8  cups assorted fresh fruit (see Note)

1. Split vanilla bean lengthwise; scrape seeds into small saucepan. (If using extract instead of bean, wait until step 2 to add extract.) Add vanilla-bean halves and next 3 ingredients. Over medium heat, stir until sugar dissolves. Cook for 5 to 7 minutes, or until consistency of light syrup.

2. Pour syrup into large serving container. (If using vanilla extract, stir into syrup at this point.) Cover and refrigerate for 30 minutes, or until well chilled. Add fruit to syrup and gently toss until coated. Cover and refrigerate for at least 30 minutes. Remove vanilla-bean halves before serving.

Makes 6 servings.

*Per serving: 148 calories, 2 g protein, 1 g fat, 36 g carbohydrate, 0 mg cholesterol, 9 mg sodium.*

*Note:* Cantaloupe cups are perfect disposable serving dishes: Cut several small cantaloupes in half. With a spoon or melon-baller, scoop out flesh, leaving about ½ inch inside the rind to form cups. Toss vanilla syrup with some of the melon balls and other cut-up fruit. Save remaining melon balls to serve another time.

## BANANA BLACK-BOTTOM CUPCAKES

These delightfully moist cupcakes start with a simple cake mix and don't even need frosting! They're perfect to take on a picnic. (Pictured, page 94.)

Cream-cheese mixture:
2 packages (3-ounce size) cream cheese, softened
¼ cup sugar
2 tablespoons (¼ stick) butter or margarine, softened
2 tablespoons all-purpose flour
1 egg

Cake mixture:
1 package (18.25 to 18.5 ounces) devil's food cake mix
2 medium bananas, very ripe, mashed
⅓ cup salad oil
3 eggs

1. Preheat oven to 350°F. Line two 12-cup muffin pans with paper liners.

2. For cream-cheese mixture: In medium bowl, with electric mixer on medium speed, beat all ingredients until smooth; set aside.

3. For cake mixture: Prepare cake-mix batter according to package directions, substituting bananas, oil, eggs and ½ cup water for ingredients specified on package. Spoon batter into prepared muffin cups; then top each with some cream-cheese mixture. (Each muffin cup should be about ⅔ full.)

4. Bake cupcakes for 20 to 25 minutes, or until toothpick inserted in center of cupcakes comes out clean (test in chocolate part, not cream cheese). Cool on wire racks.

Makes 2 dozen cupcakes.

*Per cupcake: 186 calories, 3 g protein, 10 g fat, 22 g carbohydrate, 46 mg cholesterol, 222 mg sodium.*

## PICNIC POINTERS

What would summer be without a picnic? Try these tips to ensure success:

● Bundle individual place settings (plastic knife, fork, spoon) in a few paper napkins. Bring paper plates, plenty of paper cups for hot and cold drinks, some premoistened towelettes and a big tablecloth. Pack extra trash bags to place underneath the cloth if the ground is damp. Wrap sharp knives and glass containers in thick cloths or towels.

● Bring some finger foods—sandwiches, fruit, crudités and cupcakes are all good. Wrap tender-skinned fruits such as peaches in paper towels. Take packets of salt and pepper, ketchup and mustard and other condiments.

● Use good-quality vacuum bottles and insulated containers to keep foods hot or cold. Hot foods stay hottest if you wrap the container in aluminum foil and then in several layers of newspaper.

● Transport baked goods in the pan you baked them in.

● Pack picnic fare in an insulated cooler or plastic-foam chest. If possible, divide everything between two coolers—one for food and the other for beverage.

● If you don't own a cooler, you can quickly and easily make a wicker basket leakproof if you line it with a large plastic bag and then with a table-cloth for insulation.

● Keep everything cool with blue ice packs, cans of frozen juice or ice cubes packed in self-sealing plastic bags (you can use the cubes for drinks). Pack the heaviest and most perishable foods closest to the ice. Also pack first what you will be eating last.

● Don't put the cooler in the trunk for the trip to your picnic site; once there, keep the cooler in a shady place.

● Don't let picnic fare sit out for too long. In hot weather, an hour is the maximum for safety.

● Bring insect repellent spray or citronella candles for warding off bugs. Be careful not to spray on food.

# Savannah-Style Supper

*Above: Roasted Oysters (this page) served with Vidalia Relish (page 100).*

## MENU

*Roasted Oysters*

*Vidalia Relish*

*Piglets in a Blanket*

*Low-Country Boil*

*Smoked turkey*

*Salad of mixed greens*

*Herbed Corn Bread*

*Marshmallow Burnt-Sugar Sauce*
*French vanilla ice cream*

*Chewy Chocolate Cookies*

*Chilled beer and fruit juices*

## ROASTED OYSTERS

Plan to bake these simple yet sensational oysters about 30 minutes before serving. To save time, have your fish merchant scrub the oysters. (Pictured, left.)

**3 dozen medium (select) fresh oysters in the shell, scrubbed**

1. Preheat oven to 400°F. Place oysters in single layer in 2 large shallow pans. Bake for 10 to 15 minutes, or until shells open. (Oysters will open slightly when cooked, but you may need a knife to pry shells open completely.)

*Above: Low-Country Boil (page 101), Herbed Corn Bread (page 101).*

2. Remove and discard top shells of oysters; top each oyster with a spoonful of Vidalia Relish (recipe follows), or serve with prepared cocktail sauce.

Makes 3 dozen oysters.

*Per oyster (without relish): 10 calories, 1 g protein, 0 g fat, 1 g carbohydrate, 8 mg cholesterol, 16 mg sodium.*

● *Low-Country Boil is a spicy mix of shrimp, chicken, sausage and vegetables. The dish originated in the coastal region of Georgia which "lies low" between rivers, marshes and the Atlantic Ocean. This Southern specialty is served with Herbed Corn Bread, chilled beer and juices.*

## VIDALIA RELISH

A zesty accent to the Roasted Oysters, this relish can be made a day in advance, covered and refrigerated. (Pictured, page 98.)

¼ cup olive oil
8 scallions, minced (about ½ cup)
1 medium Vidalia or Spanish onion, minced (see Note)
1 medium red onion, minced
1 small red pepper, diced
¼ cup minced parsley
¼ cup Greek olives, pitted and finely chopped
Juice of 2 small lemons (about ¼ cup)
2 tablespoons minced fresh oregano or thyme, or 1½ teaspoons dried oregano or thyme
1 tablespoon grated lemon peel
1 teaspoon black pepper
¼ teaspoon salt

1. Heat oil in large skillet over medium-high heat. Add scallions, Vidalia onion and red onion; sauté for 5 minutes, or until tender, stirring occasionally. Remove skillet from heat; add remaining ingredients.

2. Let relish cool; transfer to serving dish or storage container. Cover and refrigerate until chilled.

Makes about 3 cups.

*Per tablespoon: 17 calories, 0 g protein, 1 g fat, 1 g carbohydrate, 0 mg cholesterol, 37 mg sodium.*

*Note:* Vidalia onions are a uniquely sweet, mild variety grown in Vidalia County, Georgia. They taste delicious in salads or sandwiches; some fans even eat these onions raw, like apples.

## PIGLETS IN A BLANKET

Here's a kid-pleasing, do-ahead dish. Prepare and bake piglets the morning of the party—reheat them for 10 minutes or so just before serving.

1 sheet frozen puff pastry
12 hot dogs

1. Preheat oven to 375°F. Thaw pastry according to package directions. Cut each hot dog crosswise into thirds.

2. Unfold pastry; cut lengthwise into 9 strips. Cut each strip crosswise into 4 pieces. Place a piece of hot dog on a piece of pastry; pinch ends of pastry together to seal. Repeat with remaining hot dogs and pastry. Place seam-side down, about 1 inch apart, on jelly-roll pan. Bake for 12 to 15 minutes, or until pastry is puffed and golden.

Makes 3 dozen piglets.

*Per piglet: 89 calories, 2 g protein, 7 g fat, 3 g carbohydrate, 9 mg cholesterol, 244 mg sodium.*

### JAZZED-UP BREADS AND BUTTERS

Turn ordinary breads into party fare with a spread or flavored butter.

● Try this low-calorie, high-flavor alternative to butter as a spread for bread: Roast a whole unpeeled head of garlic in a little broth, covered with aluminum foil, in a 350°F oven for 1¼ hours, or until soft. Squeeze roasted garlic on toasted bread.

● Stir chili powder into softened butter; serve with breads or corn on the cob.

● Mix finely chopped walnuts with softened butter and a little dried oregano or marjoram. Spread on slices of French bread and broil until lightly browned.

## LOW-COUNTRY BOIL

To cut down on last minute preparation, shell and devein shrimp the day before your supper—or buy precleaned shrimp. Start this dish about two hours before you're ready to eat. (Pictured, page 99.)

2  pounds hot and/or sweet Italian sausage
4  pounds boneless, skinless chicken thighs
6  large cloves garlic, peeled
4  pounds small red-skinned potatoes, halved
3  large onions, cut into thin wedges
½  cup minced fresh herbs (oregano, basil, thyme) or 3 to 4 tablespoons dried Italian seasoning
1  teaspoon cayenne pepper
Salt to taste
2  packages frozen half-ears corn on the cob
3  pounds medium shrimp, shelled and deveined

1. Prick sausage with fork; place in large pot over medium heat. Cook until browned on all sides. With a slotted spoon, remove sausage from pot; cut into ¾-inch-thick slices. In drippings in pot, brown chicken in batches, removing to a bowl as it browns. Add salad oil if necessary; set chicken aside.

2. Drain and discard fat in pot. Return sausage to pot; add garlic, potatoes, onions, herbs, cayenne and 4 quarts water. Bring to a boil; reduce heat to medium and cook for 35 minutes. Season broth with salt to taste.

3. Add browned chicken and corn; over high heat, bring to a boil. Reduce heat to medium; cover and cook for 10 minutes, or until chicken is cooked through.

4. Just before serving, add shrimp; cook for 5 to 8 minutes, or until just cooked through. Skim any excess fat from broth in pot. Flavors will mellow nicely as dish cools slightly. Seconds taste wonderful.
Makes 12 servings.
*Per serving: 681 calories, 66 g protein, 23 g fat, 53 g carbohydrate, 308 mg cholesterol, 796 mg sodium.*

## HERBED CORN BREAD

Bake this savory corn bread in the morning and serve at room temperature—or if desired, reheat it briefly before serving. (Pictured, page 99.)

2  boxes (8½-ounce size) corn bread or corn muffin mix
½  cup cottage cheese
¼  cup minced parsley
¼  cup snipped fresh chives or scallions

1. Preheat oven to 350°F. Grease several corn-stick molds or two 8-inch square baking pans. Set aside.

2. Prepare mixes according to package directions, adding cottage cheese, parsley and chives to batter. Spoon into prepared molds. Bake for 12 to 15 minutes, or until lightly browned (corn bread baked in square pans will take about 25 minutes).
Makes 12 servings.
*Per serving: 179 calories, 4 g protein, 5 g fat, 28 g carbohydrate, 1 mg cholesterol, 455 mg sodium.*

## MARSHMALLOW BURNT-SUGAR SAUCE

If desired, make this topping a week ahead through step 2. Add the marshmallows when reheating the sauce. Reheat in the microwave or on stovetop. (Pictured, left.)

1½  cups sugar
6  tablespoons (¾ stick) butter
⅔  cup whipping cream
⅔  cup light corn syrup
¼  cup bourbon (see Note)
2  cups miniature marshmallows

1. Measure all ingredients to be able to add to pan quickly. In large, heavy skillet, slowly heat sugar over low heat until melted and amber in color. Do not stir, but swirl pan to color syrup evenly.

2. Add butter; stir constantly until mixture is almost smooth. Remove skillet from heat; stir in cream and corn syrup. Over medium heat, cook until mixture is smooth, stirring constantly. (Mixture will initially look separated.) Remove skillet from heat; stir in bourbon.

3. Cool sauce slightly before adding miniature marshmallows. Wonderful served with French vanilla, coffee or chocolate ice cream.
Makes 12 servings.

*Per serving: 275 calories, 0 g protein, 10 g fat, 45 g carbohydrate, 30 mg cholesterol, 79 mg sodium.*

*Note:* You can substitute ¼ cup additional corn syrup and 1 tablespoon vanilla extract for the bourbon.

## CHEWY CHOCOLATE COOKIES

These bite-size cookies will keep beautifully in the freezer for up to a month. Bring them out about 15 minutes before serving time. (Pictured, left.)

1  pound semisweet chocolate, chopped
2  tablespoons (¼ stick) butter or margarine
½  cup all-purpose flour
½  teaspoon baking powder
½  teaspoon ground cinnamon
**Dash of salt**
4  eggs
1½  cups sugar
1  teaspoon vanilla extract
1½  cups pecan pieces

1. Preheat oven to 375°F. Grease several large baking sheets.

2. In large, heavy saucepan over low heat, melt chocolate and butter, stirring frequently. Set aside. Sift together flour, baking powder, cinnamon and salt. In large bowl, with mixer on medium speed, beat eggs until pale and fluffy. Slowly beat in sugar, 2 tablespoons at a time. Gently fold in chocolate mixture, flour mixture and vanilla. Stir in pecans.

3. Drop batter by teaspoonfuls, about 1 inch apart, onto prepared baking sheets. Bake for 5 to 6 minutes, or until cookies are puffed and shiny. Let cookies cool on baking sheet before removing to wire racks. As cookies cool, tops will crack but insides will remain chewy.
Makes about 8 dozen cookies.

*Per cookie: 55 calories, 1 g protein, 3 g fat, 7 g carbohydrate, 12 mg cholesterol, 9 mg sodium.*

*Left: Marshmallow Burnt-Sugar Sauce (this page) over ice cream, Chewy Chocolate Cookies (this page).*

# Weekend Brunch

## MENU

*Crudités with Confetti Dip*

〜〜〜

*Shrimp Spoon Bread*

〜〜〜

*Deli-baked ham*
*and spiced crab apples*

〜〜〜

*Acorn Squash Baked in Cider*

〜〜〜

*Georgia Pecan Sticky Buns*

〜〜〜

*Fresh Fruit Ambrosia*

〜〜〜

*Juices, coffee and iced tea*

*Above: Crudités with Confetti Dip (facing page).*

*Left: Shrimp Spoon Bread (page 106).*

## CRUDITES WITH CONFETTI DIP

If desired, make this tasty dip and blanch veggies a day ahead; wrap separately and chill. (Pictured, left.)

Confetti dip:

1 large clove garlic
2 bunches radishes, trimmed
2 bunches baby carrots, trimmed
1 bunch watercress, stemmed
1 bunch scallions, cut into 2-inch pieces
2 packages (8-ounce size) cream cheese, softened
¼ cup milk
1 to 2 tablespoons minced fresh tarragon, or 1 to 2 teaspoons dried tarragon
1 teaspoon dill seed
½ teaspoon cayenne pepper
½ teaspoon salt
Juice of 1 lemon

Crudités:

1 small head broccoli
½ pound green beans
1 small head Chinese (Napa) cabbage
6 medium stalks celery
2 large red peppers
2 large yellow or green peppers
1 small head cauliflower

1. For dip: In food processor fitted with steel blade, process garlic until minced. Add 1 bunch of the radishes and 3 of the carrots; process until finely chopped. Remove mixture to a medium bowl. Set aside remaining radishes, carrots and a sprig of watercress; refrigerate. Place remaining watercress and scallions in processor bowl and process until finely chopped; add to radish mixture. Stir in cream cheese and next 6 ingredients until well combined. Cover and refrigerate for at least 6 hours to allow flavors to develop.

2. For crudités: Cut broccoli into florets; trim green beans. Blanch broccoli and green beans in boiling water; cool immediately in ice water. Drain; cover and refrigerate.

3. Line serving basket with cabbage leaves. Cut celery into 3-inch pieces and peppers into thin strips. Cut cauliflower into florets. Slice one of the radishes to garnish dip; set aside. Arrange remaining radishes and carrots, the broccoli, green beans, celery, peppers and cauliflower on top of cabbage. Cover vegetables with damp paper towels and plastic wrap; refrigerate until serving.

4. Just before serving, spoon dip into serving bowl to serve with crudités. Garnish dip with watercress sprig and sliced radish.

Makes about 12 servings.

*Per serving: 190 calories, 6 g protein, 14 g fat, 13 g carbohydrate, 42 mg cholesterol, 260 mg sodium.*

## BRUNCH BASICS

● When planning the menu, choose several dishes that can be made ahead. Sticky buns, muffins, breakfast casseroles, fruit salads—these are just some of the possibilities.

● Set the table the night before. Put out your favorite flatware and china; add coordinating napkins and a pretty tablecloth. Washable place mats are handy for the kids. Fill a pitcher with extra cutlery and serving utensils. Line baskets for rolls and breads with bright kitchen towels.

● Keep an assortment of spreads on hand. Fill small dishes or pitchers with honey, maple syrup, all-fruit spreads, jams and marmalades. Include cream cheese, peanut butter and butter or margarine for savory tastes.

● Round out the brunch with just-squeezed juices, iced tea and plenty of freshly brewed coffee served with a pitcher of hot milk. In chilly weather, kids and adults enjoy hot cocoa.

## SHRIMP SPOON BREAD

Down-home spoon bread becomes an extra-special party dish with the addition of succulent shrimp. You can make the batter a day ahead through step 2; refrigerate batter, and then finish the recipe an hour before serving. (Pictured, right.)

1  pound medium shrimp
2  cups milk
¾  teaspoon salt
2  cups yellow cornmeal
About 2 tablespoons (¼ stick) butter or
    margarine
6  eggs
2½  teaspoons baking powder
½  teaspoon baking soda
2  tablespoons chopped parsley
Parsley sprigs (optional garnish)

1. Shell and devein shrimp, leaving tails on a few shrimp; set aside shrimp with tails for garnish. Grease 3-quart casserole; place remaining shrimp in a single layer in casserole. Refrigerate if not baking immediately.

2. In large saucepan, combine milk, salt and 1½ cups water. With a whisk, slowly stir in cornmeal. Over medium heat, cook until cornmeal mixture thickens, whisking constantly. Remove saucepan from heat; stir in 2 tablespoons butter. Set cornmeal mixture aside to cool.

3. Preheat oven to 350°F. Add ½ cup water to cornmeal mixture, stirring until smooth. In large bowl, with electric mixer on high speed, beat eggs, baking powder and baking soda until thick and light. Fold egg mixture and chopped parsley into cornmeal mixture; pour batter over shrimp in casserole. Bake for 35 to 40 minutes, or until spoon bread is puffed and golden.

4. Meanwhile, sauté reserved shrimp in a little butter until just cooked through. Garnish baked spoon bread with shrimp and parsley sprigs.
Makes 12 servings.
*Per serving: 198 calories, 12 g protein, 7 g fat, 21 g carbohydrate, 194 mg cholesterol, 380 mg sodium.*

## ACORN SQUASH BAKED IN CIDER

You can slice squash and chill (wrapped in damp paper towels) the day before; then complete the dish an hour before serving. Squash can bake right along with the spoon bread. (Pictured, right.)

3  medium acorn squash (about 1 pound
    each)
2  cups apple cider or juice
2  tablespoons (¼ stick) butter or
    margarine

1. Preheat oven to 350°F. Cut each squash in half lengthwise; remove seeds. Leaving skin on, cut each half crosswise into ½-inch-thick slices. Place squash in large baking pan; add apple cider and dot with butter.

2. Bake for 35 to 45 minutes, or until squash is tender. Drain liquid in baking pan into a large saucepan. Over high heat, bring to a boil; cook until liquid is reduced to a syrupy glaze (about ½ cup). Pour glaze over squash; turn slices to coat with glaze.
Makes 12 servings.
*Per serving: 71 calories, 1 g protein, 2 g fat, 14 g carbohydrate, 5 mg cholesterol, 23 mg sodium.*

*Above: (Clockwise from top right) Deli-baked ham with spiced crab apples served with Acorn Squash Baked in Cider (facing page), Fresh Fruit Ambrosia (page 109), Georgia Pecan Sticky Buns (page 109), Shrimp Spoon Bread (facing page).*

### GEORGIA PECAN STICKY BUNS

Plan to thaw frozen bread dough in the refrigerator a day ahead. The next morning, shape sticky buns, let rise, and then bake as directed. (Pictured, right.)

2 packages (1-pound size) frozen whole-
   wheat or white bread dough
1½ cups pecan pieces
¾ cup (1½ sticks) butter or margarine,
   melted
¾ cup packed brown sugar
1 tablespoon ground cinnamon

1.  Thaw bread dough in refrigerator overnight according to package directions. Grease two 12-cup muffin pans. Place 1 teaspoon pecans, ½ teaspoon butter and ½ teaspoon brown sugar in bottom of each cup.

2.  On floured surface, roll each piece of dough into a 12-by-6-inch rectangle. Brush rectangles with some of the butter. In small bowl, combine cinnamon, remaining pecans and brown sugar; sprinkle mixture on rectangles. Starting from long side of dough, roll each rectangle into a 12-inch-long log; slice each log crosswise into 12 buns. Place buns in prepared muffin cups; brush with any remaining butter. Let rise for 1 to 1½ hours, or until doubled.

3.  Preheat oven to 350°F. Bake for 20 minutes, or until rolls are golden brown; invert immediately onto a sheet of wax paper. Spoon any pecan mixture left in cups onto sticky buns.
  Makes 24 buns.

*Per bun: 224 calories, 3 g protein, 12 g fat, 26 g carbohydrate, 17 mg cholesterol, 243 mg sodium.*

Left: Georgia Pecan Sticky Buns (facing page), Fresh Fruit Ambrosia (this page).

## FRESH FRUIT AMBROSIA

A wonderful weekend wake-up treat—this traditional Southern dish is full of refreshing flavors. (Pictured, left.)

1 medium lemon
5 large oranges
1 tablespoon sugar
2 large apples, cored and diced
1 large fresh pineapple, peeled, cored and diced
2 cups seedless green grapes
½ cup shredded coconut

Squeeze juice from lemon and 1 of the oranges into a large serving bowl. Stir in sugar until dissolved. Peel and section remaining oranges. Add oranges, apples, pineapple and grapes to juice mixture; toss until well combined. Sprinkle with coconut; cover and refrigerate until ready to serve.

Makes 12 servings.

*Per serving: 117 calories, 1 g protein, 2 g fat, 27 g carbohydrate, 0 mg cholesterol, 9 mg sodium.*

# Dazzling Dinner

## MENU

*Zucchini Turnovers*

~~~~~

*Creamy Mustard Sauce*

~~~~~

*Southern Cornish Hen Pilau*

~~~~~

*Julienned vegetables*

~~~~~

*Green Salad with Oranges and
Benne Seeds*

~~~~~

*Candied Yam Tart with Gingered
Whipped Cream*

~~~~~

*Wine and soda*

*Left: Good friends and great food make any dinner a festive occasion. In this party setting, the subtle flower arrangement allows guests to talk freely across the table.*

*Right: Zucchini Turnovers (this page) served with Creamy Mustard Sauce (facing page).*

## ZUCCHINI TURNOVERS

These flavorful turnovers are an easy, elegant appetizer you can make a day ahead—but don't bake. Pop them in the oven about 30 minutes before serving. (Pictured, right.)

Pastry:
1  cup all-purpose flour
1  package (3 ounces) cream cheese, cubed
6  tablespoons (¾ stick) chilled butter or margarine, cubed

Filling:
2  tablespoons (¼ stick) butter or margarine
1  medium onion, minced
1  small clove garlic, minced
1  large zucchini, grated and patted dry with paper towels (about 2½ cups)
2  tablespoons minced fresh basil or dill, or 1½ teaspoons dried basil or dillweed
½  teaspoon salt
Dash of cayenne pepper
2  tablespoons all-purpose flour
½  cup (2 ounces) grated cheddar cheese
Fresh basil (optional garnish)

1.  For pastry: In food processor fitted with steel blade or with pastry blender, process

cookie cutter, cut out circles. Repeat with remaining dough; gather trimmings, reroll and cut out (makes about 16 circles). Place a spoonful of filling on each circle of dough; fold to form half-moons and press edges with fork to seal. With small knife, cut decorative design on pastry tops. (Turnovers can be made a day ahead up to this point and refrigerated.)

4. Place turnovers on large baking sheet. Bake for 15 to 20 minutes, or until pastry is golden brown. Place on serving platter; garnish with basil. Serve with Creamy Mustard Sauce (recipe follows).

Makes about 16 turnovers.

*Per turnover: 122 calories, 3 g protein, 9 g fat, 8 g carbohydrate, 25 mg cholesterol, 131 mg sodium.*

flour and cubed cream cheese until mixture resembles coarse meal. Add butter; process just until mixture forms a ball of dough. Divide into 2 pieces. Wrap each in plastic wrap; refrigerate for at least 30 minutes.

2. For filling: Melt butter in medium skillet over medium-high heat. Add onion and garlic; sauté for 2 minutes. Add zucchini, minced basil, salt and cayenne; sauté for 2 minutes, stirring frequently. Sprinkle flour over mixture; stir until well combined. Remove from heat; let mixture cool. Stir in cheese and set aside.

3. Preheat oven to 400°F. On lightly floured surface, roll dough, one piece at a time, to about ⅛-inch thickness; keep remaining dough chilled. With 4-inch round

## CREAMY MUSTARD SAUCE

This tangy two-ingredient sauce can be made a day ahead—great with warm Zucchini Turnovers. (Pictured, above left.)

1 container (8 ounces) plain yogurt or sour cream
1 to 2 tablespoons grainy Dijon mustard

In small bowl, mix yogurt and mustard until well combined.

Makes about 1 cup.

*Per tablespoon (with yogurt): 11 calories, 1 g protein, 1 g fat, 1 g carbohydrate, 1 mg cholesterol, 52 mg sodium.*

## SOUTHERN CORNISH HEN PILAU

Pilau is a South Carolina version of pilaf. (Pictured, right.)

2 tablespoons (¼ stick) butter or margarine
4 Cornish hens, split in half lengthwise
1 tablespoon minced fresh thyme, or 1½ teaspoons dried thyme
1 teaspoon coarsely ground black pepper
1 teaspoon salt
3 large cloves garlic, minced
2 ounces country ham or prosciutto, diced
1 large onion, finely chopped
2 cups uncooked long-grain rice
1 large red pepper, diced
1 tablespoon curry powder
2 cans (10½-ounce size) low-sodium chicken broth
1 can (14½ to 16 ounces) tomatoes
½ cup dry vermouth
½ cup chopped parsley
¼ cup chopped pecans, toasted

1. Melt butter in large skillet over medium-high heat. Add 4 hen halves; sprinkle with half of the thyme, black pepper and salt. Cook until browned on both sides; remove from skillet. Repeat with remaining hens, thyme, pepper and salt. Set aside.

2. To drippings in skillet, add garlic, ham and onion. Reduce heat to medium; sauté for 2 minutes. Add rice, red pepper and curry powder; sauté for 2 minutes, stirring often.

3. Preheat oven to 325°F. In large roasting pan, combine rice mixture, chicken broth, tomatoes and vermouth; stir until well combined, breaking tomatoes up with a spoon. (Depending on the size of your roasting pan, you may need 2 pans—rice doubles in bulk when cooked.) Place Cornish hens on top of rice mixture, skin side up. Cover and bake for 1 to 1¼ hours, or until Cornish hens and rice are tender and liquid is absorbed. Remove Cornish hens to serving platter; toss rice mixture with parsley and pecans. Arrange rice with Cornish hens on platter.
   Makes 8 servings.
   *Per serving: 661 calories, 48 g protein, 30 g fat, 46 g carbohydrate, 147 mg cholesterol, 650 mg sodium.*

## GREEN SALAD WITH ORANGES AND BENNE SEEDS

Make salad and dressing ahead—toss the salad just before serving. (Pictured, right.)

3 large oranges
1 large bunch watercress
1 large head Belgian endive
1 large head Boston lettuce
3 scallions
2 tablespoons red-wine vinegar
½ small clove garlic, minced
¼ teaspoon black pepper
¼ teaspoon salt
¼ cup salad oil
1 tablespoon benne seeds (sesame seeds), toasted

1. Coarsely grate 2 teaspoons orange peel; reserve for dressing. With serrated knife, peel oranges, removing white membrane. Slice oranges crosswise into thin rounds and set aside. Trim tough stems from watercress. Mince enough watercress to measure 2 tablespoons; reserve for dressing. Separate leaves of endive and lettuce; tear into bite-size pieces. Cut scallions diagonally into ¼-inch pieces. Place endive, lettuce, scallions and remaining watercress in large salad bowl. Cover and

*Above: (Clockwise from right) Southern Cornish Hen Pilau (facing page), Green Salad with Oranges and Benne Seeds (facing page), julienned vegetables.*

refrigerate salad greens and oranges separately if not serving immediately.

2. In medium bowl, whisk orange peel, minced watercress, vinegar, garlic, pepper and salt. Slowly whisk in oil. Set aside.

3. Just before serving, whisk dressing again if it has separated. Gently toss salad with orange slices and dressing; sprinkle with benne seeds.

Makes 8 servings.

*Per serving: 107 calories, 2 g protein, 8 g fat, 10 g carbohydrate, 0 mg cholesterol, 84 mg sodium.*

◗ What's a Benne? Benne seeds, called sesame outside the South, were first brought to the region by West Indians, who planted them for good luck. Benne-seed cakes and candy were staple sweets in many plantation kitchens.

## CANDIED YAM TART WITH GINGERED WHIPPED CREAM

You can bake this luscious tart a day ahead but make the gingered cream and add garnish just before serving. (Pictured, right.)

3  medium yams or sweet potatoes (about 1½ pounds)
9-inch refrigerated piecrust
¾  cup sugar
2  tablespoons (¼ stick) butter or margarine, softened
½  teaspoon grated nutmeg
2  eggs, beaten
1  cup whipping cream
5  teaspoons minced crystallized ginger

1.  Preheat oven to 350°F. Bake yams for 45 to 60 minutes, or until tender. Let yams cool; remove skin and mash pulp. Measure 2 cups pulp; set aside.

2.  Line 9-inch round tart pan with removable bottom with piecrust, gently folding under any excess crust to form a thicker edge on the crust.

3.  Increase oven temperature to 400°F. In large bowl, with electric mixer on medium speed, beat mashed yams, sugar, butter, nutmeg, eggs, ½ cup of the cream and 2 teaspoons of the ginger until smooth. Spread yam mixture in pastry-lined tart pan.

4.  Place pan on baking sheet on bottom rack of oven; bake for 5 minutes. Reduce oven temperature to 350°F; bake for 35 to 40 minutes, or until knife inserted just off center comes out clean. Let tart cool completely before removing from pan. Refrigerate until ready to serve.

5.  In small bowl, with electric mixer on medium speed, whip remaining ½ cup cream with 2 teaspoons of the ginger until soft peaks form. Spoon gingered cream on top of tart; sprinkle with remaining 1 teaspoon ginger.

Makes 8 servings.

*Per serving: 404 calories, 4 g protein, 21 g fat, 50 g carbohydrate, 109 mg cholesterol, 222 mg sodium.*

## DAZZLING DINNER

Planning a party? Keep it simple! Remember, good food need not be fussy food. In fact, your best strategy is to skip anything really complicated. Do as much as possible in advance—from prepping vegetables for side dishes and salads (wrap in damp paper towels for keeping) to making salad dressings.

Some, if not all, of the recipes should be chosen with "do-ahead" in mind. Oven-baked dishes such as casseroles generally don't require any last-minute fussing. For dessert, select one you can prepare a day or two ahead.

Put your microwave and food processor to work—these appliances really do save time. Avoid labor-intensive tasks. You may, for instance, find it easier to buy already boned and skinned chicken breasts. Take advantage of bakeries and take-out gourmet shops—none of your guests will be the wiser.

Many of the steps in this menu can be done in advance and finished just before serving. The turnovers, mustard sauce and yam tart can all be made a day ahead. On the morning of your party, prepare the greens, oranges and salad dressings and refrigerate separately. The Southern Cornish Hen Pilau is an ideal main dish because you can put it in the oven and forget about it. This leaves you more time for the most important thing—to relax and enjoy your guests.

*Right: Candied Yam Tart with Gingered Whipped Cream (this page).*

# Holiday Feast

## MENU

**Lemon-Herb Turkey Breast**

~~~~~

**Onion-and-Shallot Brown Gravy**

~~~~~

**Oven-Roasted Sweet Potatoes with Maple-Pecan Butter**

~~~~~

**Rich Mashed Potatoes**

~~~~~

**Green Beans Vinaigrette**

~~~~~

**Cranberry-Raspberry Sauce**

~~~~~

**Corn Bread Stuffin' Muffins**

~~~~~

**Streusel Pumpkin Pie**

~~~~~

**Bourbon Pecan Pie**

### LEMON-HERB TURKEY BREAST

A turkey breast is perfect for a small family gathering—it cooks in about half the time of a whole bird. (Pictured, right.)

Basting mixture:
2  tablespoons lemon juice
1  tablespoon olive oil

Turkey:
1  bone-in turkey breast (7 to 8 pounds), thawed if frozen (see Note)
2  large cloves garlic, minced
1  tablespoon olive oil
1  tablespoon lemon juice
1¼  teaspoons salt
1  teaspoon grated lemon peel
1  teaspoon dried thyme
¾  teaspoon black pepper
½  teaspoon dried sage
Lemon wedges, fresh sage and thyme (optional garnish)

1. For basting mixture: In a cup, combine lemon juice and oil; set aside.

2. For turkey: Preheat oven to 350°F. Rinse turkey; pat dry with paper towels. Pull off any excess fat around neck; if necessary, cut off attached rib bones with poultry shears (save bones for making soup or stock). Partially loosen skin on turkey, starting at neck area and working your hand between skin and meat (do not detach skin along sides or at bottom of turkey breast).

3. In small bowl, mix remaining ingredients except garnish. Spoon some of lemon-herb mixture under loosened skin, spreading evenly over meat. Rub remaining mixture over outside of skin.

*Left: Turkey with all the fixings.*

*Above: Holiday Feast menu.*

4. Place turkey on rack in roasting pan. Roast turkey for about 20 minutes per pound, basting every 15 to 20 minutes with basting mixture and pan juices as they accumulate. Turkey is done when skin is brown, juices run clear and a meat thermometer inserted in thickest part of meat (but not touching bone) registers 170°F. If turkey starts to get too brown, cover loosely with a tent of aluminum foil; remove foil for last 10 to 15 minutes of roasting.

5. Transfer turkey to serving platter or carving board; reserve juices in pan for gravy, if you like. Let turkey stand for 15 minutes before thinly slicing. Garnish platter with lemon, sage and thyme.

Makes about 10 servings, 8 ounces each.

*Per serving: 468 calories, 67 g protein, 20 g fat, 1 g carbohydrate, 173 mg cholesterol, 422 mg sodium.*

*Note:* Thaw frozen turkey, still in its wrapping, on a tray in the refrigerator for 1 to 2 days. If you have dark-meat fans in your family, bake thighs and drumsticks in a separate pan for 1½ to 1¾ hours, basting occasionally with pan juices.

## ONION-AND-SHALLOT BROWN GRAVY

At last—a gravy you can make in advance to cut last-minute details. (Pictured, page 117.)

¼ cup olive oil
3 medium shallots, thinly sliced
2 medium onions, thinly sliced
1 large clove garlic, minced
3 tablespoons all-purpose flour
1 package or cube chicken-flavor instant bouillon
1 package or cube beef-flavor instant bouillon
¼ teaspoon black pepper
Pan juices reserved from turkey (optional)

1. Heat oil in large saucepan over medium heat. Add shallots, onions and garlic to pan; sauté for 10 to 12 minutes, or until vegetables are very soft and lightly browned, stirring frequently.

2. Add flour; reduce heat to low and cook for 2 minutes, stirring constantly. Stir in chicken and beef bouillon and 2 cups water. Cover; remove from heat and let stand for 1 minute.

3. Return saucepan to medium-high heat; stir gravy until well blended. Bring to a boil, stirring frequently. Reduce heat to medium-low and simmer for 10 minutes, or until thickened and bubbly, stirring occasionally. Stir in pepper.

4. For best flavor, add pan juices reserved from turkey to gravy: Strain juices through a fine sieve into a bowl. Let stand for a few minutes to allow fat to rise to the top; skim off fat with spoon or small ladle. Stir pan juices into gravy; simmer for 3 to 4 minutes, or until bubbly (see Note). Taste gravy and adjust seasonings if necessary.

*Above: This young lady can hardly wait for the Holiday Feast.*

*Make-ahead tip:* Make gravy up to 3 days ahead through step 3; cool, cover and refrigerate. Add pan juices (if using) just before serving; rewarm over medium-low heat, stirring frequently.

Makes about 3 cups.

*Per ¼-cup serving: 55 calories, 1 g protein, 5 g fat, 3 g carbohydrate, trace cholesterol, 203 mg sodium.*

*Note:* If gravy thins down too much after you've added pan juices, simmer a few minutes longer. Or thicken with a mixture of 1 tablespoon cornstarch and 2 tablespoons cold water; drizzle a little at a time into simmering gravy until of desired thickness, stirring constantly.

## OVEN-ROASTED SWEET POTATOES WITH MAPLE-PECAN BUTTER

These delicious, no-fuss potatoes bake right along with the turkey. (Pictured, page 117.)

½ cup (1 stick) unsalted butter, softened
¼ cup finely chopped pecans
2 tablespoons maple syrup
¼ teaspoon ground mace
8 small sweet potatoes

1. For maple-pecan butter: In small bowl, mix butter, pecans, maple syrup and mace until well combined. Spoon into serving container and cover (or roll into a log in a sheet of aluminum foil). Refrigerate or freeze until ready to serve with potatoes. If frozen, defrost butter in refrigerator the night before serving.

2. Scrub potatoes; place in large baking pan. Bake potatoes in 350°F oven (they can bake in same oven with turkey) for 1 hour to 1 hour and 15 minutes, or until they feel soft when squeezed. Cut potatoes in half for serving, if you like.

*Make-ahead tip:* Make Maple-Pecan Butter up to 1 month ahead, wrap tightly and freeze. Baked sweet potatoes will remain hot for 1 hour if you wrap each one loosely in a sheet of aluminum foil and return to hot baking pan (but not to oven). If they cool down, remove foil and rewarm potatoes in 350°F oven for 10 to 15 minutes.

Makes 8 servings.

*Per serving: 273 calories, 3 g protein, 14 g fat, 35 g carbohydrate, 31 mg cholesterol, 19 mg sodium.*

## RICH MASHED POTATOES

For those who think it's just not a feast without mashed potatoes—our luscious, creamy version. (Pictured, page 117.)

3 pounds baking potatoes, peeled and cut into chunks
1 can (14½ ounces) chicken broth
1 cup sour cream
½ cup milk
3 tablespoons butter or margarine, cut into small pieces
3 tablespoons snipped fresh chives (optional)
¾ teaspoon salt
½ to 1 teaspoon white pepper

1. Combine potatoes, broth and 2 cups water in large nonaluminum pot; cover and bring to a boil over high heat. Reduce heat to medium-low; simmer for 15 minutes, or until tender. Drain potatoes thoroughly.

2. Put potatoes through a ricer, letting riced potatoes fall into cooking pot, or return to cooking pot and mash with a potato masher. Add remaining ingredients; stir until thoroughly combined.

*Make-ahead tip:* Up to 2 days ahead, peel potatoes but don't cut into chunks. Place in large nonaluminum container with enough cold water to cover; keep refrigerated until ready to use. Drain, cut and cook as recipe directs. Prepare recipe up to 4 hours ahead: Spoon into large baking dish or heatproof serving dish; cool slightly, cover with aluminum foil and refrigerate. Reheat in 350°F oven for 30 minutes; stir well.

Makes 8 servings.

*Per serving: 256 calories, 5 g protein, 11 g fat, 35 g carbohydrate, 26 mg cholesterol, 495 mg sodium.*

## GREEN BEANS VINAIGRETTE

Here's a crisp make-ahead salad and a color-ful vegetable in one simple yet interesting dish! (Pictured, page 117.)

1½  pounds green and/or wax beans, trimmed
1  large red pepper, cut into thin strips
1  medium red onion, thinly sliced
⅓  cup olive oil
¼  cup red-wine vinegar
1  tablespoon Dijon mustard
¾  teaspoon salt
½  teaspoon black pepper

1. Bring large pot of lightly salted water to a boil over high heat. Add beans; stir, return to a boil and cook for 2 to 4 minutes, or until tender-crisp. Drain beans; immediately plunge into bowl of ice water to stop cooking and retain color. Drain again; then place in large serving bowl. Toss beans with red pepper and onion.

2. For vinaigrette, measure oil in 1-cup glass measure. Add remaining ingredients; whisk until well blended.

3. Pour vinaigrette over bean mixture; toss until well coated. Refrigerate for at least 3 hours. Just before serving, toss again. Adjust seasoning if necessary.

*Make-ahead tip:* Make vinaigrette up to 1 week ahead; cover and keep chilled. Whisk before using. Cook beans and slice red pepper and onion 1 day ahead; keep chilled in separate plastic bags. Recipe can be made up to 8 hours before serving; cover and refrigerate until serving.

Makes 8 servings.

*Per serving: 112 calories, 2 g protein, 9 g fat, 7 g carbohydrate, 0 mg cholesterol, 267 mg sodium.*

## CRANBERRY-RASPBERRY SAUCE

Three ingredients are all it takes to make this tangy condiment. (Pictured, page 117.)

1  package (12 ounces) cranberries
1  package (10 ounces) frozen raspberries in light syrup
½  cup sugar

In medium nonaluminum saucepan, com-bine cranberries, raspberries, sugar and ¼ cup water. Over high heat, bring mixture to a boil, stirring occasionally. Reduce heat to medium-low; simmer for 10 to 12 minutes, or just until cranberries pop, stirring occasion-ally. Cool completely; cover and refrigerate for at least 4 hours before serving.

*Make-ahead tip:* Make sauce up to 1 month ahead; cool, transfer to self-sealing freezer bag and freeze flat. Thaw frozen sauce in refrigerator the night before serving. Or make sauce up to 5 days ahead, cover and refrigerate until serving.

Makes about 2¾ cups.

*Per ¼-cup serving: 77 calories, trace protein, trace fat, 20 g carbohydrate, 0 mg cholesterol, 1 mg sodium.*

## CORN BREAD STUFFIN' MUFFINS

If you like, prepare and freeze the batter in advance. Then just pop into the oven on feast day. (Pictured, below left.)

6  tablespoons (¾ stick) butter or margarine
4  medium stalks celery, finely chopped, with some leaves
1  large onion, chopped
1  teaspoon salt
1  teaspoon dried sage
1  teaspoon dried thyme
½  teaspoon cracked black pepper
1½  cups all-purpose flour
½  cup yellow cornmeal
1  tablespoon baking powder
½  teaspoon baking soda
1½  cups sour cream
¼  cup milk
3  eggs, beaten

1. Melt butter in medium skillet over medium heat. Add celery and onion; sauté for 10 to 12 minutes, or until almost tender, stirring occasionally. Add salt, sage, thyme and pepper; cook for 30 seconds. Transfer to large bowl; cool to room temperature.

2. Preheat oven to 375°F. Lightly grease a 12-cup muffin pan or line with paper liners.

3. In medium bowl, mix flour, cornmeal, baking powder and baking soda until thoroughly combined.

4. Add sour cream, milk and eggs to celery mixture; stir until well blended. Add flour mixture; stir just until combined.

5. Spoon batter into prepared muffin cups, filling each to the top. Bake for 40 to 45 minutes, or until muffins are browned and firm to the touch. Remove muffins from pan; cool slightly on wire rack.

*Make-ahead tip:* Up to 5 days ahead, make batter and spoon into paper liners in muffin pan. Freeze unbaked batter until solid; then transfer filled liners to plastic bag and place in freezer. To bake, return batter-filled liners to muffin pan and bake at 375°F. Frozen batter takes a few minutes longer to bake.

Makes 12 muffins.

*Per muffin: 220 calories, 5 g protein, 13 g fat, 20 g carbohydrate, 82 mg cholesterol, 430 mg sodium.*

### MUFFIN-MAKING TIPS

Homemade muffins are a welcome treat on any table. Add them to your next menu. As you select your recipe and prepare the muffins, keep these hints in mind:

● Mix dry ingredients thoroughly to evenly disperse the baking powder or baking soda.

● When combining dry ingredients and liquid ones, beat batter only until it's moistened.

● If you don't have enough batter to fill all the muffin cups, fill empty ones with a little water. This creates steam for moist muffins and also keeps the pan from warping.

● Muffin pans come in all sizes—from giant to miniature. If you'd like to adapt a muffin recipe, reduce the baking time for smaller ones and increase it for larger. Tiny savory muffins make great party appetizers.

● Muffins freeze beautifully when cooled and sealed in airtight freezer bags. Rewarm frozen muffins, wrapped in aluminum foil, in a 350°F oven for about 15 minutes. Remember that you can also freeze unbaked batter right in the pan—just be sure to allow a few extra minutes cooking time.

*Left: Corn Bread Stuffin' Muffins (this page).*

## STREUSEL PUMPKIN PIE

Here's an all-time favorite with a crumbly, crunchy topping. (Pictured, right.)

**Filling:**
¾ cup packed dark-brown sugar
3 eggs
1 can (16 ounces) solid pack pumpkin
1 cup evaporated milk
1½ teaspoons ground cinnamon
1¼ teaspoons grated nutmeg
½ teaspoon ground ginger
¼ teaspoon salt
⅛ teaspoon ground cloves
9-inch unbaked pie shell

**Streusel topping:**
½ cup all-purpose flour
⅓ cup packed dark-brown sugar
3 tablespoons cold unsalted butter or
   margarine, cut into small pieces
1 teaspoon ground cinnamon
Confectioners' sugar (optional)

1. Preheat oven to 425°F. Prepare filling: In large bowl, with whisk or electric mixer, beat brown sugar and eggs until smooth. Add next 7 ingredients; beat until well combined. Pour filling into pie shell; bake for 15 minutes. (If crust starts getting too brown, shield with thin strips of aluminum foil.)

2. Meanwhile, prepare streusel topping: Combine ingredients except confectioners' sugar; mix with fingers until crumbs form.

3. After pie has baked for 15 minutes, sprinkle with topping. Reduce oven temperature to 300°F; bake for 30 to 40 minutes longer, or until pie feels firm and looks set when gently shaken and a knife inserted just off center comes out clean. Cool slightly on wire rack. Sprinkle with confectioners' sugar

(if using). Pie is best when served slightly warm; cover and refrigerate any leftovers.

*Make-ahead tip:* Use a frozen prepared 9-inch pie shell, or make a piecrust using a recipe or a packaged mix. Fit dough into pie plate; wrap in plastic bag and freeze for up to 3 weeks. If using a metal pie plate, there's no need to thaw crust before filling and baking. If using a glass pie plate, let it stand at room temperature for 15 minutes to prevent the icy-cold plate from cracking in a hot oven.

Up to 3 weeks ahead, make streusel, put in a plastic bag and freeze. Make filling up to 1 day ahead; cover and refrigerate. Stir filling before pouring into pie shell. Sprinkle streusel topping, still frozen, over partially baked filling.

Makes 8 servings.

*Per serving: 383 calories, 7 g protein, 16 g fat, 53 g carbohydrate, 100 mg cholesterol, 275 mg sodium.*

## BOURBON PECAN PIE

This Southern specialty couldn't be easier to make—just mix all ingredients in one bowl. (Pictured, right.)

¾ cup sugar
2 tablespoons all-purpose flour
¼ teaspoon salt
¾ cup dark corn syrup
⅓ cup whipping cream
1 tablespoon plus 1 teaspoon bourbon
   (or use 1 teaspoon vanilla extract)
2 eggs
1½ cups pecan halves
8- or 9-inch unbaked pie shell

1. Preheat oven to 375°F. In large bowl, mix sugar, flour and salt. Add corn syrup, cream, bourbon and eggs; with whisk or electric mixer on low speed, beat until smooth. Stir in pecans; pour filling into pie shell.

2. Bake for 45 to 50 minutes, or until pie feels almost firm, looks set when gently shaken and has puffed slightly. Cool completely on wire rack before serving. If desired, serve with Bourbon Whipped Cream (recipe follows).

*Make-ahead tip:* Make and freeze piecrust up to 3 weeks ahead (see make-ahead tip for Streusel Pumpkin Pie, left). Mix filling ingredients, except for pecans, up to 3 days ahead; cover and refrigerate. Stir filling well before adding pecans; pie may take a few minutes longer to bake.

Makes 8 servings.

*Per serving: 463 calories, 5 g protein, 26 g fat, 57 g carbohydrate, 64 mg cholesterol, 246 mg sodium.*

## BOURBON WHIPPED CREAM

Top a slice of Bourbon Pecan Pie with a dollop of this quick-fix whipped cream—great with other pies, too. (Pictured, below).

1 **cup whipping cream**
1 **tablespoon dark-brown sugar**
1 **teaspoon bourbon**

In large bowl, with electric mixer on medium speed, whip cream until it begins to thicken. Add brown sugar and bourbon; continue whipping until soft peaks form. Cover and refrigerate until ready to use. Spoon into serving dish; sift a little more brown sugar on top, if you like.

*Make-ahead tip:* Make whipped cream up to 3 hours ahead. If necessary, rewhip briefly just before serving.

Makes about 2½ cups.

*Per ¼-cup serving: 76 calories, 1 g protein, 7 g fat, 2 g carbohydrate, 27 mg cholesterol, 9 mg sodium.*

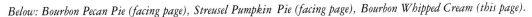

*Below: Bourbon Pecan Pie (facing page), Streusel Pumpkin Pie (facing page), Bourbon Whipped Cream (this page).*

# Dessert Buffet

## MENU
*Bourbon Pound Cake*

~~~~~

*Nutty Chocolate Tassies*

~~~~~

*Raspberry-Coconut Cookies*

~~~~~

*Lemon-Lime Tart*

~~~~~

*Brie and grapes*

~~~~~

*Champagne and liqueurs*

~~~~~

*Coffee*

### BOURBON POUND CAKE

You can freeze this a month ahead. Thaw the day before serving. (Pictured, right.)

Streusel topping:
⅓ cup all-purpose flour
⅓ cup packed brown sugar
3 tablespoons butter or margarine

Cake batter:
3 cups all-purpose flour
1½ teaspoons baking powder
½ teaspoon grated nutmeg
1½ teaspoons baking soda
1½ cups sour cream
¼ cup bourbon
1½ cups granulated sugar
¾ cup (1½ sticks) butter or margarine, softened
3 eggs

1. Preheat oven to 350°F. Grease 9- or 10-inch tube pan.

2. For streusel topping: In medium bowl, combine all ingredients; crumble with fingers until coarse crumbs form.

3. For cake batter: Sift together flour, baking powder and nutmeg; set aside. In small bowl, dissolve baking soda in 1½ teaspoons water; stir in sour cream and bourbon. In large bowl, with electric mixer on medium speed, cream granulated sugar with butter until light and fluffy. Add eggs one at a time, beating well after each addition and scraping sides of bowl occasionally with rubber spatula. Add sour-cream mixture; beat until just combined. Gently fold in flour mixture.

4. Pour batter in prepared pan; sprinkle with streusel topping. Bake for 45 to 50

*Above: (Clockwise from top) Brie and grapes, Lemon-Lime Tart (page 129), Raspberry-Coconut Cookies (page 126), Bourbon Pound Cake (facing page), Nutty Chocolate Tassies (page 126). The platter of Brie and grapes doubles as the centerpiece.*

*Right: Bourbon Pound Cake (facing page).*

minutes, or until knife inserted just off center of cake comes out clean. Cool cake in pan on wire rack for 10 minutes; remove from pan. Cool completely before serving.

Makes 16 servings.

*Per serving: 341 calories, 5 g protein, 17 g fat, 44 g carbohydrate, 90 mg cholesterol, 253 mg sodium.*

## NUTTY CHOCOLATE TASSIES

These wonderful tartlets can be baked and frozen for a month or two (without garnish). Thaw a day in advance—add whipped cream and candied violets shortly before serving. (Pictured, right.)

2  (9-inch) refrigerated piecrusts
½  cup (1 stick) butter or margarine
3  squares (1-ounce size) unsweetened chocolate
1⅓  cups sugar
3  tablespoons light corn syrup
1  teaspoon vanilla extract
4  eggs
¾  cup pecan pieces
Whipped cream and candied violets (optional garnish)

1. On lightly floured surface, roll piecrusts, one at a time, to about ⅛-inch thickness. With 4-inch round cookie cutter, cut out circles. Repeat with remaining piecrust; gather trimmings, reroll and cut out (makes about 20 circles). Press piecrust circles into 3-by-1-inch tartlet pans (see Note). Refrigerate while preparing filling.

2. Preheat oven to 350°F. In small, heavy saucepan over low heat, melt butter and chocolate, stirring frequently. Remove from heat; let cool slightly.

3. In large bowl, combine sugar, corn syrup, vanilla and eggs; beat until well combined. Add butter-chocolate mixture; beat until smooth. Stir in pecans.

4. Place tartlet pans in a jelly-roll pan for easier handling. Pour chocolate filling into shells; bake for 15 to 20 minutes, or until filling is crusty on top (inside will be moist) and pastry is lightly browned. Let cool slightly before removing from pans. When

ready to serve, garnish cooled tartlets with some whipped cream and candied violets.

Makes about 20 tartlets.

*Per tartlet: 262 calories, 3 g protein, 17 g fat, 27 g carbohydrate, 67 mg cholesterol, 187 mg sodium.*

*Note:* You can use slightly larger or smaller tartlet pans, but cooking time and yield will be different. To make a pie, press 9-inch refrigerated piecrust into 9-inch pie plate. Pour filling into crust and bake for about 30 minutes.

## RASPBERRY-COCONUT COOKIES

Baked cookies will freeze splendidly a month or more. Thaw at room temperature the day before the party. (Pictured, right.)

Crust:
1  cup all-purpose flour
½  cup (1 stick) unsalted butter
1  teaspoon baking powder
1  egg, beaten

Topping:
¼  cup raspberry preserves
⅔  cup sugar
¼  cup (½ stick) unsalted butter
1  teaspoon vanilla extract
1  egg, beaten
1  package (7 ounces) shredded coconut

1. Preheat oven to 350°F. Grease 8-inch square baking pan.

2. For crust: In food processor fitted with steel blade or with pastry blender, process or combine flour, butter and baking powder until mixture resembles coarse meal. Add egg; process just until mixture begins to form a ball (7 to 8 pulses with food processor). Press onto bottom of pan.

*Above: Nutty Chocolate Tassies (facing page), Raspberry-Coconut Cookies on platter (facing page).*

3. For topping: Spread preserves on crust to within ½ inch of edge of pan. (Preserves will melt and spread slightly while baking.) In food processor fitted with steel blade or by hand, process sugar, butter and vanilla until well combined. Add egg; process until creamy. Stir in coconut (3 to 4 pulses with food processor). Spread mixture over preserves. Bake for 30 to 35 minutes, or until browned. Cool completely before cutting.

Makes about 24 cookies.

*Per cookie: 147 calories, 1 g protein, 9 g fat, 16 g carbohydrate, 39 mg cholesterol, 47 mg sodium.*

*Right: Fruit-flavored liqueurs like Chambord and Cassis add a splash of color to champagne's sparkle.*

## LEMON-LIME TART

Bake the buttery cornmeal crust a day ahead for this delectable tart. (Pictured, left.)

**Pastry:**
1 cup all-purpose flour
3 tablespoons yellow cornmeal
2 tablespoons sugar
½ cup (1 stick) cold butter or margarine, cut into small pieces
1 egg yolk
1 tablespoon lemon juice

**Filling:**
1 cup sugar
¼ cup lime juice
2 tablespoons lemon juice
1 package unflavored gelatin
3 eggs, separated
¼ cup orange-flavor liqueur or orange juice
1 teaspoon grated lemon peel
1 teaspoon grated lime peel
½ cup whipping cream
Lemon and lime peel (optional garnish)

1. For pastry: In food processor fitted with steel blade, combine flour, cornmeal and sugar; pulse 2 to 3 times until mixed. Add butter; process about 30 seconds, or until butter is incorporated into flour mixture. (You should not see any butter pieces.) In small bowl, mix egg yolk and lemon juice. With food processor running, gradually add egg mixture; process just until mixture begins to form a ball. (Or combine flour, cornmeal and sugar in mixing bowl. With pastry blender, cut in butter until mixture resembles fine crumbs. Gradually add egg mixture.) Wrap dough in plastic wrap; refrigerate for at least 30 minutes.

2. Preheat oven to 400°F. Evenly press dough into an 18-by-11-inch rectangular or 10-inch round tart pan with removable bottom. (If working in a warm kitchen, chill crust for 5 minutes before baking.) Place pan on baking sheet; bake for 15 minutes, or until crisp and lightly browned. Cool completely on wire rack.

3. For filling: In medium nonaluminum saucepan, combine sugar, lime juice, lemon juice, gelatin and ¼ cup water; set aside. In small bowl, with electric mixer on medium speed, beat egg yolks until pale and fluffy; add to sugar mixture. Over low heat, cook until sugar and gelatin dissolve, stirring constantly. (Do not boil.) Remove from heat; stir in liqueur, grated lemon and lime peel.

4. Transfer lemon-lime filling to a bowl set over ice; stir until mixture begins to cool and set. Filling should mound slightly when dropped from spoon. Remove from ice bath. Beat egg whites until stiff peaks form; whip cream. Fold egg whites and cream into filling. (If filling doesn't mound at this point, chill slightly.) Spoon lemon-lime filling into tart shell and chill for 1 hour, or until set. Garnish with lemon and lime peel.

Makes 10 servings.

*Per serving: 310 calories, 5 g protein, 15 g fat, 37 g carbohydrate, 148 mg cholesterol, 121 mg sodium.*

♦ When grating citrus peel, grate only the colored part because the white pith is bitter.

*Left: Lemon-Lime Tart (this page).*

# No-Fuss Entertaining: Appetizers

## CREAMY GORGONZOLA DIP

This zesty dip takes five minutes to make but will last several days in the refrigerator. (Pictured, right.)

3  ounces Gorgonzola or other blue cheese
¼  cup milk
1  tablespoon finely chopped scallions
⅓  cup plain yogurt or sour cream
½  teaspoon grated lemon peel
⅛  teaspoon black pepper
Assortment of sliced fresh fruit or
    vegetables

Crumble cheese into small bowl; add milk. With fork, mash mixture until well combined. Reserve a few chopped scallions for garnish; stir remaining scallions into cheese mixture. Add yogurt, lemon peel and pepper. Spoon into serving dish; garnish with reserved scallions. Cover and refrigerate until ready to serve. Arrange fruit or vegetables on a platter and serve with dip.

Makes 1 cup.

*Per tablespoon: 24 calories, 1 g protein, 2 g fat, 1 g carbohydrate, 5 mg cholesterol, 79 mg sodium.*

*Right: (Clockwise from top left) Peppery Cheese Twists (facing page), Creamy Gorgonzola Dip with assorted fruits (this page), Turkey Mini-Muffins (this page).*

## TURKEY MINI-MUFFINS

Here's a bite-size turkey dinner—no need for a knife and fork! (Pictured, below.)

1  package (12 ounces) corn bread or corn muffin mix
¾  cup sour cream
2  teaspoons minced fresh rosemary, or ½ teaspoon dried rosemary, crushed
1  egg, beaten
5  thin slices smoked turkey (4 ounces)
About 3 tablespoons whole-berry cranberry sauce

1. Preheat oven to 400°F. Grease a 20-cup mini-muffin pan (1¾-inch-diameter cups).

2. In medium bowl, stir together corn bread mix, sour cream, rosemary and egg just until combined. Spoon batter into prepared muffin cups. Bake for 15 minutes, or until muffins are golden brown. Cool slightly in pan before turning muffins out onto wire rack to cool completely.

3. To serve, split each muffin; cut each turkey slice into quarters. Fold turkey slices to fit on bottom halves of muffins; top turkey with some cranberry sauce and remaining muffin halves.

Makes about 20 muffins.

*Per muffin: 106 calories, 3 g protein, 4 g fat, 14 g carbohydrate, 32 mg cholesterol, 260 mg sodium.*

## PEPPERY CHEESE TWISTS

Impressive and easy! (Pictured, left.)

1 **sheet frozen puff pastry, thawed**
1 **egg white, beaten**
⅓ **cup grated Parmesan cheese**
1½ **teaspoons cracked black pepper**

Preheat oven to 375°F. On lightly floured surface, roll pastry into 14-by-11-inch rectangle. Brush with egg white. Sprinkle with cheese and pepper; gently press into pastry. Cut crosswise into ¾-inch-wide strips; shape into twists. Place on baking sheet; press down ends. Bake for 15 minutes, or until crisp and browned.

Makes about 18 twists.

*Per twist: 66 calories, 1 g protein, 4 g fat, 5 g carbohydrate, 1 mg cholesterol, 95 mg sodium.*

### QUICK-FIX APPETIZERS

● Marinate olives for 30 minutes in a mixture of olive oil, lemon slices, garlic and a sprinkling of fennel seeds, rosemary or thyme.
● Cut slices of cocktail pumpernickel bread into triangles; spread with dill butter (fresh or dried dill, butter and a little lemon juice); top with smoked turkey and a sprig of dill.
● Spread whipped cream cheese on gingersnaps or wheat biscuits (or pipe cheese with a decorating bag); dab on red or green hot-pepper jelly and garnish with a little hot pepper.

## SANTA FE SALSA WITH CUMIN-SPICED CHIPS

These homemade chips are lower in fat and salt than the commercial fried variety.

### Salsa:
1 pound plum tomatoes, diced, or 1 can (28 ounces) tomatoes, drained and diced
1 large red pepper, diced
1 to 2 teaspoons seeded and minced fresh or pickled jalapeño pepper
½ small red onion, finely chopped
¼ cup coarsely chopped fresh cilantro or Italian parsley
2 tablespoons olive oil
1 tablespoon red-wine vinegar
¾ teaspoon salt
½ teaspoon ground cumin
¼ teaspoon black pepper

### Chips:
¼ cup olive oil
1 teaspoon ground cumin
⅛ teaspoon cayenne pepper
12 corn tortillas
1 teaspoon coarse (kosher) salt

1. For salsa: In large bowl, mix all ingredients. Cover and refrigerate up to 2 days.

2. For chips: Preheat oven to 350°F. In a glass measure, mix oil, cumin and cayenne; brush over both sides of each tortilla. Make two tortilla stacks; cut each stack into eighths. Arrange chips in a single layer on several baking sheets; sprinkle with salt. Bake chips for 10 minutes, or until crisp.

Makes about 12 servings.

*Per serving: 138 calories, 3 g protein, 8 g fat, 15 g carbohydrate, 0 mg cholesterol, 317 mg sodium.*

## CHEDDAR-PEPPER SPREAD

Use your food processor to make this hearty hors d'oeuvre in a flash.

1 pound cheddar cheese, cut into 1-inch pieces, at room temperature
½ cup sour cream
2 large red peppers, roasted and diced, or 1 jar (7 ounces) roasted red peppers, drained and diced (see Hot Peppers box, below)
2 teaspoons paprika
1 teaspoon dried thyme
1 teaspoon caraway seeds, crushed
¼ to ½ teaspoon cayenne pepper

In food processor fitted with steel blade or in blender, process cheese and sour cream until smooth; transfer to large bowl. Stir in remaining ingredients until well combined. Spoon into serving dish; store in refrigerator. Bring to room temperature before serving.

Makes about 3 cups.

*Per tablespoon: 44 calories, 2 g protein, 4 g fat, 0 g carbohydrate, 11 mg cholesterol, 60 mg sodium.*

### HOT PEPPERS

● Hot peppers such as jalapeño and serrano add a flavor punch to a variety of dishes. But these peppers—fresh or dried—contain oils that can irritate sensitive skin. When working with them, it's best to wear rubber kitchen gloves. Remember not to touch your face and to wash the work surface thoroughly after chopping.

● To roast peppers, preheat broiler. Place whole peppers on broiling pan about 6 inches from heat source and broil until blackened on all sides, using tongs to turn. Put peppers in brown paper bag and close tightly; let rest for 10 minutes. Remove peppers from bag; peel off skin. Cut peppers in half and remove stems and seeds.

# Entrées

*Above: (Clockwise from top) Steaks with Roasted Red-Pepper Sauce (this page), Fettuccine with Shrimp and Artichokes (page 136), Herb-and-Cheese Stuffed Chicken Breasts (page 136), Turkey-and-Stuffing Potpie (page 135).*

## STEAKS WITH ROASTED RED-PEPPER SAUCE

This Italian-style sauce is full of flavor! It takes less than 10 minutes to make and is wonderful with broiled chicken or seafood as well as steaks. (Pictured, right.)

1   tablespoon olive oil
2   large cloves garlic, minced
1   jar (7 ounces) roasted red peppers, drained and finely chopped
¼   cup chopped parsley
2   tablespoons dry white wine or water
½   teaspoon dried oregano
⅛   teaspoon cayenne pepper (optional)
4   beef shell or rib-eye steaks, trimmed (about 6 ounces each)
½   teaspoon coarsely ground black pepper

1.  Preheat broiler. Heat oil in small skillet over medium heat. Add garlic; sauté for 1 minute. Add red peppers, parsley, wine, oregano and cayenne (if using). Reduce heat to low; simmer for 5 minutes.

2.  Sprinkle steaks with black pepper; place on broiling rack 4 to 5 inches from heat source. Broil for 6 to 8 minutes for rare, or until of desired doneness, turning once. Spoon some sauce on top of each steak.

Makes 4 servings.

*Per serving: 411 calories, 32 g protein, 29 g fat, 4 g carbohydrate, 102 mg cholesterol, 93 mg sodium.*

## QUICK-FIX DISHES

● Toss just-cooked pasta with chunks of Brie cheese, sliced roasted red pepper, black pepper and parsley.

● For easy chicken cacciatore, brown chicken pieces and place in a casserole; top with a jar of mushroom-marinara sauce and bake for about an hour in a 350°F oven.

● Here's another quick pasta dish: Heat some heavy cream until reduced by half. Toss with cooked pasta, thinly sliced smoked salmon, scallions and cracked black pepper. For extra flair, top with salmon caviar.

## CHUTNEY-GLAZED LEG OF LAMB

Boning and butterflying this leg of lamb cuts cooking time from two and a half hours to 20 minutes! Have your butcher bone and butterfly the lamb for you.

¼ cup orange juice
¼ cup chopped fresh mint, or 1 tablespoon dried mint
2 tablespoons lemon juice
2 tablespoons salad oil
2 large cloves garlic, minced
1 jar (8 ounces) mango chutney, finely chopped
1 leg of lamb (about 6 pounds), boned, trimmed and butterflied

1. For marinade: In wide, shallow glass or ceramic dish, combine all ingredients except lamb. Add lamb; turn to coat with marinade. Cover and marinate lamb in refrigerator for at least 2 hours, or overnight. (If short on time, skip the marinating—you can use the chutney marinade as a glaze to brush on lamb as it broils.)

2. Preheat broiler. Place lamb on broiling rack, 4 to 5 inches from heat source. Broil lamb for 20 minutes for rare, or until of desired doneness, turning once and basting lamb occasionally with marinade remaining in glass dish.

3. Let lamb stand for 10 minutes before thinly slicing. Skim and discard fat from juices in broiling pan. Bring pan juices to a boil; pour over lamb slices. Serve with extra chutney on the side, if you like.

Makes 8 to 10 servings.

*Per serving: 414 calories, 51 g protein, 16 g fat, 14 g carbohydrate, 178 mg cholesterol, 169 mg sodium.*

## QUICK APRICOT PORK WITH MUSTARD SAUCE

Couscous or nutty wild rice is a perfect accompaniment to this tangy dish.

1½ cups apple cider or juice
½ cup dried apricots, halved
3 tablespoons dried currants or raisins
1 teaspoon grated lemon peel
1 pork tenderloin (about 1 pound)
2 tablespoons salad oil
3 large shallots, finely chopped
2 medium cloves garlic, finely chopped
3 tablespoons Dijon mustard
1 can (10½ ounces) low-sodium chicken broth
½ teaspoon dried rosemary, crushed

1. In medium bowl, stir together apple cider, apricots, currants and lemon peel until well combined; set aside.

2. Slice pork crosswise into ¼-inch-thick slices. (Meat is easier to slice if chilled in the freezer for 15 minutes.) Heat oil in large skillet over medium-high heat. Add pork in batches; sauté until lightly browned and cooked through. Remove to a platter; cover and keep warm.

3. To drippings in skillet, add shallots and garlic. Reduce heat to low; cook for 5 minutes, or until softened, stirring occasionally. Add mustard, broth and rosemary; cook for 5 minutes, or until liquid is reduced by half. Add dried-fruit mixture; simmer for 5 minutes, or until sauce is slightly thickened. Return pork to skillet; heat through.

Makes 4 servings.

*Per serving: 325 calories, 26 g protein, 11 g fat, 31 g carbohydrate, 74 mg cholesterol, 418 mg sodium.*

## TURKEY-AND-STUFFING POTPIE

This potpie is a great way to use leftover roast turkey! (Pictured, page 133.)

4 tablespoons (½ stick) butter or margarine
2 medium carrots, thinly sliced
1 medium onion, chopped
1 package (12 ounces) mushrooms, quartered
½ teaspoon dried marjoram
½ teaspoon dried sage
½ teaspoon dried thyme
¼ teaspoon salt
¼ teaspoon black pepper
¼ cup all-purpose flour
2 cans (10½-ounce size) low-sodium chicken broth
½ cup whipping cream
1½ pounds cooked turkey, cut into ¾-inch pieces
1 cup frozen green peas
1 package (12 ounces) corn bread mix or corn muffin mix
¼ cup chopped parsley

1. Preheat oven to 350°F. Grease a 3-quart or 13-by-9-inch baking dish.

2. Melt 2 tablespoons of the butter in large saucepan over medium heat. Add carrots and onion; sauté for 5 minutes. Increase heat to medium-high. Add mushrooms, marjoram, sage, thyme, salt and pepper; sauté for 5 minutes, stirring occasionally. With slotted spoon, remove vegetable mixture to prepared baking dish.

3. Melt remaining 2 tablespoons butter in same saucepan over medium heat. Add flour and cook for 1 minute, stirring constantly. Stir in broth and cream. Cook until cream sauce is thickened and reduced to about 2 cups, stirring constantly. Add cream sauce, turkey and peas to vegetables; set aside.

4. Prepare corn bread mix according to package directions; stir in parsley. Spoon batter in an even layer over turkey mixture. Bake for 40 to 50 minutes, or until topping is firm and golden and sauce is bubbling.

Makes 6 to 8 servings.

*Per serving: 577 calories, 38 g protein, 25 g fat, 48 g carbohydrate, 181 mg cholesterol, 859 mg sodium.*

### KITCHEN TRICKS

Here are some handy staples that turn meats, poultry, fish and veggies into super meals!

● Semisoft garlic herbed cheese is great dabbed on broiled chicken or fish—it will melt into a creamy sauce.

● Bottled Italian dressing makes an instant marinade for poultry or steak.

● Dried mushrooms, once reconstituted, can be tossed into meat loaves, burgers, stir-fries and sauces for meats and poultry.

● Pecans, cashews, walnuts and macadamias add crunch and taste to salads and stir-fries. Try dipping fish, meat or poultry in beaten egg, then into ground nuts before sautéing.

● Balsamic vinegar is delicious in meat and vegetable marinades or splashed on salads.

● Sun-dried tomatoes in oil are nice on burgers and grilled sandwiches, or stuffed into baked potatoes with cheddar and bacon.

● Canned mild chilies add zip to omelets, stews or cheese sauces for veggies.

● Chutney makes a simple glaze for grilled chicken or lamb. Mix with a little mustard, if you like, and brush on the meat as it cooks.

● Prepared salsa is a zesty, low-fat flavor accent—try on baked potatoes, broiled fish and lean grilled meats as well as all your favorite Mexican dishes.

## HERB-AND-CHEESE-STUFFED CHICKEN BREASTS

These oven-roasted chicken breasts are stuffed with Boursin, a soft white cheese flavored with garlic, herbs or pepper. (Pictured, page 133.)

1 package (5 ounces) Boursin cheese
2 tablespoons minced parsley
½ teaspoon cracked black pepper
¾ teaspoon dried thyme
6 boneless chicken-breast halves with skin
¼ cup (½ stick) butter or margarine, melted
2 tablespoons dry white wine

1. Preheat oven to 425°F. In medium bowl, combine cheese, parsley, pepper and ½ teaspoon of the thyme.
2. Partially loosen chicken skin (without completely detaching) on each chicken breast by carefully working your hand between meat and skin. Spread some cheese mixture evenly under the skin of each breast. Place chicken in roasting pan.
3. Combine butter, wine and remaining ¼ teaspoon thyme. Brush chicken with some of the butter mixture. Bake for 40 minutes, or until chicken is cooked through, basting occasionally with butter mixture. Skim excess fat from pan juices; discard. Serve chicken with pan juices.
Makes 6 servings.

*Per serving: 471 calories, 51 g protein, 28 g fat, 1 g carbohydrate, 171 mg cholesterol, 427 mg sodium.*

## FETTUCCINE WITH SHRIMP AND ARTICHOKES

Leftovers—if there are any—make a wonderful cold pasta salad. The robust sauce is ready in the time it takes to cook the pasta. (Pictured, page 133.)

1½ pounds large shrimp
12 ounces fettuccine or spaghetti
3 tablespoons olive oil
2 large cloves garlic, minced
1 can (14½ to 16 ounces) tomatoes
¼ cup chopped parsley
2 jars (6-ounce size) marinated artichoke hearts, drained
2 ounces feta cheese, crumbled

1. Shell and devein shrimp. Cook fettuccine according to package directions.
2. Meanwhile, heat oil in large skillet over medium-high heat. Add garlic; sauté for about 30 seconds. Add shrimp; sauté until shrimp turn pink and are just cooked through. With slotted spoon, remove shrimp to a platter.
3. To drippings in skillet, add tomatoes, breaking them up with a spoon; add 3 tablespoons of the parsley. Reduce heat to medium; simmer for 5 minutes, or until tomato mixture is slightly thickened, stirring occasionally. Add artichoke hearts; simmer mixture for 5 minutes. Return shrimp to skillet; heat through.
4. Drain pasta; place on a large serving platter. Spoon shrimp sauce on top of pasta; sprinkle with cheese and remaining 1 tablespoon chopped parsley.
Makes 6 servings.

*Per serving: 458 calories, 29 g protein, 16 g fat, 50 g carbohydrate, 202 mg cholesterol, 426 mg sodium.*

# Side Dishes

## SPICED SWEET-POTATO MUFFINS

For an appetizer, stuff miniature muffins with ham and chutney. Or bake regular-size muffins (they take a few minutes longer) for a dinner accompaniment. If desired, make muffins; then wrap tightly and freeze up to two months. (Pictured, right.)

1¾  cups all-purpose flour
1  teaspoon baking powder
½  teaspoon salt
¼  teaspoon baking soda
¼  teaspoon ground cinnamon
¼  teaspoon black pepper
½  cup (1 stick) butter or margarine, melted and cooled slightly
¼  cup packed light-brown sugar
2  eggs
1¼  cups cooked, cooled, mashed sweet potatoes (about 1 pound potatoes)
½  cup finely chopped mango chutney
6  ounces thinly sliced cooked ham
Kale leaves (optional garnish)

1. Preheat oven to 350°F. Grease 36 miniature muffin-pan cups (see Note).

2. In large bowl, mix first 6 ingredients until thoroughly combined.

3. In medium bowl, whisk butter, brown sugar and eggs. Add sweet potatoes; whisk until smooth. Add to flour mixture; stir just until combined. Spoon batter into prepared muffin cups. Bake muffins for 20 to 25 minutes, or until lightly browned. Remove from pans; cool completely on wire racks.

*Above: (Clockwise from top) Vegetable Slaw with Basil Dressing (page 143), Spiced Sweet-Potato Muffins (this page), Wild Rice and Sausage Stuffing (page 140).*

4. To serve, split muffins; spread each half with a little chutney. Sandwich ham between muffin halves. Serve muffins on kale leaves.

Makes about 36 muffins.

*Per muffin: 82 calories, 2 g protein, 3 g fat, 11 g carbohydrate, 21 mg cholesterol, 158 mg sodium.*

*Note:* If you bake muffins in batches, be sure to cool pan completely before filling with more batter.

*(Clockwise from top left) Cheddar-Pepper Quick Bread (facing page), Mustard-Chive Butter (facing page), Fresh Green Bean Casserole (page 142), Scalloped Potatoes with Mushrooms (page 141), Oranges with Chunky Cranberry Sauce (this page).*

## ORANGES WITH CHUNKY CRANBERRY SAUCE

Make the sauce for this dish in advance. Reserve some orange slices to serve plain if your kids don't like cranberries. (Pictured, above.)

1 package (12 ounces) cranberries
1 cup orange juice
½ cup granulated sugar
½ cup packed light-brown sugar
6 large navel oranges
Fresh pineapple mint or regular mint
   (optional garnish)

1. In medium, heavy nonaluminum saucepan, combine first 4 ingredients. Over high heat, bring to a boil, stirring occasionally. Reduce heat to low; simmer for 5 minutes, or just until cranberries pop, stirring occasionally. Cool completely; cover and refrigerate for at least 2 hours, or up to 1 week.

2. With serrated knife, peel oranges, removing white membrane. Slice oranges crosswise into thin rounds.

3. To serve, layer cranberry sauce and orange slices in large serving dish. Garnish with mint.

Makes about 12 servings.

*Per serving: 129 calories, 1 g protein, trace fat, 33 g carbohydrate, 0 mg cholesterol, 4 mg sodium.*

## CHEDDAR-PEPPER QUICK BREAD

You can bake and then freeze these flavorful loaves, tightly wrapped, up to two months ahead. Thaw and reheat or serve at room temperature. (Pictured, left.)

5  cups all-purpose flour
2  tablespoons sugar
2  teaspoons baking powder
1½ teaspoons salt
1½ teaspoons coarsely ground black
    pepper
1  teaspoon baking soda
2½ cups (10 ounces) shredded extra-sharp
    cheddar cheese
4  eggs
4  scallions, thinly sliced
2  cups plain low-fat yogurt
⅔  cup olive oil
2  tablespoons Dijon mustard

1. Preheat oven to 350°F. Grease two 9-by-5-inch loaf pans.

2. In large bowl, mix first 6 ingredients until thoroughly combined. Stir in 2 cups of the cheese.

3. In medium bowl, whisk eggs, scallions, yogurt, oil and mustard. Add egg mixture to flour mixture; stir just until combined (batter will be very stiff). Divide batter between prepared pans; spread evenly and smooth tops.

4. Bake for 40 to 45 minutes, or until browned and toothpick inserted in center of loaves comes out clean. Remove pans to wire rack; sprinkle loaves with remaining ½ cup cheese. Cool loaves in pans on rack.

Makes 2 loaves; each about 16 servings.

*Per serving: 170 calories, 6 g protein, 9 g fat, 17 g carbohydrate, 37 mg cholesterol, 257 mg sodium.*

## MUSTARD-CHIVE BUTTER

Serve this seasoned butter slightly softened for best flavor and spreadability. It's an ideal accompaniment for the Cheddar-Pepper Quick Bread (recipe, left)—or use to jazz up vegetables. (Pictured, left.)

¾  cup (1½ sticks) unsalted butter,
    softened
2  tablespoons (scant) grainy Dijon
    mustard
1  tablespoon snipped fresh chives or green
    part of scallion
¼  teaspoon salt
Pinch of black pepper
Fresh chives (optional garnish)

In small bowl, mix all ingredients except garnish until well combined. Spoon into serving container; cover and refrigerate or freeze until ready to use. Garnish with chives.

Makes about ¾ cup.

*Per tablespoon: 104 calories, trace protein, 12 g fat, trace carbohydrate, 31 mg cholesterol, 67 mg sodium.*

### QUICK-FIX SIDE DISHES

● Sauté walnuts in a little butter until the nuts are toasted and the butter is browned—drizzle over steamed broccoli or green beans.

● Stir a can of rinsed and drained black beans and some grated lime peel into cooked rice.

● Steam julienned carrots, turnips and rutabaga; then toss with butter and chopped parsley.

● Sauté thinly sliced zucchini and red onion in a little olive oil with just a pinch of crushed red pepper.

● Follow a traditional scalloped-potato recipe but try substituting sweet potatoes for the regular potatoes.

## WINTER FRUIT-CORN BREAD STUFFING

This kid-appealing stuffing, chock-full of fruit, starts with a packaged mix. Any combination of dried fruit works fine.

½ cup (1 stick) butter or margarine
2 medium stalks celery with leaves, diced
1 large onion, chopped
1 teaspoon dried sage
1 large apple, diced
1¾ cups chopped mixed dried fruit (raisins, prunes, apricots and dried cherries are good)
1½ cups apple juice
2 packages (8-ounce size) corn bread stuffing mix
1 can (14½ ounces) chicken broth

1. Preheat oven to 350°F. Grease 2½-quart baking dish.

2. Melt butter in medium nonaluminum saucepan over medium heat. Add celery, onion and sage; cover and cook for 8 minutes, or until almost tender, stirring occasionally. Stir in diced apple; cover and cook for 2 minutes, or until just softened. Place celery mixture in prepared baking dish.

3. In same saucepan over high heat, bring dried fruit and apple juice to a boil. Remove from heat. Let stand for 5 minutes; add to celery mixture in baking dish. Stir in corn bread mixes and broth, tossing until well combined. Cover with aluminum foil.

4. Bake stuffing for 30 minutes. Remove foil; bake for 15 minutes, or until top is lightly browned.

Makes 12 to 14 servings.

*Per serving: 278 calories, 5 g protein, 9 g fat, 47 g carbohydrate, 19 mg cholesterol, 614 mg sodium.*

## WILD RICE AND SAUSAGE STUFFING

Italian sausage adds plenty of robust flavor to this simple stuffing. Make sure the sausage is completely cooked. (Pictured, page 137.)

3 packages (4.3-ounce size) long-grain and wild-rice mix
2 cans (14½-ounce size) chicken broth
1 pound sweet Italian sausage, casing removed
2 tablespoons olive oil
2 tablespoons (¼ stick) butter or margarine
4 medium cloves garlic, minced
2 medium onions, chopped
2 medium red peppers, diced
2 medium stalks celery with leaves, diced
½ cup coarsely chopped Italian parsley
1 tablespoon chopped fresh thyme, or 1 teaspoon dried thyme

1. In large saucepan over high heat, bring rice mixes (save seasoning packets for another use or discard) and broth to a boil. Cover; reduce heat to low and simmer for 20 minutes, or until rice is tender and most of liquid is absorbed. Remove from heat. Cover and let stand for 20 minutes, or until all liquid is absorbed.

2. Meanwhile, crumble sausage in large skillet. Over medium heat, cook for 12 minutes, or until lightly browned and cooked through, stirring frequently. With slotted spoon, remove sausage to paper towels to drain. Preheat oven to 350°F.

3. In drippings in skillet, heat oil and butter. Add garlic and onions; sauté for 5 minutes, stirring frequently. Add peppers and celery; sauté for 8 minutes, or until tender, stirring frequently. Transfer vegetable mixture to 2½-quart baking dish. Stir in

rice mixture, sausage, parsley and thyme, tossing until well combined. Cover with aluminum foil. Bake stuffing for 20 to 25 minutes, or until heated through.

Makes 12 to 14 servings.

*Per serving: 234 calories, 9 g protein, 11 g fat, 24 g carbohydrate, 25 mg cholesterol, 598 mg sodium.*

## SCALLOPED POTATOES WITH MUSHROOMS

Shiitake mushrooms have a wonderful woodsy flavor, but regular button mushrooms work just fine, too. You can bake this dish in advance and reheat it in a 350°F oven. (Pictured, page 138.)

¼  cup (½ stick) butter or margarine
2  medium onions, thinly sliced
¾  pound fresh shiitake (see Note) or button mushrooms, sliced
½  teaspoon dried thyme
3½  pounds russet potatoes, peeled and very thinly sliced (about 7 medium potatoes)
1  teaspoon salt
½  teaspoon black pepper
2  cups (8 ounces) shredded Jarlsberg cheese
1  cup whipping cream
¾  cup milk
Fresh thyme (optional garnish)

1. Preheat oven to 425°F. Generously grease 3-quart baking dish.

2. Melt butter in skillet over medium-high heat. Add onions; sauté for 5 minutes, or until softened, stirring frequently. Stir in mushrooms; sauté for 5 minutes, or until liquid in skillet almost evaporates. Stir in dried thyme.

3. In prepared baking dish, layer one-third of the potatoes, a little of the salt and pepper, half of the mushroom mixture and then one-third of the cheese. Repeat layering once. Add remaining one-third of the potatoes and remaining salt and pepper; reserve remaining one-third of the cheese. Lightly press down top of potatoes.

4. In small saucepan over medium heat, bring cream and milk to a boil (this reduces curdling in finished dish); pour evenly over potatoes. Sprinkle with remaining cheese.

5. Bake for 45 to 55 minutes, or until top is browned and potatoes are very tender. (Check potatoes after about 30 minutes; if getting too brown, cover with aluminum foil.) Garnish with fresh thyme.

Makes about 12 servings.

*Per serving: 285 calories, 9 g protein, 16 g fat, 26 g carbohydrate, 50 mg cholesterol, 347 mg sodium.*

*Note:* The stems of shiitake mushrooms are tough; trim and use to flavor soups and stocks or discard.

## FESTIVE SIDE DISHES

● Italian-style mashed potatoes: Beat potatoes with olive oil instead of butter. Stir in grated Parmesan cheese and chopped Italian parsley.

● Jazz up rice by adding minced fresh ginger to the cooking water. Or, after rice is cooked, stir in chopped toasted almonds, grated citrus peel or chopped herbs such as mint, cilantro or parsley.

● Toss cooked fresh fettuccine with a little heavy cream, some grated lemon peel and cracked black pepper.

● Marinate sliced cucumbers and chopped chives or scallions in rice vinegar with a little sugar for a zesty salad.

## FRESH GREEN BEAN CASSEROLE

When you have to bring one dish to a dinner party, this casserole is sure to impress. To transport, toss the cooked green beans with the sauce. Pack the bean mixture, shallot mixture and Parmesan cheese in separate containers. Assemble and bake when you reach your destination. (Pictured, page 138.)

2½ pounds green beans, trimmed
¾ teaspoon salt
2 tablespoons olive oil
2 tablespoons (¼ stick) butter or
   margarine
8 medium shallots, thinly sliced
3 medium cloves garlic, minced
2 medium onions, thinly sliced
3 tablespoons all-purpose flour
1 cup half-and-half
¾ cup chicken broth
½ teaspoon black pepper
3 tablespoons grated Parmesan cheese

1. Preheat oven to 400°F. Grease 2½-quart baking dish.
2. Bring large pot of water, covered, to a boil over high heat. Add green beans and ½ teaspoon of the salt; cook for 3 minutes, or until tender-crisp (beans should not be completely cooked). Drain well and place in prepared baking dish.
3. Heat oil and 1 tablespoon of the butter in same pot over medium heat. Add shallots, garlic and onions; sauté for 15 minutes, or until well browned, stirring occasionally. With slotted spoon, remove shallot mixture to a plate; set aside.
4. In drippings in pot, melt remaining 1 tablespoon butter. Add flour; cook for 2 minutes, stirring mixture constantly. Stir in half-and-half and broth; bring mixture to a boil and cook until slightly thickened, stirring constantly. Remove from heat. Stir in pepper and remaining ¼ teaspoon salt. Pour sauce over beans in baking dish; toss until coated. Top with shallot mixture. Cover beans with aluminum foil.
5. Bake for 15 minutes, or until sauce is bubbly around edges. Remove foil; sprinkle beans with cheese. Bake for 5 minutes.
Makes 10 to 12 servings.
*Per serving: 125 calories, 4 g protein, 8 g fat, 12 g carbohydrate, 15 mg cholesterol, 235 mg sodium.*

## PROVENÇAL VEGETABLE GRATIN

For maximum flavor and moisture, keep this dish covered while cooking. It's great served hot or at room temperature—a few sun-dried tomatoes add real punch.

⅔ cup plus 1 tablespoon seasoned dried
   bread crumbs
¼ cup chopped oil-packed sun-dried
   tomatoes (optional)
6 tablespoons (¾ stick) butter or
   margarine, softened
3 pounds medium zucchini, cut
   diagonally into ½-inch-thick slices
2 pounds small thin eggplants, cut
   diagonally into ½-inch-thick slices
1 jar (7 ounces) roasted red peppers,
   drained and sliced
⅓ cup olive oil
4 medium cloves garlic, minced
1 tablespoon chopped fresh rosemary, or 1
   teaspoon dried rosemary, crushed
1½ teaspoons salt
¾ teaspoon black pepper

1. Preheat oven to 375°F. Grease 13-by-9-inch baking dish. Sprinkle dish with 1 tablespoon of the bread crumbs.

2. In medium bowl, mix sun-dried tomatoes (if using), butter and remaining ⅔ cup bread crumbs. Set aside.

3. In prepared baking dish, layer half of the zucchini, eggplant and red-pepper slices, alternating vegetables; brush with half of the olive oil. Sprinkle with half of the garlic, rosemary, salt, pepper and half of the bread-crumb mixture. Repeat layering, but do not add remaining bread-crumb mixture. Cover with aluminum foil.

4. Bake for 1 hour, or until vegetables are very tender. Remove foil; sprinkle vegetables with remaining bread-crumb mixture. Place dish under broiler about 3 inches from heat source; broil for 2 to 3 minutes, or until top is browned.

Makes about 12 servings.

*Per serving: 187 calories, 4 g protein, 14 g fat, 15 g carbohydrate, 16 mg cholesterol, 646 mg sodium.*

## VEGETABLE SLAW WITH BASIL DRESSING

The dressing and the veggies (wrapped in damp paper towels) can be prepared in advance and mixed together before serving. (Pictured, page 137.)

Slaw:

5 ounces snow peas
3 medium carrots
2 medium yellow summer squash
1 large cucumber
1 medium head radicchio, or ½ medium head red cabbage
½ medium head green cabbage

Basil dressing:

1¾ cups loosely packed fresh basil, or 1½ cups loosely packed Italian parsley
¾ cup cholesterol-free, reduced-calorie mayonnaise
¼ cup lemon juice
1 medium clove garlic
1 teaspoon salt
¾ teaspoon black pepper
½ cup sour cream

Red cabbage leaves (optional garnish)

1. For slaw: Cut snow peas and carrots into julienne strips. Halve squash and cucumber lengthwise. Scoop out and discard seedy centers; cut into julienne strips. Shred radicchio and green cabbage. In large bowl, toss all vegetables, except garnish, until well combined.

2. For dressing: In blender or food processor fitted with steel blade, blend all ingredients except sour cream until smooth. Stir in sour cream. (Dressing can be made up to 2 days ahead; cover and refrigerate.)

3. Just before serving, pour dressing over vegetables; toss until well coated. Serve slaw on top of cabbage leaves.

Makes 12 to 14 servings.

*Per serving: 104 calories, 2 g protein, 7 g fat, 10 g carbohydrate, 4 mg cholesterol, 264 mg sodium.*

● For a colorful, flavorful side dish, sauté chunks of zucchini and summer squash in olive oil with fresh or dried oregano. When veggies are tender-crisp, add minced garlic and chopped jarred roasted red peppers or pimientos.

# Desserts

*Above: (Clockwise from top left) Glazed Apple-and-Pear Tart (facing page), Orange Mousse with Raspberry Sauce (this page), Country Carrot-Pumpkin Cake (facing page).*

## ORANGE MOUSSE WITH RASPBERRY SAUCE

This speedy dessert is ready in less than 15 minutes! If you prefer, orange juice makes a fine substitute for the orange-flavor liqueur. (Pictured, left.)

¼ cup sweet orange marmalade
3 tablespoons orange-flavor liqueur
1 cup whipping cream
1 bag (12 ounces) frozen unsweetened raspberries, thawed
2 to 3 tablespoons sugar
Orange peel and fresh mint (optional garnish)

1. For mousse: In medium bowl, mix orange marmalade with 2 tablespoons of the orange-flavor liqueur until mixture is well combined. In another medium bowl, with electric mixer on medium speed, whip cream until soft peaks form. Gently fold whipped cream into marmalade-liqueur mixture. Spoon mousse into 4 individual dessert dishes.

2. For sauce: Strain raspberries through fine sieve into a small bowl, pressing with back of a spoon to extract as much juice as possible; discard seeds. Add remaining 1 tablespoon liqueur and sugar to taste to raspberry juice; stir until sugar dissolves. Spoon some raspberry sauce into each dessert dish around orange mousse. Garnish with orange peel and mint. Serve remaining sauce on the side. (Raspberry sauce is also delicious spooned over ice cream, pound cake, brownies, or—for a low-calorie dessert—sliced oranges.)

Makes 4 servings.

*Per serving: 359 calories, 2 g protein, 23 g fat, 37 g carbohydrate, 82 mg cholesterol, 25 mg sodium.*

## COUNTRY CARROT-PUMPKIN CAKE

You'd never know this moist and sumptuous dessert started with a cake mix! And it combines some favorite flavors: pumpkin, maple and apple cider! (Pictured, left.)

1 cup coarsely chopped walnuts
2 teaspoons all-purpose flour
1 package (18¾ ounces) carrot cake mix
   with pudding in the mix
½ can (16-ounce size) solid-pack pumpkin
½ cup apple cider or juice
¼ cup (½ stick) butter or margarine,
   melted
3 eggs
2½ cups confectioners' sugar
¼ cup milk
½ teaspoon maple extract

1. Preheat oven to 350°F. Grease and flour 10-inch tube or Bundt pan. Toss walnuts with flour; set aside.

2. In large bowl, with electric mixer on medium-low speed, beat cake mix, pumpkin, apple cider, butter and eggs until moistened. Stir in walnuts.

3. Pour batter into prepared pan; bake for 50 to 55 minutes, or until a toothpick inserted just off-center of cake comes out clean. Cool cake in pan on wire rack for 10 minutes; then invert onto rack and cool completely before serving.

4. In small bowl, mix confectioners' sugar, milk and maple extract until smooth. (If you like, add more maple extract for a stronger maple flavor.) Spoon glaze over top of cooled cake. Let glaze set before cutting cake.

Makes 10 to 12 servings.

*Per serving: 461 calories, 5 g protein, 17 g fat, 71 g carbohydrate, 87 mg cholesterol, 432 mg sodium.*

## GLAZED APPLE-AND-PEAR TART

This apple-and-pear tart is a sophisticated and simple way to use an abundance of winter fruits. (Pictured, left.)

1 sheet frozen puff pastry
2 apples
2 pears
2 tablespoons lemon juice
2 tablespoons sugar
¼ cup apple jelly or apricot jam

1. Preheat oven to 350°F. Thaw pastry according to package directions.

2. With sharp knife, core and thinly slice apples and pears (do not peel). In medium glass or ceramic bowl, gently toss apple and pear slices with lemon juice; set aside.

3. Unfold pastry on ungreased baking sheet. With floured rolling pin, roll pastry into 14-by-11-inch rectangle. Brush edges of rectangle with water. Carefully roll edges of pastry toward center to form a rim and make an 11-by-8½-inch rectangle. Crimp pastry rim lightly with fork to seal; prick bottom with fork.

4. Tightly overlap apple and pear slices in tart shell. Sprinkle slices with sugar. Bake tart for 40 minutes, or until fruit is tender and pastry is golden. Carefully remove to wire rack and cool.

5. In small saucepan over low heat, melt apple jelly with 1 tablespoon water. (If using jam, heat jam and strain into a small bowl. Return unstrained portion to jar for another use.) With pastry brush, coat fruit with jelly glaze; let glaze set before serving.

Makes 8 servings.

*Per serving: 215 calories, 2 g protein, 9 g fat, 33 g carbohydrate, 0 mg cholesterol, 147 mg sodium.*

# Elegant Desserts

3. Bake for 45 to 50 minutes, or until pudding is browned and puffy and knife inserted in center comes out clean.

Makes about 12 servings.

*Per serving: 239 calories, 5 g protein, 12 g fat, 28 g carbohydrate, 100 mg cholesterol, 190 mg sodium.*

## CRANBERRY-ORANGE BREAD PUDDING

For down-home comfort with a touch of class, offer this elegant dessert. Use day-old bread for best results and be sure to serve with scrumptious Hot Fudge Sauce (recipe follows). (Pictured, right.)

1  loaf (24 inches) French bread (about 8 ounces)
¼  cup (½ stick) butter or margarine, softened
4  eggs
2½  cups half-and-half
⅓  cup orange-flavor liqueur or orange juice
¾  cup sugar
1  cup cranberries

1.  Preheat oven to 350°F. Grease shallow 2½-quart casserole. Cut bread diagonally into ½-inch-thick slices. Lightly butter 1 side of each bread slice. Arrange bread, butter side up, in prepared casserole, overlapping slices slightly.

2.  In bowl, whisk eggs, half-and-half, liqueur and ½ cup of the sugar until well combined. Gradually pour egg mixture over bread slices in casserole. Let stand for at least 20 minutes. (Or cover and refrigerate mixture for up to 2 hours.) With a fork, gently press bread into egg mixture. Sprinkle bread mixture with cranberries, and then with remaining ¼ cup sugar.

## HOT FUDGE SAUCE

Rich in fudgy flavor, this quick-cooking sauce has only five ingredients! Serve it with Cranberry-Orange Bread Pudding or over your favorite ice cream.

½  cup unsweetened cocoa powder
½  cup whipping cream
¼  cup packed brown sugar
¼  cup (½ stick) butter or margarine
1  tablespoon orange-flavor liqueur or brandy (optional)

In medium, heavy saucepan, combine first 4 ingredients. Over medium heat, bring to a boil, stirring frequently. Boil for 1 minute. Remove from heat; stir in liqueur (if using). Serve warm or refrigerate until ready to use. Can be reheated in the microwave or on stovetop.

Makes about 1½ cups.

*Per tablespoon: 64 calories, trace protein, 4 g fat, 8 g carbohydrate, 12 mg cholesterol, 24 mg sodium.*

*Right: (Clockwise from top right) Southern Lemon Chess Pie (page 148), Chocolate-Raspberry Temptation (page 148), Cranberry-Orange Bread Pudding (this page).*

## CHOCOLATE-RASPBERRY TEMPTATION

This is a chocoholic's dream. Cut into very thin slices and serve with the accompanying raspberry sauce. Keep both in the freezer for last-minute guests. (Pictured, page 147.)

1 cup hazelnuts
2 packages (8-ounce size) semisweet chocolate, chopped
2½ cups whipping cream
1 teaspoon vanilla extract
½ cup confectioners' sugar
3 tablespoons raspberry-flavor liqueur (optional)
2 cups coarsely broken butter cookies
1 package (10 ounces) frozen raspberries in light syrup, thawed
Fresh raspberries (optional garnish)

1. Preheat oven to 350°F. Grease 9-by-5-inch loaf pan; line with wax paper. Spread hazelnuts on baking sheet; bake for 10 minutes, or until skins blister. Wrap hazelnuts in a kitchen towel; rub together to remove most of skins. Cool hazelnuts; then chop.

2. In medium, heavy saucepan over low heat, melt chocolate, stirring frequently. Remove from heat; let cool.

3. In large bowl, with electric mixer on medium speed, whip cream, vanilla extract, ¼ cup of the confectioners' sugar and 2 tablespoons of the liqueur (if using) until soft peaks form. Gently fold in cooled chocolate; then add hazelnuts and cookies. Spoon mixture into prepared loaf pan, smoothing top. Lightly tap pan on counter to eliminate air pockets. Cover and freeze for at least 3 hours or refrigerate overnight until firm.

4. For sauce: In blender or food processor fitted with steel blade, puree raspberries in syrup with remaining ¼ cup confectioners' sugar and remaining 1 tablespoon liqueur (if using). Cover and refrigerate until ready to serve.

5. To serve, invert loaf onto serving plate; remove wax paper. Let stand at room temperature for about 20 minutes before slicing. (It's easier to cut into thin slices with a serrated knife.) Serve with raspberry sauce; garnish with raspberries.

Makes 18 to 20 servings.

*Per serving: 344 calories, 3 g protein, 26 g fat, 30 g carbohydrate, 51 mg cholesterol, 57 mg sodium.*

## SOUTHERN LEMON CHESS PIE

This classic recipe comes from the files of our food editor's grandmother. We used a petal-shaped tart ring. (Pictured, page 147.)

1 package (10 to 11 ounces) piecrust mix
1¼ cups granulated sugar
2 tablespoons yellow cornmeal
1 tablespoon all-purpose flour
¼ teaspoon salt
3 eggs
½ cup (1 stick) butter or margarine, melted and cooled slightly
3 tablespoons fresh lemon juice
2 teaspoons grated lemon peel
Confectioners' sugar and fresh lavender or candied violets (optional garnish)

1. Position rack in lower third of oven; preheat to 325°F. Prepare pastry according to package directions; use pastry to line 9-inch pie plate. Or, if time is tight, use a frozen prepared unbaked 9-inch pie shell.

2. In large bowl, mix granulated sugar, cornmeal, flour and salt until well combined.

*Above: (Clockwise from top left) Spiced Sweet-Potato Tart (page 150), Snowdrift Sundaes (page 159), Honey Gingersnap Cheesecake (page 151), Brownie Berry Shortcakes (page 150).*

Whisk in eggs, butter, lemon juice and grated lemon peel until well combined; pour mixture into pie shell.

3. Bake for 40 minutes, or until knife inserted just off center of pie comes out clean. Cool completely on wire rack. Garnish with confectioners' sugar and lavender. Cut into very thin slices.

Makes 8 to 10 servings.

*Per serving: 443 calories, 4 g protein, 26 g fat, 48 g carbohydrate, 104 mg cholesterol, 430 mg sodium.*

## SPICED SWEET-POTATO TART

Pulverize chocolate wafers in your blender or food processor; wipe out the work bowl and whip up the filling. (Pictured, page 149.)

1 cup chocolate-wafer or graham-cracker crumbs
3 tablespoons butter or margarine, melted
1 can (17 ounces) sweet potatoes or yams in syrup, drained
1 cup half-and-half
¾ cup packed light-brown sugar
1½ teaspoons ground cinnamon
½ teaspoon grated orange peel
¼ teaspoon grated nutmeg
¼ teaspoon salt
2 eggs
Candied orange peel (optional garnish)

1. Preheat oven to 350°F. In 9-inch square or round tart pan with removable bottom or 9-inch pie plate, mix chocolate-wafer crumbs and butter. Press into bottom and up sides of pan. Place pan on baking sheet.

2. In blender or food processor fitted with steel blade, puree remaining ingredients except garnish until smooth; pour mixture into crust in pan.

3. Bake for 40 to 45 minutes, or until knife inserted just off center of tart comes out clean. Cool slightly on wire rack. Cover and refrigerate for at least 4 hours. Remove sides of pan; garnish with candied peel.

Makes 8 to 10 servings.

*Per serving: 255 calories, 4 g protein, 10 g fat, 39 g carbohydrate, 67 mg cholesterol, 236 mg sodium.*

## BROWNIE BERRY SHORTCAKES

Cocoa whipped cream makes these fruit-filled desserts a double chocolate treat. Grease muffin cups well; to keep brownies from crumbling, cool them completely before removing from pan. (Pictured, page 149.)

1 package (12.9 to 14.1 ounces) brownie mix
¾ cup coarsely chopped walnuts
2 pints strawberries, sliced
2 tablespoons granulated sugar
1 cup whipping cream
½ cup confectioners' sugar
¼ cup unsweetened cocoa powder
1 teaspoon vanilla extract

1. Preheat oven to 350°F. Generously grease eight 3-inch muffin-pan cups.

2. Prepare brownie mix according to package directions, adding ½ cup of the walnuts to batter. Spoon batter into prepared muffin cups; sprinkle tops with remaining ¼ cup walnuts. Half-fill any empty muffin cups with water. Bake brownies for 30 to 35 minutes, or until toothpick inserted in center comes out clean. Cool completely in pan.

3. Meanwhile, in medium bowl, mix strawberries and granulated sugar; let stand while brownies cool. In large bowl, with electric mixer on medium speed, whip cream, confectioners' sugar, cocoa and vanilla extract until soft peaks form.

4. Remove brownies from pan; cut each in half. Place bottom halves on dessert plates; top with strawberries and cocoa whipped cream. Replace brownie tops.

Makes 8 servings.

*Per serving: 518 calories, 6 g protein, 30 g fat, 57 g carbohydrate, 67 mg cholesterol, 191 mg sodium.*

## HONEY GINGERSNAP CHEESECAKE

We tested crowd reaction by serving this at an office baby shower. It got raves! (Pictured, page 149.)

1¾ cups gingersnap-cookie crumbs
6 tablespoons (¾ stick) butter or margarine, melted
5 packages (8-ounce size) cream cheese, softened
5 eggs
2 egg yolks
2 teaspoons grated lemon peel
2 teaspoons vanilla extract
1½ teaspoons ground ginger
1 cup honey
1 cup sour cream (optional topping)
Assorted fresh fruit, such as blueberries, grape halves and carambola (star fruit) slices (optional)

1. Position rack in lower third of oven; preheat to 325°F. In 10-inch springform pan, mix cookie crumbs and butter; press into bottom and partially up sides of pan.

2. In large bowl, with electric mixer on medium speed, beat cream cheese until smooth. Add eggs, egg yolks, lemon peel, vanilla extract, ginger and ¾ cup of the honey. Beat for 5 minutes, scraping sides of bowl occasionally with rubber spatula. Pour batter into crust in pan.

3. Bake cheesecake for 1 hour and 5 minutes. (If you'd like a sour-cream topping, remove cheesecake from oven after baking 1 hour; cool for 10 minutes. Spread sour cream over top of cake; bake for 5 to 10 minutes longer.) Turn off oven; with door slightly ajar, cool cheesecake in oven—this helps prevent cracking. Cover and refrigerate for at least 4 hours.

4. Carefully take off removable rim of pan. Top cheesecake with fruit, if you like. In small saucepan over low heat, warm remaining ¼ cup honey; brush fruit with warm honey to glaze.

Makes about 20 servings.

*Per serving: 343 calories, 7 g protein, 26 g fat, 23 g carbohydrate, 149 mg cholesterol, 270 mg sodium.*

## QUICK-FIX DESSERTS

● Soften a pint of vanilla ice cream and stir in coarsely crushed peppermint candy or candy canes. Serve with hot-fudge sauce. Or spoon ice cream into a chocolate-cookie piecrust and freeze. Serve with whipped cream and chocolate sauce.

● Brush pineapple slices with melted butter and sprinkle with a little brown sugar. Broil until sugar melts. Serve plain or topped with your favorite ice cream.

● Fill miniature chocolate shells (sold in specialty stores and candy shops, often in gold-foil cups) with whipped cream flavored with vanilla or almond extract or your favorite liqueur. Serve with after-dinner coffee.

● For a simple fruit split, top vanilla ice cream with chunks of cantaloupe and some minced crystallized ginger.

● Mash fresh raspberries with a little raspberry jam; then fold in fresh blueberries. Spoon over frozen yogurt, ice cream or slices of angel food or pound cake.

● Beat whipping cream with a spoonful of apricot or peach jam—spoon on top of thinly sliced fresh peaches tossed with a little brown sugar. (Also wonderful made into shortcakes: Split biscuits or cut slices of pound cake; top with peaches and whipped cream.)

## PUMPKIN-SPICE FROZEN SOUFFLE

Simple and impressive! (Pictured, right.)

2  packages (3-ounce size) ladyfingers
4  tablespoons orange-flavor liqueur
1  can (30 ounces) pumpkin-pie mix
1  can (14 ounces) sweetened condensed
   milk
2  teaspoons grated orange peel
1  teaspoon ground cinnamon
½  teaspoon ground ginger
⅛  teaspoon ground cloves
2  cups whipping cream
Cinnamon sticks and long curls of orange
   peel (optional garnish)

1. Line bottom and sides of 9-inch spring-form pan with enough ladyfingers to cover pan completely; brush with 2 tablespoons of the liqueur. Crumble remaining ladyfingers into medium bowl and toss with remaining 2 tablespoons liqueur; set aside.

2. In large bowl, mix next 6 ingredients until smooth. In another large bowl, with electric mixer on medium speed, whip cream until soft peaks form. Gently fold whipped cream into pumpkin mixture.

3. Spoon half of pumpkin mixture into lined pan; sprinkle evenly with reserved lady-finger crumbs. Top with remaining pumpkin mixture, swirling surface with a knife. Cover and freeze for at least 8 hours.

4. Remove soufflé from freezer 15 minutes before serving; set aside on a serving plate. Carefully remove rim of pan. Garnish with cinnamon sticks and orange curls.

Makes 14 to 16 servings.

*Per serving: 290 calories, 4 g protein, 13 g fat, 39 g carbohydrate, 85 mg cholesterol, 170 mg sodium.*

*Above: (Clockwise from top left) Pumpkin-Spice Frozen Soufflé (this page), Double-Chocolate Raspberry Cake (page 156), Festive Fruit Tart (page 154), Pear-and-Cranberry Crumb Pie (page 154).*

## PEAR-AND-CRANBERRY CRUMB PIE

Make crust two days ahead (or freeze three weeks ahead). (Pictured, pages 152 and 153.)

6 ripe pears (about 3 pounds), peeled, cored and thinly sliced
⅓ cup all-purpose flour
2 tablespoons quick-cooking tapioca
1 tablespoon lemon juice
1 teaspoon ground ginger
¾ cup packed brown sugar
⅓ cup old-fashioned oats
¼ teaspoon ground cinnamon
3 tablespoons butter or margarine
⅓ cup slivered almonds or chopped walnuts
1 package (10 to 11 ounces) piecrust mix
1 cup cranberries

1. In large bowl, gently toss first 5 ingredients and ½ cup of the brown sugar. Let stand for 30 minutes, or until tapioca is softened, stirring occasionally.

2. Meanwhile, preheat oven to 425°F. In small bowl, combine oats, cinnamon and remaining ¼ cup brown sugar. With pastry blender or 2 knives, cut in butter until mixture resembles coarse crumbs. Stir in almonds. Prepare pastry according to package directions; use to line 9-inch pie plate.

3. Stir cranberries into pear mixture; spoon into pie shell. Bake for 20 minutes. Sprinkle with crumb mixture; continue baking for 15 to 20 minutes, or until pears are tender. Cool on wire rack for about 1 hour. Serve warm with ice cream or whipped cream, or cool completely to serve later.

Makes about 8 servings.

*Per serving: 524 calories, 5 g protein, 24 g fat, 75 g carbohydrate, 18 mg cholesterol, 326 mg sodium.*

## FESTIVE FRUIT TART

The tart shell with its chocolate and cream-cheese layers can be made the day before and refrigerated. Top with fruit and glaze before serving. (Pictured, pages 152 and 153.)

1 package (10 to 11 ounces) piecrust mix (see Note)
2 ounces milk chocolate
1 package (8 ounces) cream cheese, softened
⅓ cup confectioners' sugar
2 tablespoons sweet Marsala or orange juice
2 kiwis, sliced
1 pint strawberries, sliced
2 tablespoons red-currant jelly

1. Preheat oven and prepare pastry according to package directions. On lightly floured surface, roll pastry about 1 inch larger than 13-by-4-inch rectangular or 9-inch round tart pan with removable bottom. Line pan with pastry, pressing into bottom and up sides; trim edges. Prick pastry with a fork. Place pan on baking sheet. Bake for 8 to 10 minutes, or until golden; cool completely on wire rack.

2. In small, heavy saucepan over low heat, melt chocolate, stirring constantly. Spread melted chocolate in cooled tart shell; chill in refrigerator for 10 minutes, or until set.

3. Meanwhile, with electric mixer or a wooden spoon, beat cream cheese, confectioners' sugar and Marsala until mixture is smooth; spread evenly over chocolate. Arrange kiwi and strawberry slices over cream-cheese layer.

4. In small saucepan over low heat, melt jelly, stirring frequently. With pastry brush, coat fruit with jelly glaze. Chill tart for

about 1 hour before serving. Remove sides of pan; set tart on serving plate.

Makes about 8 servings.

*Per serving: 432 calories, 5 g protein, 28 g fat, 39 g carbohydrate, 39 mg cholesterol, 367 mg sodium.*

*Note:* You can use a frozen prepared 9-inch pie shell, if you like.

## CHOCOLATE CHIP-CREAM PUFF WREATH

The ricotta filling can be made up to two days ahead. (Pictured, page 157.)

½  cup (1 stick) butter or margarine
½  teaspoon salt
1  cup all-purpose flour
5  eggs
2  containers (15- to 16-ounce size) part-skim ricotta cheese
¾  cup confectioners' sugar
¾  teaspoon almond extract
½  cup miniature chocolate chips
1  pint strawberries
½  cup seedless green grapes

1. Heat butter, salt and 1 cup water in medium saucepan over medium heat until mixture boils. Immediately remove from heat; add flour all at once and stir vigorously with a wooden spoon. Return to low heat and cook for 1 minute, or until mixture forms a ball and leaves sides of pan, stirring constantly. Remove from heat; cool for 5 minutes. Add 4 of the eggs, one at a time; beat well after each addition, until mixture is smooth, shiny and stiff enough to hold its shape.

2. Preheat oven to 400°F. Grease and flour large baking sheet. Using 9-inch plate or pot lid as guide, trace a circle in flour on prepared baking sheet. Drop batter by heaping tablespoons into mounds on top of circle to form a wreath, allowing mounds to just touch one another. Beat remaining egg and brush over wreath.

3. Bake wreath for 40 minutes. With sharp knife, make several small cuts in side of wreath to allow steam to escape. Reduce oven temperature to 325°F. Continue baking for 10 minutes, or until lightly browned. Remove to wire rack and cool completely.

4. Meanwhile, in large bowl, with electric mixer on low speed, beat ricotta, confectioners' sugar and almond extract until combined. Increase speed to medium; continue beating until smooth. Stir in chocolate chips. (Cover and refrigerate mixture if not using right away.)

5. Slice most of the strawberries, reserving several large berries for garnish. Cut each grape in half. With serrated knife, cut wreath horizontally in half; remove and discard any soft dough inside. Fill bottom half of wreath with ricotta mixture; top with sliced strawberries and grapes. Cover with top half of wreath; garnish with reserved strawberries. Tie a ribbon into a large bow and attach to wreath, if you like.

Makes about 10 servings.

*Per serving: 377 calories, 15 g protein, 21 g fat, 32 g carbohydrate, 159 mg cholesterol, 348 mg sodium.*

## DOUBLE-CHOCOLATE RASPBERRY CAKE

If you wish, prepare frosting and cake in advance—then assemble an hour or two before serving. (Pictured, pages 152 and 153.)

1 package (18.25 to 18.5 ounces) chocolate cake mix
1 package (12 ounces) semisweet-chocolate chips
1 cup sour cream
4 tablespoons raspberry-flavor liqueur
½ cup raspberry spreadable fruit or raspberry preserves
Raspberries, rose geranium or mint leaves and confectioners' sugar (optional garnish)

1. Preheat oven and prepare and bake cake mix according to package directions, using 2 greased and floured 9-inch square or round cake pans. Invert layers onto wire rack; cool completely before frosting. (Cake layers can be made a day or two ahead; wrap securely and store at room temperature.)

2. In medium, heavy saucepan over low heat, melt chocolate, stirring frequently. Remove from heat; let cool. Whisk in sour cream until smooth; then whisk in 2 table-spoons of the liqueur. Cover and refrigerate for 30 minutes, or until of good spreading consistency. (Frosting can be made a day or two ahead; cover and refrigerate. Let stand at room temperature until spreadable before frosting cake.)

3. In small bowl, mix spreadable fruit and remaining 2 tablespoons liqueur. Set 1 cake layer, top side down, on a cake plate; spread with raspberry mixture. Top with second layer, top side up. Spread frosting over top and sides of cake. Garnish with raspberries

and rose geranium leaves; sift confectioners' sugar over raspberries.

Makes about 12 servings.

*Per serving: 524 calories, 5 g protein, 29 g fat, 61 g carbohydrate, 62 mg cholesterol, 388 mg sodium.*

## GOLDEN APRICOT FRUITCAKE

It's easy to turn pound cake mix into a fantastic fruitcake by adding nuts and mixed dried fruit. (Pictured, right.)

¾ cup chopped pecans
½ cup diced mixed dried fruit
¼ cup golden raisins
¼ cup diced crystallized ginger or candied citrus peel
1 tablespoon all-purpose flour
1 package (16 ounces) pound cake mix
¼ cup brandy
½ cup plus 1 tablespoon apricot nectar
¼ cup apricot jam or apple jelly

1. Preheat oven according to cake-mix package directions. Grease and flour tall 2-quart tube mold or 9-cup Bundt pan.

2. In small bowl, mix first 5 ingredients until well combined. In medium bowl, prepare cake mix according to package directions, substituting brandy and ½ cup of the apricot nectar for liquid specified on package. Stir fruit mixture into batter; pour into prepared pan.

3. Bake for 1 to 1¼ hours, or until toothpick inserted just off center of cake comes out clean. Cool cake in pan on wire rack for 15 minutes; invert onto rack and cool completely.

4. Set cake on serving plate. (If cake will not sit evenly, remove a thin slice from bottom with serrated knife.) In small saucepan

over low heat, melt jam with remaining 1 tablespoon apricot nectar. With pastry brush, coat cake with jam glaze.

Makes 10 to 12 servings.

*Per serving: 346 calories, 3 g protein, 15 g fat, 52 g carbohydrate, 39 mg cholesterol, 181 mg sodium.*

*Above: (Clockwise from top left) Chocolate Chip-Cream Puff Wreath (page 155), Golden Apricot Fruit Cake (facing page), Caramelized Apple Shortcakes (page 158).*

## CARAMELIZED APPLE SHORTCAKES

Shortcake can be enjoyed long after summer has gone. (Pictured, page 157.)

4  medium tart red cooking apples (McIntosh or Rome Beauties), cored and thinly sliced (do not peel)
3  tablespoons dried currants
10  tablespoons butter or margarine
⅓  cup plus 2 tablespoons packed brown sugar
1  tablespoon bourbon (optional)
2  cups all-purpose flour
3  teaspoons baking powder
½  teaspoon salt
⅔  cup plus 1 teaspoon milk
1  tablespoon coarse (pearl) sugar or granulated sugar
½  teaspoon ground cinnamon
3  tablespoons finely chopped pecans
1  cup whipping cream

1.  In large skillet over medium heat, combine apples, currants, 4 tablespoons of the butter and ⅓ cup of the brown sugar. Cook for 5 to 8 minutes, or until apples are tender, stirring occasionally. Stir in bourbon (if using) and cook for 1 minute; set aside. (Apple mixture can be prepared a day in advance; cover and refrigerate until serving time.)

2.  Preheat oven to 425°F. In large bowl, mix flour, baking powder, salt and remaining 2 tablespoons brown sugar. With pastry blender or 2 knives, cut in remaining 6 tablespoons butter until mixture resembles coarse crumbs. Add ⅔ cup of the milk to mixture; with fork, quickly stir just until flour mixture forms a soft dough and leaves sides of bowl. With floured hands, knead dough 10 times.

3.  On floured surface, roll dough to about ½-inch thickness. With 3-inch biscuit cutter, cut out rounds; reroll trimmings (makes about 8 shortcakes). Place on baking sheet.

4.  In a cup, mix coarse sugar and cinnamon. Brush tops of shortcakes with remaining 1 teaspoon milk; sprinkle with pecans and cinnamon-sugar. Bake for 12 to 15 minutes, or until golden. Remove shortcakes to wire rack and cool slightly. Split warm shortcakes in half with a fork.

5.  If necessary, reheat apple mixture over low heat. In medium bowl, with electric mixer on medium speed, whip cream until soft peaks form. Place bottom halves of shortcakes on dessert plates; top with apple mixture, and then replace shortcake tops. Serve with whipped cream.

Makes 8 servings.

*Per serving: 462 calories, 5 g protein, 27 g fat, 53 g carbohydrate, 75 mg cholesterol, 468 mg sodium.*

---

### EASY ENDINGS

● Super-simple chocolate fondue: Warm prepared fudge sauce with a little ground cinnamon. Serve with banana chunks, fresh pineapple spears, sliced mangoes and apples, or cubes of angel food cake.

● For a colorful fruit parfait, layer your favorite sliced fruit or berries with honey-sweetened yogurt and chopped pistachios or macadamias in clear dessert glasses. Garnish with mint sprigs.

● Plump dried apricots, dried cherries, prunes or raisins in a little fruit juice or liqueur for about 30 minutes. Delicious served over lemon sherbet or gingerbread.

● Marinate fresh strawberries in a splash of tequila, some sugar and a little grated lime peel.

## SNOWDRIFT SUNDAES

Delightful festive fare! (Pictured, page 149.)

Mango ice cream:
1  ripe mango, peeled, pitted and halved
3  tablespoons shredded coconut
1  tablespoon chopped crystallized ginger
1  quart vanilla ice cream, softened

Phyllo cups:
¼  cup macadamia nuts
1  tablespoon sugar
2  teaspoons ground ginger
4  sheets phyllo dough, thawed if frozen
3  tablespoons butter or margarine, melted

Optional Toppings: shredded coconut,
    macadamia nuts, minced crystallized
    ginger and mango slices

1.  For mango ice cream: In food processor fitted with steel blade, puree mango with coconut and crystallized ginger. Place vanilla ice cream in large bowl; stir in mango puree just until swirled. Cover and freeze for at least 2 hours, or until firm.

2.  For phyllo cups: In clean, dry food processor fitted with steel blade, grind nuts with sugar and ground ginger, using short on/off pulses; stop and check frequently to avoid overprocessing.

3.  Preheat oven to 375°F. Grease eight 3-inch muffin-pan cups. Stack phyllo sheets; cut lengthwise in half, and then crosswise in thirds to make 24 rectangles. Cover phyllo with slightly damp paper towels.

4.  Arrange 3 phyllo rectangles in 1 muffin cup, brushing melted butter and sprinkling a little nut mixture between layers. Brush top layer of phyllo with butter, but not with nut mixture. Repeat with remaining ingredients to make 8 cups. Bake for 8 to 10 minutes,

or until golden. Carefully remove from pan; cool on wire rack.

5.  To serve, scoop mango ice cream into phyllo cups. Garnish with toppings.
    Makes 8 servings.
    *Per serving: 302 calories, 4 g protein, 16 g fat, 39 g carbohydrate, 42 mg cholesterol, 155 mg sodium.*

Sundae Variations:
● **Hot Fudge-Walnut:** Substitute walnuts for macadamias and omit ginger in phyllo cups. Scoop your favorite flavor of ice cream into phyllo cups; top with Hot Fudge Sauce (see recipe, page 146) and chopped walnuts.
● **Cherry Almond:** Substitute almonds for macadamias and ground cinnamon for ginger in phyllo cups. Heat canned pitted dark sweet cherries with a little brandy; spoon over vanilla ice cream in phyllo cups. Top with toasted slivered almonds.
● **Fruit 'n' Nut:** Stir crushed pineapple, blueberries or strawberries into softened vanilla ice cream; scoop into phyllo cups. Top with chopped nuts and miniature marshmallows.
● **Toffee-Coffee Crunch:** Substitute almonds for macadamias and omit ginger in phyllo cups. Stir chopped chocolate-covered toffee bars into softened coffee ice cream; scoop into phyllo cups. Top ice cream with prepared caramel sauce.
● **Sherbet Rainbow:** Scoop a little raspberry, orange and lime sherbet into phyllo cups; top with rainbow sprinkles.
● **Peanut Split:** Substitute unsalted peanuts for macadamias and omit ginger in phyllo cups. Stir chopped chocolate-covered peanut-butter cups into softened vanilla ice cream; scoop into phyllo cups. Top with banana chunks and chopped unsalted peanuts.

# Build-a-Meal Recipes

*Planning a menu is easy if you build the meal around the main dish. Choose from the four family-pleasing categories listed below. Whatever you're looking for, you'll find it in this creative section. (Pictured from front, Hot Chicken-and-Vegetable Salad Oriental, page 174; Creamy Corn-and-Shrimp Chowder, page 164; Sautéed Pork Tenderloin with Chutney Glaze, page 201.)*

Soups, Salads &
  Sandwiches
Italian Favorites
Oven Dishes
Skillet Suppers

# Soups, Salads & Sandwiches

## SUMMER VEGETABLE SOUP

Serve this with grilled-cheese sandwiches.

1 medium Spanish onion, quartered
2 tablespoons olive oil
2 medium red and/or green peppers, halved
1 medium zucchini, halved crosswise
⅓ cup packed fresh basil
1 large clove garlic
5 medium tomatoes, quartered
2 cans (13¾- to 14½-ounce size) chicken broth

1. In food processor fitted with grating disk, process onion. Heat oil in large pot over medium-low heat; add onion and sauté for 5 minutes, stirring occasionally.

2. With grating disk, process peppers and zucchini; add to pot with onion and cook for 5 minutes, stirring occasionally.

3. Insert steel blade. Process basil and garlic until finely chopped; add tomatoes (in batches, if necessary) and pulse 5 or 6 times until coarsely chopped. Add mixture and broth to pot. Increase heat to high and bring to a boil. Reduce heat to low; simmer for 12 to 15 minutes. Serve hot or chilled.

Makes 6 servings.

*Per serving: 98 calories, 3 g protein, 6 g fat, 10 g carbohydrate, 0 mg cholesterol, 586 mg sodium.*

## TOMATO-CARROT SOUP WITH DILL GREMOLATA

Be sure to use the freshest vegetables you can find for the most vibrant summer flavor. The soup tastes equally good chilled—just remember to substitute olive oil for the butter. (Pictured, right.)

2 tablespoons (¼ stick) butter or margarine
1 tablespoon olive oil
1 large carrot, finely chopped
1 medium onion, finely chopped
2 pounds tomatoes, chopped
2 cups chicken broth
½ teaspoon black pepper
3 tablespoons chopped fresh dill
1 tablespoon coarsely grated lemon peel
1 tablespoon minced parsley
Fresh dill and lemon slices (optional garnish)

1. Heat butter and oil in large saucepan over medium heat. Add carrot and onion; sauté for 15 minutes, stirring occasionally. Stir in tomatoes, broth, pepper and 2 tablespoons of the chopped dill; bring to a boil. Reduce heat to low; simmer for 20 minutes.

2. Meanwhile, prepare gremolata: In a cup, mix lemon peel, parsley and remaining 1 tablespoon chopped dill. Set aside.

3. In blender or food processor fitted with steel blade, puree soup (in batches, if necessary). Return soup to saucepan and heat through. Ladle soup into serving bowls; sprinkle with gremolata. Garnish with dill and lemon.

Makes 4 servings.

*Per serving: 144 calories, 4 g protein, 10 g fat, 12 g carbohydrate, 16 mg cholesterol, 575 mg sodium.*

*Above: (Clockwise from top right) Takeout Roast Chicken-and-Bread Salad (page 172), Tex-Mex Stuffed Steak (page 190), Tomato-Carrot Soup with Dill Gremolata (facing page), Smoked Mozzarella Crostini (page 177).*

## MINTED PEA SOUP

You can serve this delicately flavored soup warm—or refreshingly chilled. Follow the same procedure, simply substitute salad oil for the butter.

2 tablespoons (¼ stick) butter or margarine

1 medium onion, chopped

3 cups shelled fresh peas (about 2½ pounds unshelled peas), or 2 packages (10-ounce size) frozen baby green peas

2 cans (13¾- to 14½-ounce size) chicken broth

½ cup half-and-half

2 tablespoons minced fresh mint, or 1 teaspoon dried mint

¼ teaspoon black pepper

1. Melt butter in large saucepan over medium heat. Add chopped onion and sauté for 8 to 10 minutes, or until lightly browned, stirring onion mixture frequently. Add fresh peas and chicken broth to sautéed onion in saucepan; bring chicken-broth mixture to a boil. Reduce heat to low; cover and simmer chicken-broth mixture for 15 minutes.

2. In blender or food processor fitted with steel blade, puree soup mixture (in batches, if necessary). Return soup mixture to saucepan over low heat. Stir in half-and-half, mint and black pepper; heat through.

Makes 4 to 6 servings.

*Per serving: 178 calories, 7 g protein, 10 g fat, 16 g carbohydrate, 21 mg cholesterol, 969 mg sodium.*

## CREAMY CORN-AND-SHRIMP CHOWDER

For a lighter version of this chowder, use equal parts of milk and half-and-half. (Pictured, pages 160 and 161.)

1 tablespoon butter or margarine
1 small bunch scallions, chopped
2 packages (10-ounce size) frozen corn, thawed
2 cups half-and-half
1 pound medium shrimp, shelled, deveined and halved lengthwise
Salt and black pepper to taste

1. Melt butter in large saucepan over medium-high heat. Add chopped scallions; cook for 3 to 5 minutes, or until softened, stirring frequently.

2. Reserve 1 cup of the corn kernels. In food processor fitted with steel blade, puree remaining corn. Add reserved corn kernels, pureed corn and half-and-half to scallions; bring to a boil, stirring. Reduce heat to low; simmer for 2 to 3 minutes.

3. Add shrimp, salt and pepper; simmer for 2 to 3 minutes, or until shrimp are just cooked through.

Makes 4 servings.

*Per serving: 411 calories, 27 g protein, 19 g fat, 37 g carbohydrate, 192 mg cholesterol, 220 mg sodium.*

### CANNED SOUP—PLUS
● Add a splash of dry sherry to beef bouillon.
● Accent vegetable soups with sautéed pepperoni or crumbled bacon.
● Top any cream soup with grated cheese, crunchy croutons or chopped parsley.
● Add prepared tortellini, peas and a sprinkling of Parmesan to chicken broth.

## CORN CHOWDER WITH SPINACH AND BASIL

To cut short your kitchen duty, buy cleaned spinach from a supermarket salad bar. (For a refreshing summertime meal, serve chilled chowder; just substitute olive or salad oil for the bacon in step 1.)

3 strips bacon, diced
2 to 3 fresh jalapeño peppers, finely chopped (optional)
2 medium cloves garlic, minced
1 large onion, diced
6 large ears corn, husked
¼ pound fresh spinach, coarsely chopped
½ cup coarsely chopped fresh basil
4 cups milk
Salt and white pepper to taste

1. In large pot over medium heat, cook bacon until crisp. Remove to paper towels to drain; set aside. To drippings in pot, add jalapeños (if using), garlic and onion; cook until vegetables are tender, stirring occasionally.

2. Meanwhile, use a sharp knife to cut kernels from corn (about 3 cups). Add corn, spinach and basil to onion mixture in pot; cook for 1 minute. Add milk; bring to a boil. Reduce heat to low; simmer for 5 minutes. Add salt and white pepper to mixture. Sprinkle chowder with bacon.

Makes 6 servings.

*Per serving: 251 calories, 10 g protein, 13 g fat, 27 g carbohydrate, 30 mg cholesterol, 186 mg sodium.*

## TEX-MEX MICROWAVE CHILI

The perfect choice for a weeknight dinner—quick, thick and delicious. It's a filling one-dish meal you can prepare from start to finish after work.

1 medium onion, chopped
1 large clove garlic, minced
1 small green pepper, chopped
1 fresh or pickled jalapeño pepper, seeded and minced
1 tablespoon salad oil
1 pound lean ground beef
1 can (15¼ to 16 ounces) red kidney beans, undrained
1 can (14½ to 16 ounces) tomatoes, drained and chopped
2 to 3 tablespoons chili powder
2 tablespoons tomato paste
1 teaspoon ground cumin
½ teaspoon cayenne pepper
¼ teaspoon salt

1. In 2-quart microwaveproof dish, combine onion, garlic, green pepper, jalapeño and oil. Microwave on High for 1 to 2 minutes. Crumble beef into onion mixture; stir. Microwave on High for 3 minutes, or until beef has lost most of its pink color.

2. Drain and discard drippings; stir in remaining ingredients. Microwave on High for 4 minutes, stirring once. Cover tightly with lid or with plastic wrap turned back slightly on one side. Microwave on Medium for 5 to 6 minutes. Let chili stand, covered, for about 5 minutes. Serve with oyster crackers, if you like.

Makes 4 servings.

*Per serving: 406 calories, 28 g protein, 21 g fat, 29 g carbohydrate, 66 mg cholesterol, 866 mg sodium.*

## GREAT WAYS WITH LEFTOVER CHILI

### FIESTA CHILI PIE

3 cups corn chips, coarsely crushed
1 small onion, finely chopped
1 cup (4 ounces) shredded American or cheddar cheese
2 cups homemade or canned chili

Preheat oven to 350°F. Spread 2 cups of the corn chips in bottom of 9-inch pie plate; sprinkle with onion and half of the cheese. Top with chili, then remaining corn chips and cheese. Bake for 15 minutes, or until heated through.

Makes 4 to 6 servings.

*Per serving: 302 calories, 13 g protein, 21 g fat, 18 g carbohydrate, 39 mg cholesterol, 701 mg sodium.*

### SUPER-FAST CHILI NACHOS

1 bag (12 ounces) tortilla chips
2 cups homemade or canned chili
1 cup (4 ounces) shredded Monterey Jack cheese with jalapeño peppers

Preheat oven to 450°F. On large baking sheet, arrange tortilla chips in single layer. Top each chip with some chili and cheese. Bake for 5 minutes, or until cheese melts.

Makes 8 servings.

*Per serving: 308 calories, 10 g protein, 17 g fat, 31 g carbohydrate, 26 mg cholesterol, 502 mg sodium.*

## CINCINNATI CHILI

Spoon a healthy serving of this specially spiced favorite over pasta. (Pictured, right.)

2 pounds lean ground beef
1 medium onion, chopped
3 tablespoons chili powder
1 teaspoon ground cinnamon
1 teaspoon ground cumin
¾ teaspoon salt
¼ teaspoon cayenne pepper
⅛ teaspoon ground allspice
⅛ teaspoon ground cloves
2 tablespoons distilled white vinegar
1 can (15 ounces) tomato sauce
1 bay leaf
1 pound spaghetti
**Parsley and chopped red onion (optional garnish)**

1. In large pot over medium heat, brown beef; with slotted spoon, remove beef to a bowl. Discard all but 1 tablespoon drippings in pot.

2. To drippings in pot, add onion; sauté until tender, stirring occasionally. Add chili powder, cinnamon, cumin, salt, cayenne, allspice and cloves; cook for 1 minute, stirring constantly. Add beef, vinegar, tomato sauce, bay leaf and ½ cup water; bring to a boil. Reduce heat to low; cover and simmer for 30 minutes.

3. Meanwhile, cook spaghetti according to package directions; drain and place on a serving platter.

4. Discard bay leaf; spoon chili on spaghetti. Garnish with parsley and red onion.
   Makes 6 to 8 servings.

*Per serving: 548 calories, 33 g protein, 21 g fat, 57 g carbohydrate, 76 mg cholesterol, 533 mg sodium.*

*Left: (Clockwise from top right) Vegetable Chili with Herbed Cheese Dumplings (page 168), No-Tomato Chicken Chili (this page), Cincinnati Chili (facing page).*

## NO-TOMATO CHICKEN CHILI

This light yet satisfying chili cooks in less than 30 minutes. (Pictured, left.)

1  tablespoon salad oil
6  boneless, skinless chicken-breast halves, cut into ¾-inch cubes
2  medium green and/or red peppers, diced
1  large clove garlic, minced
1  medium onion, diced
1  fresh or pickled jalapeño pepper, seeded and minced
1  tablespoon chili powder
2  teaspoons ground cumin
1  package or cube chicken-flavor instant bouillon
½  teaspoon salt
½  teaspoon black pepper
1  can (16 to 19 ounces) white kidney beans (cannellini), drained
1  can (12 ounces) no-salt-added whole-kernel corn, drained

1.  Heat oil in large saucepan over medium heat. Add chicken; sauté for 2 to 3 minutes, stirring frequently. Add next 4 ingredients; cook for 5 minutes, or until tender.

2.  Add chili powder, cumin, bouillon, salt, black pepper and 1 cup water; bring to a boil. Reduce heat to low; cover and simmer for 15 minutes. Add beans and corn; heat through.

Makes 6 servings.

*Per serving: 267 calories, 32 g protein, 5 g fat, 25 g carbohydrate, 66 mg cholesterol, 744 mg sodium.*

## VEGETABLE CHILI WITH HERBED CHEESE DUMPLINGS

Super-easy dumplings taste great with chili. (Pictured, pages 166 and 167.)

Chili:

2 tablespoons salad oil
2 large onions, chopped
2 large cloves garlic, minced
1 medium eggplant, cut into ½-inch cubes
1 large green pepper, coarsely chopped
2 tablespoons chili powder
2 teaspoons ground cumin
1 teaspoon dried oregano
½ teaspoon cayenne pepper
3 cans (14½- to 16-ounce size) tomatoes in tomato puree
2 cans (15¼- to 16-ounce size) red kidney beans, drained

Dumplings:

¾ cup all-purpose flour
½ cup yellow cornmeal
2 teaspoons baking powder
¼ teaspoon salt
½ cup (2 ounces) shredded cheddar cheese
½ cup milk
1 egg, beaten
1 tablespoon minced fresh cilantro or parsley

1. For chili: Heat oil in large pot over medium heat. Add onions and garlic; sauté until tender, stirring occasionally. Stir in eggplant and ¼ cup water; cover and simmer for 10 minutes.

2. Add green pepper and next 4 ingredients; cook for 1 minute, stirring constantly. Add tomatoes with liquid, breaking tomatoes up with a spoon, and then beans. Bring to a boil. Reduce heat to low; cover and simmer for 10 minutes.

3. Meanwhile, prepare dumplings: In medium bowl, mix flour, cornmeal, baking powder and salt. Add ¼ cup of the cheese; toss until well combined. Add milk, egg and cilantro; stir until just combined. Drop batter by spoonfuls on top of chili; cover and simmer for 15 minutes. Sprinkle remaining ¼ cup cheese over dumplings; cover and simmer for 5 minutes, or until dumplings are cooked and cheese is melted.

Makes 6 to 8 servings.

*Per serving: 379 calories, 16 g protein, 9 g fat, 61 g carbohydrate, 50 mg cholesterol, 1,053 mg sodium.*

## ITALIAN THREE-BEAN CHILI

You can adjust the heat in this chili to suit your family's taste. (Pictured, right.)

1½ pounds lean ground beef
½ pound hot or sweet Italian sausage, casing removed and sausage crumbled
2 large cloves garlic, minced
1 large onion, chopped
1 can (28 ounces) tomatoes in tomato puree
2 tablespoons chili powder
1 teaspoon dried oregano
1 bay leaf
¾ teaspoon fennel seeds, crushed
½ to 1 teaspoon crushed red pepper
1 can (15¼ to 16 ounces) red kidney beans
1 can (16 to 19 ounces) garbanzo beans (chick-peas)
1 package (10 ounces) frozen Italian green beans, thawed
Salt to taste
Parmesan cheese shavings (optional)

1. In large pot over medium heat, brown beef and sausage. With slotted spoon, remove meat mixture to a bowl. Discard all but 1 tablespoon drippings in pot.

2. To drippings in pot, add garlic and onion; sauté until tender, stirring occasionally. Add meat mixture, tomatoes with liquid, chili powder, oregano, bay leaf, fennel seeds and pepper; bring to a boil. Reduce heat to low; cover and simmer for 30 minutes.

3. Add kidney beans with liquid, garbanzo beans with liquid and green beans; simmer for 10 to 15 minutes. Discard bay leaf; add salt. Top with cheese (if using).

Makes 8 servings.

*Per serving: 418 calories, 27 g protein, 20 g fat, 34 g carbohydrate, 67 mg cholesterol, 770 mg sodium.*

*Above: Italian Three-Bean Chili (facing page), Two-Alarm Pork Chili (this page).*

## TWO-ALARM PORK CHILI

Fresh jalapeño peppers give this feisty, fiery version its spark. (Pictured, left below.)

1 tablespoon salad oil
2 pounds lean boneless pork loin, trimmed and cut into ¾-inch cubes
3 to 4 fresh jalapeño peppers, seeded and minced
1 large green pepper, coarsely chopped
1 large clove garlic, minced
1 medium onion, coarsely chopped
2 tablespoons chili powder
1 tablespoon ground cumin
½ teaspoon black pepper
½ teaspoon crushed red pepper
2 cans (28-ounce size) tomatoes
2 cans (15- to 16-ounce size) black beans, rinsed and drained
Salt to taste
Sour cream, avocado slices and diced tomato (optional)

1. Heat oil in large pot over medium-high heat. Add pork; sauté until browned. Add jalapeños, green pepper, garlic and onion; cook for 5 minutes, stirring occasionally.

2. Add chili powder, cumin, black pepper and crushed pepper; cook for 1 minute, stirring constantly. Add tomatoes with liquid, breaking tomatoes up with a spoon; bring to a boil. Reduce heat to low; partially cover and simmer for 1 to 1½ hours, or until pork is tender, stirring occasionally.

3. Add black beans and salt; heat through. Top chili with sour cream, avocado and tomato (if using).

Makes 6 to 8 servings.

*Per serving: 409 calories, 39 g protein, 13 g fat, 35 g carbohydrate, 82 mg cholesterol, 977 mg sodium.*

*Above: Italian Veal Salad (this page).*

1. Arrange greens and radishes on a large serving platter.

2. Heat 1 tablespoon of the oil in large skillet over medium-high heat. Add veal in batches with garlic; sauté for 2 minutes, or until lightly browned and just cooked, turning once. Place veal on top of greens.

3. To drippings in skillet, add onion, vinegar, thyme, pepper, salt and remaining 2 tablespoons oil; bring to a boil. Pour over veal and greens; toss until well coated.

Makes 4 servings.

*Per serving: 302 calories, 24 g protein, 21 g fat, 5 g carbohydrate, 81 mg cholesterol, 171 mg sodium.*

*Note:* If you prefer, use thin chicken cutlets instead of the veal.

## ITALIAN VEAL SALAD

You'll get rave reviews when you serve this refreshing main-dish salad. Served on a bed of greens, the sautéed veal gets a splash of tangy dressing prepared in the same skillet. (Pictured, above.)

8 cups mixed salad greens
1 small bunch radishes, trimmed and thinly sliced
3 tablespoons olive oil
1 pound veal scaloppine, cut into serving-size pieces (see Note)
1 large clove garlic, minced
1 small red onion, thinly sliced
2 tablespoons balsamic or red-wine vinegar
¼ teaspoon dried thyme
¼ teaspoon cracked black pepper
⅛ teaspoon salt

## WARM SESAME CHICKEN SALAD

Serve with steamed rice tossed with chopped toasted almonds. (Pictured, right.)

1 medium clove garlic, minced
1 tablespoon cornstarch
1 tablespoon lemon juice
1 tablespoon reduced-sodium soy sauce
2 teaspoons chicken-flavor instant bouillon
2 teaspoons minced fresh ginger
⅛ to ¼ teaspoon crushed red pepper
¼ teaspoon oriental sesame oil (optional)
1 egg white
⅓ cup sesame seeds
⅓ cup plain dried bread crumbs
1 pound chicken cutlets, cut lengthwise into 1-inch-wide strips
4 tablespoons salad oil (preferably peanut oil)
1 large bunch watercress, stemmed
½ medium head iceberg lettuce, shredded

*Above: (From front) Warm Sesame Chicken Salad (facing page), Turkey Tandoori (page 205).*

1. For dipping sauce: In small saucepan, mix first 8 ingredients with ¾ cup water until thoroughly combined. Over medium-high heat, cook for 2 to 3 minutes, or until mixture is slightly thickened, stirring constantly. Set aside.

2. In shallow dish, beat egg white with fork until foamy. In second shallow dish, mix sesame seeds and bread crumbs. Add chicken to egg white, tossing to coat; then roll each strip in sesame-seed mixture.

3. Heat 2 tablespoons of the salad oil in skillet over medium-high heat. Add half of the chicken; cook for 3 to 4 minutes, or until browned and cooked through, turning chicken once and removing to a serving platter when done. Discard any sesame seeds in skillet; then repeat with remaining 2 tablespoons oil and chicken. Remove chicken to serving platter.

4. Increase heat to high. To drippings in skillet, add watercress and lettuce; stir-fry for 1 to 2 minutes, or until just wilted. Arrange greens on platter with chicken, and then drizzle with a little dipping sauce. Serve chicken with remaining sauce.

Makes 4 servings.

*Per serving: 385 calories, 33 g protein, 22 g fat, 15 g carbohydrate, 66 mg cholesterol, 808 mg sodium.*

## TAKEOUT ROAST CHICKEN-AND-BREAD SALAD

This timesaving recipe starts with roast chicken from the deli. If you'd like the chicken warm, heat it in the oven for about 20 minutes. (Pictured, page 163.)

½ loaf Italian bread, cut into 1-inch cubes
2 tablespoons red-wine vinegar
2 teaspoons grainy Dijon mustard
1 large clove garlic, minced
½ teaspoon salt
¼ teaspoon cracked black pepper
⅓ cup olive oil
6 cups mixed salad greens
1 pint cherry and/or yellow pear tomatoes, halved
1 cucumber, peeled and diced
1 cup torn fresh basil leaves
½ small red onion, cut into thin slivers
1 deli roast chicken (about 2½ pounds), cut into serving pieces

1. Preheat oven to 350°F. Spread bread cubes on baking sheet. Bake for 5 minutes, or until lightly toasted.

2. Meanwhile, in small bowl, whisk vinegar, mustard, garlic, salt and pepper. Slowly whisk in oil.

3. In large serving bowl, combine bread cubes, greens, tomatoes, cucumber, basil and onion; gently toss with dressing. Let salad stand for 15 minutes. Arrange chicken on top of salad.

Makes 6 servings.

*Per serving: 443 calories, 28 g protein, 24 g fat, 29 g carbohydrate, 74 mg cholesterol, 533 mg sodium.*

## SEAFOOD SALAD WITH MUSTARD-THYME DRESSING

The seafood, potatoes and dressing can be prepared ahead of time; assemble the salad just before serving. (Pictured, right.)

2 tablespoons olive oil
½ pound medium shrimp, shelled and deveined
3 scallions, thinly sliced
½ teaspoon salt
½ pound sea scallops
1 pound small red-skinned potatoes
½ cup milk
½ cup reduced-calorie, reduced-cholesterol mayonnaise
¼ cup plain nonfat yogurt
3 tablespoons grainy Dijon mustard
2 teaspoons minced fresh thyme, or ½ teaspoon dried thyme
3 cups mixed salad greens
2 ounces snow peas, trimmed and thinly sliced lengthwise (about ½ cup)

1. Heat oil in medium skillet over medium heat. Add shrimp, scallions and ¼ teaspoon of the salt; sauté for 3 minutes, or until shrimp turn pink and are just cooked through. With slotted spoon, remove shrimp mixture to a bowl. To oil in skillet, add scallops and remaining ¼ teaspoon salt; sauté for 3 minutes, or until scallops are opaque and just cooked through. Remove to bowl with shrimp. Cover; refrigerate for 30 minutes.

2. Meanwhile, place potatoes in medium saucepan; add water to cover. Bring to a boil; reduce heat to low. Cover and simmer

*Right: (From top) Seafood Salad with Mustard-Thyme Dressing (this page), Skillet Pizza Alfresco (page 180).*

for 15 minutes, or until potatoes are tender but slightly resistant when pierced. Drain and cool; cut into thin slices.

3. For dressing: In small bowl, mix milk, mayonnaise, yogurt, mustard and thyme.

4. Arrange salad greens on a serving platter; top salad greens with shrimp-scallop mixture and potato slices. Sprinkle top of salad with snow peas. Serve salad with mustard-thyme dressing.

Makes 4 servings.

*Per serving: 387 calories, 24 g protein, 18 g fat, 31 g carbohydrate, 94 mg cholesterol, 970 mg sodium.*

## HOT CHICKEN-AND-VEGETABLE SALAD ORIENTAL

Try this main-dish salad for a change of pace at dinnertime—it's ready in less than 10 minutes! (Pictured, pages 160 and 161.)

¼ cup oriental sesame oil
½ pound snow peas, trimmed
2 cups shredded cooked chicken
2 tablespoons reduced-sodium soy sauce
6 cups shredded Chinese (Napa) or savoy cabbage
Salt and black pepper to taste

1. Heat oil in large skillet over medium-high heat. Add snow peas; stir-fry for 2 to 3 minutes, or until tender-crisp.
2. Add chicken, soy sauce and 1 cup of the cabbage; stir-fry for 2 to 3 minutes, or until heated through. Season with salt and pepper. Place remaining 5 cups cabbage on a serving platter; top with chicken mixture.
Makes 4 servings.

*Per serving: 300 calories, 24 g protein, 19 g fat, 9 g carbohydrate, 62 mg cholesterol, 373 mg sodium.*

## TUNA-AND-ORZO GREEK SALAD

Serve this easy main-dish salad on a bed of lettuce or in pita pockets.

½ cup orzo or other small pasta
2 cans (6½-ounce size) water-packed tuna, drained
2 ounces feta cheese, crumbled
2 medium tomatoes, coarsely chopped
⅔ cup bottled herb vinaigrette dressing

Cook orzo according to package directions. Drain orzo; rinse with cold water and drain again thoroughly. In large bowl, mix all ingredients; gently toss to combine.
Makes 4 servings.

*Per serving: 433 calories, 30 g protein, 23 g fat, 26 g carbohydrate, 47 mg cholesterol, 766 mg sodium.*

## SALADS WITH SPARKLE

When buying salad greens, be sure to choose a head or bunch that feels heavy for its size and has good color.

Keep in mind that greens can be cleaned several days in advance if properly stored: Wash greens thoroughly and then dry them completely. Wrap the dried greens loosely in paper towels and place in large plastic bags. Press the air out of the bags and store them in the refrigerator crisper.

Here are some special types to try:
● Arugula: This tender green with a tart, mustardy taste is delicious drizzled with balsamic or red-wine vinegar and olive oil.
● Belgian endive: Use this slightly sharp-tasting green to pep up salads.
● Chicory (curly endive): A head of chicory has dark-green outer leaves and a pale center. Its strong flavor works best combined with milder lettuces.
● Radicchio: Ruby-colored radicchio has a wonderfully peppery taste. It's expensive, but a little goes a long way.
● Escarole: This cousin of chicory has a pleasantly bitter taste. Escarole is great with hot bacon dressings.

## SAUSAGE-AND-PEPPER HEROES

A bounty of tasty vegetables makes these simple-to-fix sandwiches a crunchy treat. Red and yellow peppers, together with red onion and zucchini, add extra color to the sausage heroes. (Pictured, right.)

¾  pound sweet and/or hot Italian sausage
1  tablespoon olive oil
2  large cloves garlic, minced
1  small bulb fennel, cored and thinly sliced (optional)
1  small red onion, thinly sliced
2  small red and/or yellow peppers, cut into thin strips
1  small zucchini, halved lengthwise and thinly sliced
1  can (16 to 19 ounces) garbanzo beans (chick-peas), drained
½  teaspoon dried basil
2  tablespoons balsamic or red-wine vinegar
4  to 6 braided or hero rolls, split

*Above: Sausage-and-Pepper Heroes (this page).*

1.  Prick sausage with a fork. Heat oil in large skillet over medium-high heat. Add sausage; cook for 8 to 10 minutes, or until browned on all sides. With slotted spoon, remove sausage from skillet. Cut into ½-inch-thick slices; set aside.

2.  Reduce heat to medium. To drippings in skillet, add garlic, fennel (if using) and onion; sauté for 3 minutes, or until tender-crisp, stirring frequently. Add peppers and next 3 ingredients; cook for 5 minutes, stirring frequently. Add sausage and vinegar; cook for 2 minutes. Serve on rolls.

Makes 4 to 6 servings.

*Per serving: 530 calories, 20 g protein, 26 g fat, 52 g carbohydrate, 53 mg cholesterol, 1,072 mg sodium.*

### CUSTOM SANDWICHES

Start at the deli—and make your own custom sandwich!

● Mix honey, mustard and a bit of tarragon for a great spread on a ham-and-cheese sandwich.

● Combine a little prepared horseradish with light sour cream—scrumptious on roast beef.

● Stir chopped chutney into softened butter for a sassy sandwich spread to serve with smoked turkey or baked ham.

● Mix drained oil-packed sun-dried tomatoes with mayo to accent a turkey sandwich.

## MONTEREY TURKEY SUBS

A guacamole-type topping is the flavorful secret to these quick-fix sandwiches.

Avocado topping:
1 medium avocado, peeled and pitted
1 scallion, chopped
2 teaspoons minced fresh cilantro
2 teaspoons lime juice
⅛ teaspoon salt

Turkey:
¾ pound turkey cutlets
½ teaspoon salt
2 tablespoons salad oil
1 large clove garlic, minced
2 teaspoons ground cumin
4 small whole-grain rolls, split
Fresh spinach leaves
½ cup (2 ounces) shredded Monterey Jack cheese (optional)

1. For avocado topping: In small bowl, lightly mash avocado. Stir in remaining topping ingredients; set aside.

2. For turkey: Sprinkle cutlets with salt. Heat oil in large skillet over medium-low heat. Add garlic and cumin; sauté for 5 minutes, stirring frequently. Increase heat to medium-high. Add cutlets; cook for 4 minutes, or until lightly browned and just cooked through, turning once. Remove cutlets to cutting board; cut to fit rolls.

3. Layer bottom halves of rolls with spinach, cutlets, cheese (if using) and avocado topping. Sandwich with tops of rolls.

Makes 4 servings.

*Per serving: 348 calories, 26 g protein, 17 g fat, 25 g carbohydrate, 54 mg cholesterol, 631 mg sodium.*

## PRESTO PESTO-AND-PEPPER SANDWICHES

Pesto—a rich mix of basil, Parmesan, garlic, nuts and olive oil—is available in most supermarket refrigerated sections.

1 loaf Italian bread
¾ cup store-bought pesto
1 jar (7 ounces) roasted red peppers, drained and cut into strips
¾ pound part-skim mozzarella cheese, thinly sliced
½ teaspoon black pepper
Fresh basil (optional garnish)

1. Preheat broiler. Cut loaf horizontally in half; then cut each half crosswise into thirds to make 6 pieces. Place on baking sheet cut sides up, 3 to 5 inches from heat source; broil until lightly browned.

2. Spread each piece of bread on toasted side with about 2 tablespoons of the pesto. Top with pepper strips and cheese; then sprinkle with black pepper. Broil until cheese melts and sandwiches are heated through. Garnish with basil.

Makes 6 servings.

*Per serving: 416 calories, 23 g protein, 19 g fat, 40 g carbohydrate, 39 mg cholesterol, 731 mg sodium.*

### WRAP IT UP!

Tired of the same sandwich bread? Why not wrap sandwich fillings in flour tortillas or even lettuce leaves? Or toast and fill a couple of frozen waffles or toaster corn cakes. For smaller, kid-size appetites—stuff a muffin or biscuit! Ham salad on a corn muffin is terrific. Pitas, bagels, rice cakes, croissants and hearty whole-grain breads are other ideas to give you a break from the same-old-sandwich routine.

## SMOKED MOZZARELLA
## CROSTINI

If your grocer doesn't stock smoked mozzarella, the regular variety makes a fine substitute. If you need a tasty alternative to the Italian parsley sprigs, try fresh basil. (Pictured, page 163.)

2 tablespoons olive oil
1 large clove garlic, minced
¼ teaspoon cracked black pepper
8 slices (cut diagonally ½ inch thick) Italian bread
¼ pound smoked or regular mozzarella cheese, thinly sliced
8 large sprigs Italian parsley

1. Preheat oven to 450°F. In a cup, mix olive oil, minced garlic and cracked black pepper. Brush garlic-oil mixture over 1 side of each bread slice.

2. Place 4 of the bread slices on baking sheet, garlic-oil side down. Top each slice with some cheese and 2 sprigs parsley. Sandwich with remaining bread slices, garlic-oil side up. Bake for 5 to 10 minutes, or until cheese melts and bread slices are lightly toasted.

Makes 4 servings.

*Per serving (with regular mozzarella): 299 calories, 11 g protein, 13 g fat, 33 g carbohydrate, 23 mg cholesterol, 439 mg sodium.*

## MICROWAVE GREEK-STYLE
## CHICKEN PITAS

Greek olives, crisp radishes and bread-and-butter pickles are delicious go-alongs for this hearty meal-in-a-sandwich.

4 chicken cutlets (about ¾ pound)
¼ cup prepared Italian dressing
1 medium tomato, diced
1 small cucumber, peeled and thinly sliced
1 small red onion, thinly sliced
⅔ cup plain nonfat yogurt
⅓ cup crumbled feta cheese
2 teaspoons minced fresh mint, or ½ teaspoon dried mint
1 teaspoon red-wine vinegar
¼ teaspoon salt
¼ teaspoon black pepper
4 sesame or plain pitas

1. Place cutlets in a single layer in 13-by-9-inch microwaveproof baking dish. Drizzle with dressing, turning to coat. Let stand for at least 15 minutes. (Or cover and place in refrigerator to marinate for up to a day.)

2. Meanwhile, combine remaining ingredients except pitas; set aside.

3. Cover cutlets in baking dish with wax paper; microwave on High for 2 minutes. Rotate dish and rearrange less-cooked cutlets toward outside of dish. Microwave on High for 2 to 3 minutes, or until cooked through.

4. Wrap each pita in a paper towel; microwave two at a time on High for 20 to 30 seconds, or until warm. Stuff pitas with chicken cutlets and tomato mixture.

Makes 4 servings.

*Per serving: 406 calories, 30 g protein, 12 g fat, 45 g carbohydrate, 60 mg cholesterol, 833 mg sodium.*

## CALIFORNIA-STYLE TURKEY CROISSANTS

If you wish, you can substitute 1 small avocado, peeled and thinly sliced, for the guacamole in this recipe.

4 croissants
8 slices cooked turkey (about ½ pound)
8 slices Muenster cheese (about ½ pound)
½ cup homemade or frozen, thawed guacamole
1 small tomato, thinly sliced

Preheat broiler. Split croissants without cutting all the way through. Open croissants and place cut side up on baking sheet. Place 2 turkey slices on each bottom half and 2 cheese slices on other half. Spread 2 tablespoons guacamole on turkey. Broil for 2 minutes, or until cheese melts. Top with tomato; place croissant halves together.

Makes 4 servings.

*Per serving: 544 calories, 35 g protein, 35 g fat, 24 g carbohydrate, 94 mg cholesterol, 825 mg sodium.*

*Left: (From top) Turkey Sloppy Joes (this page), Beef Burgers Stroganoff (page 198).*

## TURKEY SLOPPY JOES

This family favorite gets its zest from herbs, spices and chili sauce. (Pictured, left.)

2 tablespoons salad oil
3 medium cloves garlic, minced
2 medium onions, diced
2 medium red and/or green peppers, diced
¼ teaspoon ground cumin
¼ teaspoon dried thyme
1 pound ground turkey
½ cup chili sauce
½ cup beer
1 tablespoon Worcestershire sauce
4 large seeded rolls, split and toasted

1. Heat 1 tablespoon of the oil in large skillet over medium heat. Add garlic, onions and peppers; sauté for 8 to 10 minutes, or until tender, stirring occasionally. Add cumin and thyme; cook for 2 minutes, stirring constantly. Remove to a plate; set aside.

2. Heat remaining 1 tablespoon oil in same skillet over medium-high heat. Add turkey; cook for 3 to 4 minutes, or until lightly golden, stirring to break up turkey. Stir in vegetable mixture, chili sauce, beer and Worcestershire. Reduce heat to low; partially cover and simmer for 8 to 10 minutes, or until sauce thickens slightly, stirring occasionally. Spoon over toasted rolls; serve with coleslaw, if you like.

Makes 4 servings.

*Per serving: 471 calories, 27 g protein, 20 g fat, 46 g carbohydrate, 78 mg cholesterol, 920 mg sodium.*

## FOOD-PROCESSOR SPREADS

### CUMIN CHEESE SPREAD

4 ounces Monterey Jack cheese, cut into chunks
4 ounces Muenster cheese, cut into chunks
¼ cup mayonnaise
½ teaspoon ground cumin
¼ teaspoon ground coriander

In food processor fitted with steel blade, process all ingredients until smooth.
Makes 1¼ cups.

*Per tablespoon: 62 calories, 3 g protein, 6 g fat, 0 g carbohydrate, 12 mg cholesterol, 82 mg sodium.*

### CARROT-CREAM CHEESE SPREAD

2 large carrots, halved crosswise
1 package (8 ounces) cream cheese, softened
1 teaspoon brown sugar (optional)
½ teaspoon ground cinnamon
¼ teaspoon ground ginger
2 tablespoons raisins

In food processor fitted with grating disk, process carrots; remove disk and transfer carrots to small bowl. Insert metal blade. Process cheese, sugar (if using), cinnamon and ginger until smooth. Add raisins and carrots, pulsing 5 or 6 times to combine.
Makes about 1½ cups.

*Per ¼ cup: 156 calories, 3 g protein, 13 g fat, 7 g carbohydrate, 42 mg cholesterol, 124 mg sodium.*

### BARBECUED HAM SPREAD

½ pound cooked ham, cut into chunks
3 tablespoons mayonnaise
2 tablespoons barbecue sauce
1 teaspoon chili powder

In food processor fitted with steel blade, process all ingredients until ham is finely chopped.
Makes 1¼ cups.

*Per ¼ cup: 151 calories, 10 g protein, 11 g fat, 3 g carbohydrate, 32 mg cholesterol, 834 mg sodium.*

# Italian Favorites

## SKILLET PIZZA ALFRESCO

The ready-made crust will stay crisp if you partially bake it before adding toppings. (Pictured, page 173.)

2 tablespoons olive oil
1 large clove garlic, minced
1 large red pepper, thinly sliced
1 medium zucchini, coarsely shredded
1 tablespoon minced fresh thyme, or ½ teaspoon dried thyme
1 package (10 ounces) all-ready pizza crust
1 cup (4 ounces) shredded mozzarella cheese
2 tablespoons grated Parmesan cheese

1. Preheat oven to 450°F. Heat oil in medium skillet over medium heat. Add garlic and pepper; sauté for 5 minutes, stirring frequently. Add zucchini and thyme; sauté for 5 minutes, stirring occasionally. Remove skillet from heat.

2. Lightly grease 12-inch ovenproof skillet; unroll pizza crust in skillet. Press dough into bottom and halfway up sides of skillet; roll corners of dough to form a rounded edge. Bake on bottom rack of oven for 10 to 12 minutes, or until bottom is browned.

3. Sprinkle crust with mozzarella; top with vegetable mixture and sprinkle with Parmesan. Bake for 5 to 10 minutes.

Makes 4 to 6 servings.

*Per serving: 276 calories, 11 g protein, 13 g fat, 29 g carbohydrate, 19 mg cholesterol, 396 mg sodium.*

## SPINACH-AND-MUSHROOM PIZZA

Here's an easy spinach-mushroom pizza.

2 tablespoons olive oil
1 tablespoon pine nuts or chopped almonds
½ pound mushrooms, sliced
¾ pound spinach
¼ teaspoon salt
¼ teaspoon crushed red pepper
1 ounce sliced pepperoni, cut into strips
1 package (10 ounces) all-ready pizza crust
1 cup (4 ounces) shredded Fontina cheese

1. Preheat oven to 450°F. Heat oil in medium skillet over medium heat. Add pine nuts; sauté for 2 to 3 minutes, or until toasted, stirring frequently. With slotted spoon, remove nuts. To oil in skillet, add mushrooms; sauté for 5 minutes. Add spinach, salt and pepper; cook for 10 minutes, or until liquid evaporates, stirring frequently. Remove skillet from heat; stir in nuts and pepperoni.

2. Lightly grease 12-inch ovenproof skillet; unroll pizza crust in skillet. Press dough into bottom and halfway up sides of skillet; roll corners of dough to form a rounded edge. Bake on bottom rack of oven for 10 to 12 minutes, or until bottom is browned.

3. Sprinkle crust with cheese; top with spinach mixture. Bake for 5 to 10 minutes.

Makes 4 to 6 servings.

*Per serving: 340 calories, 15 g protein, 18 g fat, 30 g carbohydrate, 31 mg cholesterol, 718 mg sodium.*

⬧ An ovenproof skillet is handy for making pizzas, frittatas and other stovetop-to-oven dishes. If you don't own an ovenproof skillet, wrap the handle of a regular skillet in aluminum foil.

*Above: Pronto Pizza (this page).*

## PRONTO PIZZA

Toppings are a snap to prep in a food processor—let your family pick their favorites. (Pictured, left.)

1 recipe Quick Pizza Dough (see recipe, page 182)
2 cups (8 ounces) shredded part-skim mozzarella cheese
¾ cup prepared pizza sauce (or ¾ cup tomato sauce mixed with 1 teaspoon dried oregano)
Additional toppings:
3 ounces mushrooms, thinly sliced
3 ounces pepperoni, thinly sliced
1 medium green pepper, thinly sliced
1 small red onion, thinly sliced (sauté for 5 minutes in a little olive or salad oil)

1. Preheat oven to 500°F. Grease large baking sheet. Place dough on prepared baking sheet; roll into a 14-inch circle. Roll edges of dough toward center until circle measures 12 inches in diameter.

2. Sprinkle dough with 1 cup of the cheese; drizzle with pizza sauce. Top with remaining 1 cup cheese and sprinkle with additional toppings, if you like. Bake on bottom rack of oven for 15 to 20 minutes, or until cheese melts and crust is brown.

Makes 6 servings.

*Per serving (without additional toppings): 344 calories, 17 g protein, 7 g fat, 51 g carbohydrate, 22 mg cholesterol, 487 mg sodium.*

## MEXICAN PIZZA

This pizza is a sure-fire winner with kids!

1 recipe Quick Pizza Dough (recipe
   follows)
2 cups (8 ounces) shredded Monterey Jack
   cheese (plain or with jalapeños)
¾ cup prepared chunky salsa
1 cup shredded cooked chicken, or
   drained cooked ground beef
1 teaspoon dried oregano
½ teaspoon ground cumin

1. Preheat oven to 500°F. Grease large baking sheet. Place dough on prepared baking sheet; roll into a 14-inch circle. Roll edges of dough toward center until circle measures 12 inches in diameter.

2. Sprinkle dough with 1 cup of the cheese; drizzle with salsa. Top with chicken, remaining 1 cup cheese, and then oregano and cumin. Bake on bottom rack of oven for 15 to 20 minutes, or until cheese melts and crust is brown.

Makes 6 servings.

*Per serving: 430 calories, 23 g protein, 14 g fat, 52 g carbohydrate, 54 mg cholesterol, 627 mg sodium.*

1. In small bowl, stir yeast, sugar and 1 cup very warm water (between 110°F and 120°F) until yeast dissolves. Let mixture stand until it begins to foam.

2. In food processor fitted with steel blade, combine 3 cups flour and salt (2 to 3 pulses). With machine running, pour yeast mixture and oil through feed tube; process until dough begins to pull away from side of bowl and form a ball. To knead dough, process for 45 to 60 seconds, until smooth and elastic. (Add more flour, 2 tablespoons at a time, if dough seems wet.) Cover dough and let rest for 10 minutes. Shape as directed in pizza recipes.

Makes 6 servings.

*Per serving: 251 calories, 7 g protein, 3 g fat, 48 g carbohydrate, 0 mg cholesterol, 184 mg sodium.*

*Note:* One package regular active dry yeast can be substituted for fast-rising yeast; after kneading in processor, cover dough and let rest for 30 minutes before shaping.

## QUICK PIZZA DOUGH

With fast-rising yeast, this dough is ready in 15 minutes! Use in Pronto Pizza (page 181) and Mexican Pizza (above).

1 package fast-rising active dry yeast (see
   Note)
¼ teaspoon sugar
About 3 cups all-purpose flour
½ teaspoon salt
1 tablespoon olive or salad oil

◗ Many yeast-bread recipes call for sprinkling yeast over a little warm water (about 110°F) and letting the mixture stand until foamy. This is called proofing—the test is done to "prove" the yeast is alive. Within 10 minutes after mixing the yeast and water, you should see bubbling and foam on the surface. If not, discard yeast mixture and try again with a fresh package. Luckily, most yeast is reliable and, if used within the expiration date on the package, will rarely fail you.

## THYME-SCENTED GARDEN PIZZA

Frozen pizza dough is a real timesaver. Put it in the refrigerator to thaw before you leave for work.

1 large clove garlic, minced
4 tablespoons olive oil
1 tablespoon cornmeal
1 package (1 pound) frozen pizza dough or bread dough, thawed
1 cup part-skim ricotta cheese
2 tablespoons grated Parmesan cheese
1 tablespoon chopped parsley
2 teaspoons minced fresh thyme, or 1 teaspoon dried thyme
½ teaspoon black pepper
1 large green or yellow pepper, cut into ¼-inch-thick rings
1 medium tomato, thinly sliced
1 small zucchini, cut into ¼-inch-thick slices

1. Preheat oven to 500°F. In a cup, combine garlic with 3 tablespoons of the oil; set aside. Brush large baking sheet or 12-inch pizza pan with remaining 1 tablespoon oil; sprinkle with cornmeal. On lightly floured surface, roll dough into a 14-inch circle; transfer to prepared baking sheet. Roll edges of dough toward center until circle measures 12 inches in diameter.

2. In small bowl, combine ricotta, Parmesan, parsley, thyme and black pepper. Evenly spread ricotta mixture on pizza dough. Top with vegetables; brush with garlic-oil mixture. Bake on bottom rack of oven for 20 to 25 minutes, or until crust is brown.

Makes 4 servings.

*Per serving: 530 calories, 19 g protein, 23 g fat, 60 g carbohydrate, 21 mg cholesterol, 673 mg sodium.*

## THREE-CHEESE PITA PIZZAS

A delight for cheese and veggie lovers.

4 (6-inch) whole-wheat pitas
1 package (10 ounces) frozen Italian-style vegetables in seasoned sauce
1 container (15 to 16 ounces) part-skim ricotta cheese
⅓ cup grated Parmesan cheese
1 cup (4 ounces) shredded part-skim mozzarella cheese

1. Preheat oven to 400°F. For pizza crusts: Split each pita horizontally in half; place cut side up on large baking sheet. Bake for 5 minutes, or until crisp.

2. Meanwhile, cook Italian-style vegetables according to package directions. Drain vegetables, reserving 3 tablespoons of the cooking liquid. In medium bowl, combine reserved liquid, ricotta, Parmesan and ⅔ cup of the mozzarella.

3. Spread cheese mixture on pitas. Top with vegetables and remaining ⅓ cup mozzarella. Bake for 10 minutes, or until hot and bubbly.

Makes 4 servings.

*Per serving: 492 calories, 29 g protein, 20 g fat, 50 g carbohydrate, 55 mg cholesterol, 995 mg sodium.*

### PERSONALIZED PIZZA TOPPINGS!
• Shredded American cheese, crumbled bacon and chopped tomatoes
• Sautéed Italian sausage and red peppers
• Shredded cheddar and minced ham
• Ricotta, grated Parmesan and a little minced red onion
• Thin slices of smoked mozzarella and coarsely chopped fresh basil

## PASTA WITH VEAL, PEPPERS AND BASIL

A salad of arugula and Boston lettuce tossed with olive oil and lemon juice is a tangy accent to this dish. (Pictured, left.)

¾ pound spaghetti
3 tablespoons olive oil
¾ pound veal cutlets, cut crosswise into 2-inch-wide strips
2 to 3 medium cloves garlic, minced
¾ teaspoon salt
¾ teaspoon coarsely ground black pepper
2 large red and/or green peppers, cut into thin strips
1 can (28 ounces) tomatoes
1 bunch fresh basil or Italian parsley, coarsely chopped (about ¾ cup)
Grated Parmesan cheese (optional)

1. Cook spaghetti according to package directions. Drain; return spaghetti to pot and toss with 1 tablespoon of the olive oil. Cover to keep warm.

2. Meanwhile, heat 1 tablespoon of the olive oil in large skillet over high heat. Add veal, garlic, ¼ teaspoon of the salt and ¼ teaspoon of the black pepper; cook for 2 to 3 minutes, or until veal is lightly browned but still pink in center, stirring frequently. With slotted spoon, carefully remove veal to a serving bowl.

3. Reduce heat to medium. To drippings in skillet, add pepper strips and remaining 1 tablespoon oil. Sauté for 5 minutes, or until peppers are lightly browned, stirring occasionally. Stir in tomatoes with liquid,

breaking tomatoes up with a spoon, and then remaining ½ teaspoon salt and remaining ½ teaspoon black pepper. Increase heat to high; cook for 3 to 5 minutes, or until bubbly. In skillet, stir in veal and any meat juices in bowl; heat through.

4. In serving bowl, combine pasta, veal sauce and fresh basil; toss mixture until well combined. Sprinkle top with grated Parmesan cheese (if using).

Makes 4 to 6 servings.

*Per serving: 445 calories, 25 g protein, 11 g fat, 62 g carbohydrate, 53 mg cholesterol, 635 mg sodium.*

## ROBUST PASTA WITH NO-COOK TOMATO-AND-BASIL SAUCE

Leftovers make a terrific chilled pasta salad—simply add a splash of vinegar.

2 pounds plum tomatoes, chopped
½ pound part-skim mozzarella cheese, diced
¾ cup thinly sliced fresh basil (or a combination of fresh herbs)
⅓ cup olive oil
⅓ cup grated Parmesan cheese
½ teaspoon black pepper
½ teaspoon salt, or to taste
1 pound perciatelli or spaghetti

1. In large serving bowl, combine all ingredients except pasta; set aside.

2. Cook pasta according to package directions; drain and toss with tomato sauce. Serve with additional Parmesan, if you like.

Makes 4 to 6 servings.

*Per serving: 642 calories, 27 g protein, 25 g fat, 79 g carbohydrate, 31 mg cholesterol, 546 mg sodium.*

*Left: Pasta with Veal, Peppers and Basil (this page).*

### CRISPY RAVIOLI WITH PESTO DIPPING SAUCE

You don't even have to boil the ravioli for this easy dish—just coat with Parmesan bread crumbs and sauté! This delicious entrée with its dipping sauce also makes a fine appetizer.

½ cup light sour cream
¼ cup store-bought pesto
3 tablespoons milk
½ teaspoon cracked black pepper
1 egg
⅓ cup plain dried bread crumbs
2 tablespoons grated Parmesan cheese
1 tablespoon minced parsley
1 package (9 ounces) fresh cheese-filled ravioli
2 tablespoons olive oil

1. For sauce: In small bowl, mix sour cream, pesto, milk and pepper until smooth; set mixture aside.

2. In shallow dish, beat egg with 1 tablespoon water. On wax paper, mix bread crumbs, cheese and parsley. Dip each ravioli in egg, letting excess egg drip back into dish; then roll in crumb mixture to coat.

3. Heat 1 tablespoon of the oil in medium skillet over medium heat. Add half of the ravioli; cook for 3 to 4 minutes, or until golden brown, turning once. Remove to a serving platter; cover to keep warm. Repeat with remaining 1 tablespoon oil and ravioli. Serve ravioli with dipping sauce. (Ravioli can also be served with heated prepared spaghetti sauce.)

Makes 4 main-dish or 8 appetizer servings.

*Per main-dish serving: 423 calories, 17 g protein, 25 g fat, 30 g carbohydrate, 120 mg cholesterol, 538 mg sodium.*

### TOMATO-ZUCCHINI TORTELLINI TOSS

Cheese-filled tortellini add protein and calcium to this healthful dish.

1 pound fresh or frozen cheese tortellini
2 tablespoons olive oil
2 large cloves garlic, minced
2½ pounds red or yellow tomatoes, chopped
½ teaspoon salt, or to taste
¼ to ½ teaspoon crushed red pepper
3 small zucchini, coarsely chopped
4 cups stemmed and coarsely chopped arugula or watercress (about 2 bunches) (optional)
Arugula leaves (optional garnish)

1. Cook tortellini according to package directions.

2. Meanwhile, heat oil in large skillet over medium heat. Add garlic; sauté for 1 minute. Stir in tomatoes, salt and pepper. Over high heat, bring to a boil. Reduce heat to low and simmer for 5 minutes. Add zucchini; cook for 3 minutes. Remove skillet from heat; stir in arugula to wilt (if using).

3. Drain tortellini and place in serving bowl with sauce; toss until well combined. Garnish with arugula.

Makes 4 to 6 servings.

*Per serving: 375 calories, 18 g protein, 13 g fat, 49 g carbohydrate, cholesterol data unavailable, 566 mg sodium.*

# ITALIAN PRONTO!

When you're hungry for Italian food but don't have time for slow-simmering sauces, try one of the following favorites.

These easy dishes were developed for the microwave—on steamy days there's no need to heat up the kitchen! The simple recipe for Garden-Fresh Tomato Sauce yields enough to freeze for another great meal. It's also the basis for 3 tasty variations.

Choose one of these quick-fix sauces and start it in the microwave. While the sauce cooks, prepare the pasta. The result? An Italian-style specialty in minutes.

## GARDEN-FRESH TOMATO SAUCE

3  tablespoons olive oil
3  medium cloves garlic, minced
1  large onion, diced
1  large carrot, diced
4  pounds large tomatoes, chopped
1½ teaspoons salt
¾  teaspoon black pepper
3  tablespoons chopped parsley

1. In 3-quart microwaveproof bowl or casserole, microwave olive oil on High for 2 minutes. Stir in minced garlic, diced onion and diced carrot; microwave vegetable mixture on High for 8 minutes, stirring once.

2. Add chopped tomatoes, salt and black pepper. Microwave on High for 15 to 20 minutes, stirring twice.

3. Place tomato mixture, one-third at a time, in blender or food processor fitted with steel blade; blend until smooth. Stir in parsley. If necessary, microwave briefly before tossing with some cooked pasta.

Makes about 6 cups.

*Per ½-cup serving: 68 calories, 2 g protein, 4 g fat, 9 g carbohydrate, 0 mg cholesterol, 290 mg sodium.*

## SPICY-HOT TOMATO SAUCE

Prepare Garden-Fresh Tomato Sauce as directed, adding 2 to 3 tablespoons seeded and minced hot peppers, such as jalapeño, or ¾ teaspoon crushed red pepper to the garlic-onion mixture in step 1.

Makes about 6 cups.

*Per ½-cup serving: 69 calories, 2 g protein, 4 g fat, 9 g carbohydrate, 0 mg cholesterol, 290 mg sodium.*

## LIGHT BASIL-CREAM SAUCE

Prepare Garden-Fresh Tomato Sauce as directed in steps 1 through 3. Stir in ½ cup whipping cream and ⅓ cup loosely-packed thinly sliced fresh basil; microwave on High for 4 minutes.

Makes about 6½ cups.

*Per ½-cup serving: 96 calories, 2 g protein, 7 g fat, 9 g carbohydrate, 13 mg cholesterol, 272 mg sodium.*

## RED CLAM SAUCE

Prepare Garden-Fresh Tomato Sauce or the spicy-hot variation as directed in steps 1 through 3. Stir in ¾ teaspoon dried oregano. With stiff brush, scrub 18 littleneck clams under cold running water. Arrange clams, hinge ends down, in tomato sauce. Cover tightly with plastic wrap turned back slightly on one side. Microwave on High for 8 to 9 minutes, or until clams open. Discard any unopened clams. (Or use a 6½-ounce can chopped clams. Add canned clams and oregano to tomato sauce and microwave on High for 3 to 5 minutes, or until heated through.)

Makes about 6½ cups sauce.

*Per ½-cup serving: 79 calories, 4 g protein, 4 g fat, 9 g carbohydrate, 7 mg cholesterol, 279 mg sodium.*

## SAUSAGE, PEPPER AND ONION PASTA

Italian sausage makes a robust addition to this change-of-pace no-tomato pasta sauce.

½ pound hot and/or sweet Italian sausage
1 large yellow or green pepper, cut into 1-inch pieces
1 medium red onion, cut into thin wedges
1 small eggplant (about ¾ pound), cut into ¾-inch pieces
1 tablespoon olive oil
1 can (10½ ounces) low-sodium chicken broth
¾ teaspoon crushed fennel seed
¾ teaspoon black pepper
¼ teaspoon salt
¾ pound rigatoni or penne pasta
2 tablespoons chopped parsley
2 ounces Parmesan cheese

1. Prick sausage with a fork. In large skillet over medium heat, bring sausage and ¼ cup water to a boil; cover and cook for 5 minutes. Remove cover; cook for 10 minutes, or until sausage is browned, turning frequently. With slotted spoon, remove sausage to paper towels to drain; cut diagonally into thin slices and set aside.

2. Increase heat to medium-high. In drippings in skillet, sauté yellow pepper and onion for 5 minutes, or until tender and lightly browned, stirring frequently. With slotted spoon, remove to a bowl; set aside.

3. To drippings in skillet, add eggplant and oil; toss to coat eggplant with oil. Add ¼ cup of the chicken broth; cover and cook for 5 minutes, or until tender, stirring occasionally. Add sausage, pepper-onion mixture, fennel, black pepper, salt and remaining chicken broth; bring to a boil. Reduce heat to low; cover and heat through.

4. Meanwhile, cook pasta according to package directions. Drain pasta and place in serving bowl with sauce; toss until well combined. Sprinkle with parsley. Grate cheese and sprinkle some on top of each serving. (Or, if you like, draw blade of vegetable peeler across surface of cheese to make curls. Pile curls on top of pasta for garnish.)
Makes 6 servings.
*Per serving: 435 calories, 18 g protein, 18 g fat, 49 g carbohydrate, 36 mg cholesterol, 559 mg sodium.*

## SIMPLE SHRIMP RISOTTO

In the microwave, this Northern Italian classic doesn't need the constant, careful stirring that conventional cooking methods require.

¼ cup olive oil
8 scallions, chopped
2 cups Arborio or long-grain rice (see Note)
2 bottles (8-ounce size) clam juice
½ cup dry white wine
1 pound medium shrimp, shelled and deveined
½ cup fresh or frozen (thawed) green peas
½ teaspoon saffron threads (optional)
1 tablespoon chopped parsley
½ teaspoon salt
½ teaspoon black pepper

1. In 2-quart microwaveproof bowl or casserole, microwave oil on High for 3 minutes. Add scallions and rice, stirring to coat with oil. Microwave on High for 4 minutes.

2. Stir in clam juice, wine and 2 cups water; microwave on High for 12 minutes. Stir in remaining ingredients; microwave on

High for 5 minutes, or until shrimp are just cooked through and liquid is absorbed.

Makes 4 servings.

*Per serving: 579 calories, 27 g protein, 16 g fat, 80 g carbohydrate, 140 mg cholesterol, 676 mg sodium.*

*Note:* Arborio rice is a short-grain rice imported from Italy and primarily used in risottos. Look for it in specialty food stores or in the gourmet food section of supermarkets.

## ZUCCHINI FRITTATA

This recipe will work with zucchini of any size, even overgrown ones. If you use a huge zucchini, however, peel off most of the skin and scoop out the seeds.

3  cups coarsely shredded zucchini
3  tablespoons olive or salad oil
1  medium onion, chopped
8  eggs
½  cup (2 ounces) grated Parmesan, Swiss or cheddar cheese
⅓  cup coarsely chopped parsley
2  teaspoons minced fresh thyme, or ¾ teaspoon dried thyme
½  teaspoon black pepper
¼  teaspoon salt

1.  Preheat broiler. In cheesecloth or with hands, squeeze zucchini to remove excess liquid. Heat oil in large ovenproof skillet (preferably nonstick) over medium-high heat. (To ovenproof skillet, wrap handle in aluminum foil.) Add zucchini and onion; cook until tender, stirring frequently.

2.  In medium bowl, beat eggs; stir in cheese, parsley, thyme, black pepper and salt. Pour egg mixture into skillet, stirring

to distribute evenly through zucchini mixture. Reduce heat to medium; cook frittata for 5 to 7 minutes, or until bottom is set and slightly browned.

3.  Transfer skillet to broiler; cook for 1 to 2 minutes, or until top of frittata is browned. Cut into wedges and serve.

Makes about 5 servings.

*Per serving: 253 calories, 14 g protein, 20 g fat, 5 g carbohydrate, 445 mg cholesterol, 372 mg sodium.*

### PASTA, PLEASE!

● Sauté several cloves of minced garlic in olive oil; then stir in chopped fresh spinach or escarole until wilted. Toss with cooked linguine or spaghetti, grated Parmesan cheese and coarsely ground black pepper.

● Sauté Italian sausage with sliced red and green peppers; drain off fat. Stir in a little minced garlic and some canned tomato puree; cook until sauce thickens. Toss with cooked ziti; sprinkle with chopped parsley.

● Toss cooked fusilli with chunks of room-temperature Brie until cheese melts. Sprinkle with toasted chopped walnuts.

● Combine lots of chopped fresh tomatoes with olive oil, chopped fresh parsley or basil, minced garlic and thinly sliced Genoa salami; let stand for 15 minutes for flavors to combine. Toss with cooked corkscrew or bow-ties.

● Sauté chopped onions and sliced mushrooms, then stir in ground beef; cook until browned. Drain off fat. Stir in bottled marinara sauce and simmer; toss with cooked spaghetti. Sprinkle with shredded cheddar cheese.

● Toss cooked wagon wheels with crumbled, cooked bacon, ricotta, chopped oil-packed sun-dried tomatoes, cracked black pepper and a little pasta cooking water.

# Oven Dishes

### TEX-MEX STUFFED STEAK

You can marinate the steak ahead of time; then just stuff with the pepper-cilantro filling and broil or grill for a hearty supper. (Pictured, page 163.)

1 boneless beef sirloin steak (about 2½ pounds), trimmed, 1½ inches thick
¼ cup lime juice
2½ teaspoons ground cumin
3 tablespoons salad oil
2 large cloves garlic, minced
3 medium red, yellow and/or green peppers, thinly sliced
1 fresh jalapeño pepper, seeded and minced
¾ teaspoon salt
2 tablespoons chopped fresh cilantro
Fresh cilantro (optional garnish)

1. Holding a knife parallel to work surface, cut into 1 short side of steak as deeply as possible to make a pocket (do not pierce long sides of meat). Repeat from second short side of steak to make 1 continuous pocket.

2. In large shallow glass baking dish, mix lime juice, cumin, 1 tablespoon of the oil and half of the garlic. Add steak, turning to coat. Cover and let stand for about 1 hour. (Or marinate in refrigerator for up to a day.)

3. Heat remaining 2 tablespoons oil in medium skillet over medium heat. Add pepper slices, jalapeño, salt and remaining garlic. Sauté for 12 to 15 minutes, or until peppers are very tender, stirring frequently. Remove from heat; stir in chopped cilantro.

4. Preheat broiler. Remove steak to work surface, reserving marinade. Spoon pepper mixture into both sides of steak pocket, pushing mixture toward center to fill pocket evenly. Place steak on broiling rack about 6 inches from heat source. Broil for 15 to 20 minutes for rare, or until of desired doneness, brushing steak occasionally with reserved marinade and turning once. (Steak is also delicious grilled.)

5. Cut steak into ½-inch-thick slices. Serve on pieces of toasted French bread with fresh sweet corn, if you like. Garnish with cilantro.
Makes 6 to 8 servings.
*Per serving: 253 calories, 24 g protein, 15 g fat, 3 g carbohydrate, 70 mg cholesterol, 302 mg sodium.*

### FLORENTINE STEAK WITH ITALIAN CORN

Pungently spiced steaks and Italian-seasoned corn make the perfect summer combo!

3 medium cloves garlic, minced
⅓ cup lemon juice
¼ cup olive oil
3 tablespoons chopped parsley
2 tablespoons chopped fresh oregano, or 1 tablespoon dried oregano
4 teaspoons grated lemon peel
2 to 3 teaspoons cracked black pepper
½ teaspoon salt
4 small beef rib-eye or T-bone steaks, trimmed, ½ inch thick
1 tablespoon butter or margarine
4 large ears corn, husked

1. In small bowl, mix first 8 ingredients. Place steaks in large glass casserole and pour

*Above: Chili-Stuffed Potatoes (this page).*

two-thirds of lemon mixture over steaks, turning to coat. Let stand for 10 minutes.

2. In small saucepan, combine butter and remaining lemon mixture. Over low heat, cook for 3 to 5 minutes; set aside.

3. Preheat broiler. Bring large pot of water to a boil; add corn and cook for 5 minutes. Drain corn and place on a serving platter; brush with butter-lemon mixture.

4. Place steaks on broiling rack 3 to 5 inches from heat source; brush with some of the lemon mixture remaining in casserole. Broil steaks for 6 to 8 minutes for rare, or until of desired doneness, turning once. Place steaks on platter with corn.

Makes 4 servings.

*Per serving: 622 calories, 35 g protein, 43 g fat, 26 g carbohydrate, 110 mg cholesterol, 405 mg sodium.*

## CHILI-STUFFED POTATOES

This mild yet tasty beef chili bakes in the oven alongside the potatoes—what could be simpler? (Pictured, left.)

6 medium baking potatoes
1 pound lean ground beef
2 medium onions, chopped
1 medium clove garlic, minced
1 can (15 ounces) tomato sauce
2 tablespoons chili powder
1 teaspoon cumin seeds, crushed
1 teaspoon dried oregano
½ teaspoon cayenne pepper
Shredded cheddar cheese, ripe olives
  and cilantro (optional toppings)

1. Preheat oven to 425°F. Prick medium baking potatoes with a fork and bake for 20 minutes.

2. Meanwhile, in large ovenproof skillet over medium-high heat, brown beef. With slotted spoon, remove beef to a medium bowl. Discard all but 1 tablespoon drippings in skillet.

3. To drippings, add chopped onions and minced garlic; sauté until tender. Add browned beef, tomato sauce, chili powder, cumin, oregano, cayenne and 1 cup water; stir until well combined.

4. Reduce oven temperature to 350°F. Cover skillet and place in oven. Bake for 40 minutes, or until chili is thick and potatoes are tender, stirring chili occasionally. Split each potato and top with a hefty serving of chili. Top with cheddar cheese, olives and cilantro (if using).

Makes 6 servings.

*Per serving: 359 calories, 20 g protein, 11 g fat, 47 g carbohydrate, 44 mg cholesterol, 503 mg sodium.*

## OREGANO CHICKEN AND POTATOES

Oven-roasted to perfection, this savory dish just needs a green vegetable or salad to complete the meal.

¼ cup olive oil
Juice of 2 lemons
5 large cloves garlic, unpeeled
1½ teaspoons dried oregano
¾ teaspoon salt
¾ teaspoon coarsely ground black
  pepper
½ teaspoon ground cumin
5 whole chicken legs, or 5 chicken-breast
  halves
1½ pounds small red-skinned potatoes,
  halved or quartered
Lemon peel and fresh oregano (optional
  garnish)

1. Preheat oven to 425°F. In roasting pan, mix first 7 ingredients. If using whole chicken legs, cut thighs and drumsticks apart at joint. Add chicken and red-skinned potatoes to roasting pan; toss until chicken and potatoes are well coated with olive-oil mixture. Arrange chicken skin side up. Bake for 50 minutes, stirring occasionally, or until chicken and potatoes are tender.

2. With slotted spoon, remove chicken and potatoes to a serving platter. Place pan on stovetop over medium-high heat; add ½ cup water. Bring to a boil, stirring to loosen brown bits. Cook until liquid is slightly reduced; pour mixture over chicken and potatoes. Garnish chicken with lemon peel and fresh oregano.

Makes 5 servings.

*Per serving: 527 calories, 33 g protein, 31 g fat, 26 g carbohydrate, 139 mg cholesterol, 473 mg sodium.*

## CHICKEN BREASTS GREMOLATA AND ROSEMARY VEGETABLES

Gremolata is a fragrant Italian mixture of parsley, garlic and grated lemon peel.

10 medium cloves garlic, unpeeled
3 tablespoons chopped parsley
1 tablespoon grated lemon peel
4 chicken-breast halves
1 large red pepper, cut into 1-inch pieces
1 medium zucchini, cut lengthwise in
  half; then crosswise into 1-inch pieces
1 medium yellow squash, cut lengthwise
  in half; then crosswise into 1-inch pieces
1 pound mushrooms
1 tablespoon olive oil
1 tablespoon minced fresh rosemary, or 1
  teaspoon dried rosemary, crushed
¾ teaspoon salt
½ teaspoon cracked black pepper
Fresh rosemary (optional garnish)

1. Preheat oven to 400°F. Peel and mince 2 of the garlic cloves. In a cup, combine minced garlic, parsley and lemon peel. Partially loosen skin on each chicken breast by working your hand between meat and skin. Place some garlic mixture under skin of each chicken breast.

2. Place chicken skin side up in large roasting pan; bake for 10 minutes. Add red pepper, zucchini, squash, mushrooms and remaining unpeeled garlic. Drizzle vegetables with oil and sprinkle with rosemary, salt and pepper. Bake for 30 to 40 minutes, or until chicken is cooked through and vegetables are tender. Garnish with rosemary.

Makes 4 servings.

*Per serving: 223 calories, 30 g protein, 6 g fat, 14 g carbohydrate, 66 mg cholesterol, 496 mg sodium.*

## BAKED CHUTNEY CHICKEN

This kid pleaser has just four ingredients!

½ cup peanuts
½ cup cornflakes or similar cereal
⅔ cup chutney
4 boneless, skinless chicken-breast halves

1. Preheat oven to 400°F. Lightly grease 2-quart baking dish.

2. In food processor fitted with steel blade, process peanuts for 15 seconds. Add cereal; process for 10 seconds, or until mixture resembles crumbs. Remove to a plate.

3. Add chutney to food processor; blend for 15 seconds, or until smooth. Coat each chicken breast with some chutney, and then roll in peanut mixture. Place chicken in prepared baking dish; bake for 20 minutes, or until cooked through, turning once.

Makes 4 servings.

*Per serving: 351 calories, 32 g protein, 10 g fat, 34 g carbohydrate, 66 mg cholesterol, 201 mg sodium.*

## CREAMY CHICKEN-BROCCOLI BAKE

A four-pound broiler-fryer will yield enough chicken for this recipe.

½ pound spinach or egg fettuccine
2 tablespoons (¼ stick) butter or margarine
2 medium cloves garlic, minced
1 medium onion, chopped
1 can (28 ounces) crushed tomatoes
½ cup sour cream
¾ teaspoon salt
½ teaspoon crushed red pepper
2 packages (10-ounce size) frozen chopped broccoli, thawed
3 cups coarsely chopped cooked chicken

1. Preheat oven to 350°F. Grease 3-quart casserole. Bring large pot of lightly salted water to a boil. Add pasta and cook for 7 minutes; drain and set aside.

2. Meanwhile, melt butter in large skillet over low heat. Add garlic and onion; sauté for 5 minutes, or until tender, stirring occasionally. Remove from heat; stir in tomatoes, sour cream, salt and crushed pepper. Squeeze excess water from broccoli. Add broccoli and chicken to tomato mixture.

3. Spread half of the pasta in prepared casserole. Top with half of the chicken mixture; repeat layering. Cover loosely with lid or aluminum foil. Bake for 30 to 40 minutes, or until heated through.

Makes 6 to 8 servings.

*Per serving: 353 calories, 26 g protein, 13 g fat, 33 g carbohydrate, 100 mg cholesterol, 535 mg sodium.*

### CHICKEN TIPS

● At the market, choose chicken that has a fresh smell and doesn't have liquid accumulated on the tray or in the bag. Check the "sell date" on the label. Fresh poultry should be used within a day or two of purchase, or frozen immediately.

● Thaw frozen chicken, still in its wrapping, in the refrigerator overnight. Never thaw poultry on the kitchen counter.

● Thin-sliced chicken cutlets (usually about ¼ inch thick) take minutes to cook and are readily available in supermarkets. When they're on sale, stock up and then freeze them, wrapped between layers of waxed paper.

● Raw poultry can harbor bacteria. After working with chicken, wash hands, cutting boards and knives with hot water and dishwashing detergent; then rinse thoroughly. (Because plastic and acrylic cutting boards are nonabsorbent, they are safer than wood boards.)

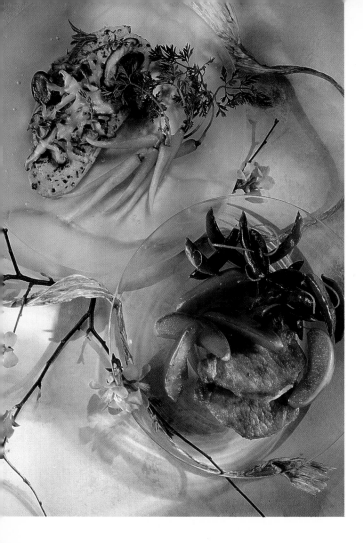

## MICROWAVE TURKEY CUTLETS WITH MUSHROOMS AND CHEESE

Add sweet spring carrots and a basket of crusty rolls to this supper. (Pictured, above.)

1 pound turkey cutlets
1 medium clove garlic, minced
1 tablespoon lemon juice
½ teaspoon black pepper
¼ teaspoon salt
¼ teaspoon dried thyme
⅛ teaspoon dried sage
2 tablespoons olive oil
1 small onion, finely chopped
10 ounces fresh shiitake and/or button mushrooms, trimmed and sliced
¾ cup (3 ounces) shredded Swiss or Fontina cheese
Fresh thyme and sage (optional garnish)

1. Place cutlets in a single layer in 13-by-9-inch microwaveproof baking dish. In a cup, mix next 6 ingredients and 1 tablespoon of the oil; drizzle mixture over cutlets, turning to coat. Let stand for about 30 minutes. (Or cover and place in refrigerator to marinate for up to a day.)

2. Meanwhile, in 2-quart microwaveproof bowl, combine onion and remaining 1 tablespoon oil. Cover with lid or with plastic wrap turned back slightly on one side; microwave on High for 3 minutes, stirring once. Add mushrooms; cover again and microwave on High for 3 to 4 minutes, or until tender, stirring once. Set aside, covered.

3. Cover cutlets in baking dish with lid or with plastic wrap turned back slightly on one side; microwave on High for 2 minutes. Rotate dish and rearrange less-cooked cutlets toward outside of dish. Microwave on High for 1 to 2 minutes, or until just cooked through. Spoon off and discard liquid.

4. With slotted spoon, place mushroom mixture on top of cutlets; sprinkle with cheese. Cover again and microwave on High for 30 seconds, or just until cheese melts. Garnish with thyme and sage.

Makes 4 servings.

*Per serving: 378 calories, 39 g protein, 22 g fat, 5 g carbohydrate, 120 mg cholesterol, 215 mg sodium.*

*Left above: (From top) Microwave Turkey Cutlets with Mushrooms and Cheese (this page), Skillet-Pork-and-Apple Sauté (page 202).*

*Right: (From top) Light Lemon-Mint Chicken (page 203), Fish Steaks Amandine with Dijon Cream (page 196).*

## FISH STEAKS AMANDINE WITH DIJON CREAM

This high-protein dish is ready in 20 minutes in a conventional oven or 10 minutes in the microwave. (Pictured, page 195.)

1½ pounds halibut or cod steaks or fillets
3 tablespoons whipping cream
2 tablespoons Dijon mustard
⅓ cup finely chopped almonds, toasted
2 tablespoons chopped parsley
Parsley sprigs (optional garnish)

1. Preheat oven to 400°F. Place fish in 11-by-7-inch baking dish. (If using fillets, tuck under about 1½ inches of the thinner tail-ends for even cooking.)

2. In a cup, mix cream and mustard; spread evenly over fish. Sprinkle with almonds and chopped parsley. Bake for 12 to 15 minutes, or until fish flakes when tested with a fork. Garnish with parsley sprigs. Serve with steamed new potatoes, if you like.

*Microwave Instructions:* Using a microwave-proof dish, prepare fish as above up to the point of baking. Cover with wax paper; microwave on High for 6 minutes. Let stand, covered, for 1 minute before serving.

Makes 4 to 6 servings.

*Per serving: 239 calories, 30 g protein, 18 g fat, 3 g carbohydrate, 56 mg cholesterol, 258 mg sodium.*

### PERFECT FISH—EVERY TIME
Fish cooks very quickly, so take care not to overdo it. Here's a foolproof rule: Measure fish at its thickest point before cooking; then allow 10 minutes of cooking time per inch of thickness. When the fish has just turned from translucent to opaque (test with a fork or knife), it's done!

## ORANGE-ROSEMARY FISH KABOBS

To ensure even cooking, leave some space between the fish, orange and onion when threading the skewers.

2 large oranges
2 tablespoons (¼ stick) butter or margarine
1½ tablespoons minced fresh rosemary, or 1½ teaspoons dried rosemary, crushed
1 teaspoon salt
½ teaspoon cracked black pepper
1½ pounds swordfish or tuna steaks, 1 inch thick
1 medium red onion

1. For marinade: Grate peel and squeeze juice from 1 of the oranges (you should have about 1 tablespoon peel and about ½ cup juice). In small saucepan, combine peel, juice, and next 4 ingredients. Over low heat, cook for 5 minutes. Pour into shallow glass baking dish; refrigerate for 10 minutes.

2. Meanwhile, remove skin from fish; cut steaks into 1½-inch chunks. Add fish to orange-rosemary marinade, turning to coat. Cover and refrigerate for 1 hour.

3. Preheat broiler. Cut onion and remaining orange into 12 wedges each. Alternate onion wedges, fish chunks and orange wedges on 4 to 6 skewers, reserving marinade. Place skewers on broiling rack 3 to 4 inches from heat source; brush with some marinade. Broil for 6 to 8 minutes, or until fish is cooked through, brushing with remaining marinade and turning once.

Makes 4 to 6 servings.

*Per serving: 226 calories, 25 g protein, 10 g fat, 9 g carbohydrate, 60 mg cholesterol, 597 mg sodium.*

# Skillet Suppers

## SIMPLE SKILLET SUKIYAKI

For easier slicing, freeze steak 25 minutes.

2 tablespoons salad oil
1 medium onion, very thinly sliced
1 bunch scallions, cut into 2-inch pieces
1 cup finely shredded Chinese (Napa) or Savoy cabbage
1 pound boneless beef sirloin, thinly sliced, each slice cut into 3-inch pieces
¾ pound mushrooms, thinly sliced
½ pound tofu, cut into ½-inch cubes
4 cups Swiss chard or spinach
1 cup fresh bean sprouts
½ cup dry vermouth or sake
3 to 4 tablespoons reduced-sodium soy sauce
2 tablespoons brown sugar
1 package or cube beef-flavor instant bouillon
1 tablespoon sesame seeds, toasted

1. Heat oil in large skillet over medium heat. Add onion and scallions; stir-fry for 2 minutes. Add cabbage; stir-fry for 2 minutes. Layer beef, mushrooms, tofu, Swiss chard and bean sprouts on top of onion mixture.

2. In small bowl, mix next 4 ingredients; stir until sugar and bouillon dissolve. Pour over vegetables and meat; cover and cook for 3 minutes. Uncover and stir-fry for 2 to 3 minutes. Top with sesame seeds.
Makes 4 servings.
*Per serving: 611 calories, 34 g protein, 43 g fat, 26 g carbohydrate, 81 mg cholesterol, 872 mg sodium.*

## PAN-FRIED STEAK WITH BURGUNDY SAUCE

Use a hot skillet with no added oil to sear the steak and seal in the juices.

2 pounds boneless beef shell or strip steaks, trimmed, 1 inch thick
¼ cup finely chopped shallots
4 tablespoons (½ stick) butter or margarine
¾ cup Burgundy or other dry red wine
1 package or cube beef-flavor instant bouillon
Salt and black pepper

1. Heat a heavy, well-seasoned skillet, preferably cast iron, over high heat until very hot. Add steaks; cook for 6 minutes for medium-rare, or until of desired doneness, turning once. Transfer steaks to a cutting board; discard excess fat in skillet.

2. Add shallots and 1 tablespoon of the butter to skillet; cook for 10 to 15 seconds. Add wine, bouillon and ½ cup water; bring to a boil, stirring to loosen brown bits. Cook until sauce is reduced to about 3 tablespoons. Remove skillet from heat; swirl in remaining butter, 1 tablespoon at a time. Season with salt and pepper. Thinly slice steaks on diagonal, across the grain; place on a serving platter. Spoon sauce over meat.
Makes 6 to 8 servings.
*Per serving: 285 calories, 26 g protein, 18 g fat, 1 g carbohydrate, 82 mg cholesterol, 274 mg sodium.*

## BEEF BURGERS STROGANOFF

A savory sauce makes all the difference in this burger variation. (Pictured, page 178.)

6 ounces egg noodles
1 medium zucchini, coarsely shredded
1 pound lean ground beef
1 tablespoon salad oil
1 medium onion, diced
¼ pound mushrooms, sliced
1 package or cube beef-flavor instant bouillon
1 tablespoon minced parsley
½ teaspoon dried dill or tarragon
¼ teaspoon black pepper
¼ cup light sour cream
Fresh dill (optional garnish)

1. Cook noodles according to package directions; add zucchini 30 seconds before draining. Drain; place on a serving platter.

2. Meanwhile, shape beef into 4 oval patties. Heat oil in large skillet over medium heat. Add burgers; cook for 8 to 10 minutes for medium-rare, or until of desired doneness, turning once. Place burgers on top of noodle mixture; cover to keep warm.

3. To drippings in skillet, add onion; cook for 3 to 5 minutes, or until tender and browned, stirring occasionally. Add mushrooms; cook for 2 minutes, stirring frequently. Add bouillon, parsley, dried dill, pepper and ¾ cup water; bring to a boil. Cook for 2 minutes, stirring constantly.

4. Remove skillet from heat; stir in sour cream. Spoon sauce over burgers and noodle mixture. Garnish with dill.

Makes 4 servings.

*Per serving: 534 calories, 27 g protein, 30 g fat, 36 g carbohydrate, 129 mg cholesterol, 291 mg sodium.*

## SAGED VEAL CUTLETS AND SUMMER TOMATO SAUTE

If fresh sage is unavailable, just add ½ teaspoon dried sage to the bread-crumb mixture in step 1.

1 egg
½ cup plain dried bread crumbs
¼ cup grated Parmesan cheese
1 pound veal cutlets
2 tablespoons olive oil
1 large clove garlic, minced
1½ pints cherry and/or yellow pear tomatoes
2 tablespoons butter or margarine
¼ cup loosely packed fresh sage leaves

1. In pie plate, beat egg with 1 tablespoon water. On wax paper, mix bread crumbs and cheese. Dip cutlets into egg mixture, and then into bread-crumb mixture to coat; set aside.

2. Heat 1 tablespoon of the oil in large skillet over medium-high heat. Add garlic; sauté for 30 seconds. Add tomatoes; cook for 3 to 4 minutes, or until heated through, stirring frequently. Remove tomato mixture to a serving platter. Wipe out skillet.

3. Heat butter and remaining 1 tablespoon oil in same skillet. Add ¼ cup sage; sauté for 1 to 2 minutes, or until crisp, stirring frequently. With slotted spoon, remove sage from skillet; set aside.

4. In sage butter in skillet, cook cutlets, half at a time, for 3 to 5 minutes, or until browned and just cooked through, turning once. Remove cutlets to platter with tomato mixture; sprinkle with sautéed sage.

Makes 4 servings.

*Per serving: 396 calories, 28 g protein, 25 g fat, 13 g carbohydrate, 169 mg cholesterol, 345 mg sodium.*

## VEAL WITH BRANDIED MUSTARD SAUCE

To complete this tasty meal, serve veal cutlets with quartered roasted new potatoes and string beans tossed with butter and toasted pine nuts.

1 pound veal cutlets
½ teaspoon salt
¼ teaspoon black pepper
1 tablespoon olive or salad oil
1 tablespoon butter or margarine
2 tablespoons brandy
1 tablespoon minced shallot or white part of scallion
⅔ cup whipping cream
1 teaspoon grainy mustard
1 tablespoon snipped fresh chives (optional)

1. Sprinkle veal cutlets with salt and pepper. Heat olive oil and butter in large skillet over high heat just until butter melts. Add veal cutlets (in batches, if necessary). Cook for 2 to 3 minutes, or until cutlets are browned and just cooked through, turning once. Remove to a serving platter; cover cutlets to keep warm.

2. Reduce heat to medium-high. To drippings in skillet, add brandy and shallot. Bring to a boil and cook for 30 seconds, or until liquid has almost evaporated. Add cream; return sauce to a boil and cook for 2 minutes, or until slightly thickened, stirring constantly. Remove from heat. Stir in mustard and chives (if using); spoon sauce over cutlets.

Makes 4 servings.

*Per serving: 297 calories, 25 g protein, 21 g fat, 2 g carbohydrate, 141 mg cholesterol, 402 mg sodium.*

*Above: Skillet Veal Burgers Parmigiana (this page).*

## SKILLET VEAL BURGERS PARMIGIANA

Use leftover homemade spaghetti sauce—or try a jarred variety. (Pictured, above.)

1 pound ground veal or lean ground beef
2 tablespoons chopped fresh basil, or ¾ teaspoon dried basil
1 teaspoon olive or salad oil
1 cup spaghetti sauce
1 cup (4 ounces) coarsely shredded part-skim mozzarella cheese

1. Preheat broiler. In medium bowl, mix veal and half of the basil until just combined. Shape into 4 patties about ¾ inch thick.

2. Heat oil in large ovenproof skillet over medium-high heat. Add burgers; sauté for 8 minutes, or until cooked through, turning once. Discard fat in skillet.

3. Spoon sauce over burgers in skillet; cook until sauce is heated. Top with cheese and remaining basil. Place under broiler for 1 to 2 minutes, or until cheese is bubbling.

Makes 4 servings.

*Per serving: 347 calories, 30 g protein, 20 g fat, 11 g carbohydrate, 97 mg cholesterol, 518 mg sodium.*

## BRAISED LAMB WITH VEGETABLES

When browning meat, use medium-high or high heat. Don't overcrowd the pan, or meat will steam instead of brown.

2 tablespoons salad oil
1¼ pounds trimmed, boneless lamb for stew (from leg or shoulder), cut into 1-inch cubes
6 large celery stalks, cut into 1-inch pieces (see Note)
3 medium shallots, minced
2 large carrots, cut into 1-inch pieces
1 large red onion, coarsely chopped
1 can (14½ to 16 ounces) tomatoes
½ teaspoon salt
½ teaspoon celery seed
Black pepper to taste
1 can (16 to 19 ounces) garbanzo beans (chick-peas), drained

1. Heat oil in large pot over medium-high heat. Add half of the lamb cubes and sauté until well browned, removing to a bowl when done. Repeat with remaining lamb. Discard excess fat; return browned lamb to pot. Add 2 cups water; bring mixture to a boil. Reduce heat to low; cover and simmer lamb for 40 minutes. Skim any excess fat from surface of mixture.

2. Add remaining ingredients except garbanzo beans; cover and cook for 30 minutes, or until lamb is tender. Add garbanzo beans; heat through.
Makes 5 servings.
*Per serving: 366 calories, 29 g protein, 13 g fat, 33 g carbohydrate, 79 mg cholesterol, 780 mg sodium.*

*Note:* If your kids don't like cooked celery, you can substitute 3 to 4 potatoes, peeled and cut into large chunks.

## LAMB-AND-APRICOT RAGOUT

This ragout is excellent made a day or two ahead and reheated. Serve with couscous or rice pilaf and a salad.

3 tablespoons butter or margarine
1¼ pounds trimmed, boneless lamb for stew (from leg or shoulder), cut into 1-inch cubes
1 medium onion, chopped
1 large clove garlic, minced
½ teaspoon salt
1 cup dried apricot halves, each cut in half
⅓ cup raisins (preferably golden)
½ teaspoon ground cinnamon
¼ teaspoon ground cardamom (optional)

1. Melt butter in large skillet over medium-high heat. Add half of the lamb; sauté until browned, removing to a bowl when done. Repeat with remaining lamb. Discard all but 1 tablespoon drippings in skillet. To drippings, add onion and garlic; sauté until lightly browned, stirring frequently.

2. Return browned lamb to skillet. Add salt and 2¼ cups water; bring to a boil. Reduce heat to low; cover and simmer for 40 minutes. Skim any excess fat from surface.

3. Add remaining ingredients; cover and cook for 30 minutes, or until lamb is tender.
Makes 5 servings.
*Per serving: 303 calories, 24 g protein, 13 g fat, 23 g carbohydrate, 98 mg cholesterol, 371 mg sodium.*

*Right: Santa Fe Pork Stir-Fry (facing page).*

## SANTA FE PORK STIR-FRY

Pork tenderloin is very lean and can be cooked in minutes. (Pictured, below.)

2   tablespoons salad oil
1   pork tenderloin (about ¾ pound), trimmed, thinly sliced and cut into ½-inch strips
1   to 2 tablespoons chili powder
1   small bunch scallions, cut into 1-inch pieces
1   medium clove garlic, minced
1   can (15 to 16 ounces) black beans, rinsed and drained
1   bunch watercress, stemmed
1   pint cherry tomatoes, halved
1   cup frozen corn, thawed
1   tablespoon lime juice
¼   teaspoon salt

1. Heat oil in large skillet over medium-high heat. Add pork with chili powder in batches; stir-fry for 2 to 3 minutes, or until pork is lightly browned and cooked through. With slotted spoon, remove to a plate.

2. To drippings in skillet, add scallions and garlic; stir-fry for 30 seconds. Add remaining ingredients; stir-fry for 2 to 3 minutes. Stir in pork; heat through.

Makes 4 servings.

*Per serving: 358 calories, 30 g protein, 10 g fat, 40 g carbohydrate, 55 mg cholesterol, 669 mg sodium.*

## SAUTEED PORK TENDERLOIN WITH CHUTNEY GLAZE

Serve this 20-minute entrée on top of rice. (Pictured, pages 160 and 161.)

1   tablespoon salad oil
1   pork tenderloin (about 1 pound), trimmed, cut into ½-inch-thick slices
¼   cup dry Madeira
⅓   cup chutney, chopped
1   large lime
Salt and black pepper

1. Heat oil in large skillet over high heat. Add pork; cook until browned on both sides, removing to a platter when done. To drippings in skillet, add Madeira. Bring to a boil, stirring to loosen brown bits. Cook until liquid is reduced by half.

2. Reduce heat to medium. Return browned pork to skillet; add chutney. Cover and simmer for 6 to 8 minutes, or until pork is cooked through, stirring occasionally.

3. Meanwhile, cut several slices of lime for garnish; squeeze 1 tablespoon juice from rest of lime. Add juice to pork; season with salt and pepper. Garnish with lime slices.

Makes 4 servings.

*Per serving: 220 calories, 24 g protein, 6 g fat, 16 g carbohydrate, 74 mg cholesterol, 102 mg sodium.*

## SKILLET-PORK-AND-APPLE SAUTE

Steamed sugar snap peas with a little orange zest make a perfect side dish. (Pictured, page 194.)

1¼ pounds pork cutlets
1 teaspoon ground cumin
¾ teaspoon salt
½ teaspoon black pepper
¼ teaspoon ground cinnamon
¼ teaspoon ground ginger
2 large apples, preferably 1 Golden Delicious and 1 Red Delicious
2 tablespoons (¼ stick) butter or margarine
1 teaspoon sugar

1. Place cutlets on wax paper. In a cup, mix cumin, salt, pepper, cinnamon and ginger; sprinkle over both sides of cutlets. Let stand while you core apples and cut into ½-inch-thick wedges.

2. Melt butter in skillet over medium-high heat. Add cutlets (in batches, if necessary). Cook for 4 to 5 minutes, or until browned and cooked through, turning once. Remove to a platter; cover to keep warm.

3. Reduce heat to medium. To drippings in skillet, add apples; sprinkle with sugar. Cook for 6 to 7 minutes, or until tender, turning frequently. Stir in any meat juices on cutlet platter; cook for 30 seconds, or until mixture thickens slightly and apples are glazed. Spoon apples over cutlets.

Makes 4 servings.

*Per serving: 335 calories, 32 g protein, 16 g fat, 15 g carbohydrate, 105 mg cholesterol, 565 mg sodium.*

## SAVORY PORK PICCATA

Serve this easy and elegant dish with spaghetti tossed with sautéed spinach, olive oil, minced garlic and chopped parsley.

1¼ pounds pork cutlets
½ teaspoon black pepper
1 tablespoon olive oil
2 tablespoons (¼ stick) unsalted butter or margarine
1 tablespoon lemon juice
1 teaspoon chicken-flavor instant bouillon
2 tablespoons chopped parsley
1½ teaspoons capers, coarsely chopped
Lemon wedges (optional)

1. Sprinkle cutlets with pepper. Heat olive oil and 1 tablespoon of the butter in large skillet over high heat just until butter melts. Add cutlets (in batches, if necessary). Cook for 2 minutes, or until browned on bottom. Turn cutlets; reduce heat to medium-high and cook for 2 minutes, or until cutlets are browned and cooked through. Remove to a platter; cover to keep warm. Discard excess fat in skillet.

2. Add lemon juice, bouillon and ¾ cup water to skillet; bring to a boil, stirring to loosen brown bits. Boil mixture rapidly for 3 to 4 minutes, or until reduced and syrupy.

3. Stir in any meat juices accumulated on cutlet platter. Remove skillet from heat, and then whisk in remaining 1 tablespoon butter until sauce thickens slightly. Add parsley and capers; spoon sauce over cutlets. Serve with lemon wedges (if using).

Makes 4 servings.

*Per serving: 310 calories, 32 g protein, 19 g fat, 1 g carbohydrate, 105 mg cholesterol, 336 mg sodium.*

## FRESH TOMATO-CHIVE CHICKEN BREASTS

The colorful, light tomato sauce in this dish cooks in just five minutes—wonderful with turkey, veal or fish fillets, too.

4 boneless, skinless chicken-breast halves
¼ teaspoon black pepper
¾ teaspoon salt
2 tablespoons olive oil
2 bay leaves
3 tablespoons snipped fresh chives
1 large clove garlic, minced
1 pound tomatoes, chopped
2 teaspoons grated lemon peel

1. Sprinkle chicken with pepper and ¼ teaspoon of the salt. Heat oil in medium skillet (preferably nonstick) over medium-high heat. Add chicken and bay leaves; cook for 8 minutes, or until chicken is cooked through, turning once. Discard bay leaves. With slotted spoon, remove chicken to a serving platter; cover and keep warm.

2. Reduce heat to low. To drippings in skillet, add chives and garlic; cook for 1 minute. Add tomatoes, lemon peel and remaining ½ teaspoon salt; cook for 5 minutes, or until just heated through, stirring occasionally (sauce should be chunky). Spoon tomato sauce over chicken.

Makes 4 servings.

*Per serving: 212 calories, 28 g protein, 8 g fat, 5 g carbohydrate, 68 mg cholesterol, 496 mg sodium.*

> ● White-wine Worcestershire sauce is terrific for poaching fish or chicken breasts; experiment by adding your favorite herb.

## LIGHT LEMON-MINT CHICKEN

A brief marinating period brings out the flavor of the mint. (Pictured, page 195.)

4 boneless, skinless chicken-breast halves
1 small bunch fresh mint, or 2 teaspoons dried mint
3 medium cloves garlic, minced
3 tablespoons olive oil
2 lemons

1. Place chicken between sheets of wax paper; pound to about ¼-inch thickness. Chop enough mint to measure 2 tablespoons; reserve remaining mint for garnish. In medium bowl, combine chopped mint, garlic and oil; add chicken to bowl, tossing to coat. Let chicken stand for 30 minutes.

2. Meanwhile, grate 1 teaspoon peel and squeeze 2 tablespoons juice from 1 of the lemons; set aside. Cut remaining lemon into wedges for garnish.

3. In large skillet over medium-high heat, sauté chicken, half at a time, in mint marinade until chicken is lightly browned and just cooked through. Remove chicken to a serving platter.

4. To drippings in skillet, add lemon peel and juice; bring mixture to a boil, stirring to loosen brown bits. Pour sauce over chicken. Garnish chicken with remaining mint and lemon wedges.

Makes 4 servings.

*Per serving: 222 calories, 26 g protein, 12 g fat, 2 g carbohydrate, 66 mg cholesterol, 74 mg sodium.*

## CHICKEN AND SPRING VEGETABLE RAGOUT

Parslied noodles are a great accompaniment. They soak up the creamy sauce! (Pictured, right.)

1¼ pounds chicken cutlets
½ teaspoon salt
¼ teaspoon black pepper
1 tablespoon olive or salad oil
1 tablespoon butter or margarine
2 medium carrots, cut diagonally into ½-inch-thick slices
1 medium leek, cut diagonally into ½-inch-thick slices, then rinsed
1 medium clove garlic, minced
2 tablespoons dry white wine (optional)
1 teaspoon chicken-flavor instant bouillon
½ pound asparagus, trimmed, cut diagonally into 2-inch pieces
1 teaspoon cornstarch dissolved in 1 tablespoon cold water
¼ cup sour cream
1 tablespoon chopped fresh dill

1. Sprinkle cutlets with salt and pepper. Heat oil and butter in large skillet over high heat just until butter melts. Add cutlets, in batches if necessary. Cook for 2 minutes, or until browned on bottom. Turn cutlets; reduce heat slightly and cook for 2 minutes, or until lightly browned and just cooked through. Remove to a platter; cover to keep warm. Discard half of the drippings in skillet.

2. Reduce heat to medium. To drippings in skillet, add carrots, leek and garlic; sauté for 3 minutes, or until leek begins to wilt, stirring frequently. Add wine (if using), bouillon and ¾ cup water; bring to a boil, stirring to loosen brown bits. Cover and cook for 5 minutes. Add asparagus; cover and cook for 3 to 4 minutes, or just until asparagus is tender-crisp.

3. Pour any meat juices accumulated on platter into skillet, and then add cornstarch mixture, stirring constantly. Increase heat to high; bring to a boil and cook for 1 minute, or until mixture thickens slightly, stirring constantly. Remove from heat; stir in sour cream and dill. Spoon vegetable ragout onto platter with cutlets.

Makes 4 servings.

*Per serving: 283 calories, 35 g protein, 12 g fat, 8 g carbohydrate, 96 mg cholesterol, 664 mg sodium.*

*Left: Chicken and Spring Vegetable Ragout (facing page).*

## QUICK CHICKEN PAPRIKA

Look for packaged chicken-breast tenders in the supermarket, or use boneless, skinless chicken breasts sliced into two-inch strips.

3 tablespoons salad oil
2 medium onions, coarsely chopped
3 medium carrots, thinly sliced
1 large red pepper, cut into thin strips
1 pound chicken-breast tenders
   (tenderloins of chicken breasts)
1 tablespoon paprika
½ teaspoon caraway seeds
1 cup vegetable or tomato juice
½ cup light sour cream
1 tablespoon chopped parsley

1. Heat oil in large skillet over medium-high heat. Add onions; sauté for 3 to 5 minutes, or until tender. Add carrots and red pepper; cook for 3 minutes, or until tender, stirring frequently.

2. Add chicken; cook for 3 minutes, stirring frequently. Stir in paprika and caraway seeds until well combined. Add vegetable juice; bring to a boil. Reduce heat to low; cover and simmer for 5 minutes, or until chicken is cooked through. Remove skillet from heat; stir in sour cream and sprinkle with parsley. Serve over rice or noodles.

Makes 4 servings.

*Per serving: 309 calories, 29 g protein, 14 g fat, 15 g carbohydrate, 74 mg cholesterol, 341 mg sodium.*

## TURKEY TANDOORI

Serve with pappadums (an Indian bread) or pitas and steamed summer squash. (Pictured, page 171.)

½ cup plain nonfat yogurt
2 large cloves garlic, minced
1 tablespoon distilled white vinegar
¾ teaspoon salt
¾ teaspoon ground cumin
½ teaspoon black pepper
½ teaspoon ground ginger
¼ teaspoon ground coriander
⅛ teaspoon cayenne pepper
1¼ pounds turkey cutlets
2½ tablespoons salad oil
1 large onion, thinly sliced
1 medium tomato, diced
1 tablespoon chopped fresh cilantro or
   parsley

1. In 13-by-9-inch baking dish, mix first 9 ingredients. Add cutlets in 1 layer; turn to coat. Cover; refrigerate 6 hours or overnight.

2. Heat 1 tablespoon of the oil in large nonstick skillet over medium-high heat. Add onion; sauté for 8 to 10 minutes, or until well browned, stirring frequently. With slotted spoon, remove onion from skillet.

3. To oil in skillet, add remaining 1½ tablespoons oil and heat until very hot. Add cutlets (in batches, if necessary). Cook for 2 minutes, or until browned on bottom. Turn cutlets; reduce heat slightly and cook for 1 minute, or until lightly browned and just cooked through. Remove to a platter. Top with sautéed onion, tomato and cilantro.

Makes 4 servings.

*Per serving: 278 calories, 36 g protein, 11 g fat, 8 g carbohydrate, 89 mg cholesterol, 546 mg sodium.*

# Kid Pleasers

*We know a secret—how to prepare food winners for kids. They'll flip over the whimsical yet nutritious creations you make with these recipes, menus and ideas. Some of the quick snacks they can even make themselves. (Pictured, Kid-Pleasing Pasta; recipes begin on page 208.)*

**Kid-Pleasing Pasta**
**Pleasing Picky Eaters**
**Food To Grow On**
**Lunchbox Express**
**Recipes for Junior**
  **Chefs**
**Snacktime Specials**
**Cook-Together Cookie**
  **Collection**

# Kid-Pleasing Pasta

*Every child loves macaroni and cheese! This creamy classic—and all of our delicious pasta casseroles—will have your family begging for seconds. These down-home dishes, loaded with calcium and protein, are so simple to prepare—and most recipes are ample for two nights' worth of satisfying suppers!*

### THREE-CHEESE MACARONI

We made it mild to suit kids' taste. For a sharper flavor, increase the cheddar and decrease the Monterey Jack. (Pictured, right.)

1  pound elbow macaroni
5  tablespoons butter or margarine
¼  cup all-purpose flour
1  tablespoon dry mustard
4  cups milk
2  cups (8 ounces) shredded part-skim mozzarella cheese
1  cup (4 ounces) shredded sharp cheddar cheese
1  cup (4 ounces) shredded Monterey Jack cheese
4  slices white bread, torn into small pieces

1. Preheat oven to 375°F. Grease deep 2-quart baking dish. In large pot of lightly salted boiling water, cook macaroni for 6 minutes; drain and return to pot. Set aside.

2. Meanwhile, melt 3 tablespoons of the butter in large saucepan over medium-high heat. Add flour and mustard; cook for 2 minutes, stirring constantly. Stir in milk; bring to a boil and cook for 5 minutes, or until sauce thickens, stirring constantly. Pour sauce over macaroni; add cheeses and toss until well combined. Spoon mixture into prepared baking dish.

3. Melt remaining 2 tablespoons butter in small saucepan over medium heat; add bread and toss to coat. Sprinkle bread on top of macaroni mixture. Bake for 20 to 25 minutes, or until bubbly around edges and bread is lightly browned. (Check macaroni after 15 minutes; if getting too brown, cover with aluminum foil.)

Makes 8 servings.

*Per serving: 579 calories, 27 g protein, 26 g fat, 58 g carbohydrate, 81 mg cholesterol, 491 mg sodium.*

**Variation:** Thaw one package (16 ounces) frozen mixed vegetables. Stir into macaroni mixture in step 2. Bake as directed, using a slightly larger baking dish.

### TEX-MEX WAGON-WHEEL CASSEROLE

Green chilies add a lot of flavor but not a lot of heat. (Pictured, right.)

½  pound wagon-wheel pasta
1¾  pounds lean ground beef
1  medium onion, chopped
2  tablespoons chili powder
1  large green pepper, chopped
1  large clove garlic, minced
2  teaspoons dried oregano
1  can (16 ounces) crushed tomatoes
1  can (12 ounces) whole-kernel corn, drained
1  can (4 ounces) chopped green chilies, drained
3  cups (¾ pound) shredded Monterey Jack cheese

*Above: (Clockwise from top) Tex-Mex Wagon-Wheel Casserole (facing page), Chicken-Pasta Mini-Casseroles (this page), Three-Cheese Macaroni (facing page).*

## CHICKEN-PASTA MINI-CASSEROLES

Cook in individual baking dishes—or serve up family style. (Pictured, left.)

6  ounces tricolor radiatore or corkscrew pasta
1  tablespoon butter or margarine
1  small onion, chopped
2  cups chopped cooked chicken
1  package (10 ounces) frozen green peas, thawed
3  tablespoons chopped parsley
1½  teaspoons dried basil
½  teaspoon salt
½  teaspoon black pepper
⅛  teaspoon grated nutmeg
1  container (15 to 16 ounces) part-skim ricotta cheese
½  cup grated Parmesan cheese
2  eggs
1  cup milk

1.  Preheat oven to 375°F. Grease four 2-cup baking dishes (or grease a 2½-quart baking dish). In pot of lightly salted boiling water, cook pasta for 6 minutes. Drain; set aside.

2.  Meanwhile, melt butter in large skillet over medium heat. Add onion; sauté for 5 minutes, or until tender, stirring occasionally. Stir in pasta and next 7 ingredients. Divide pasta mixture among prepared dishes.

3.  In medium bowl, mix ricotta, Parmesan and eggs until well combined. Stir in milk; pour over pasta mixture. Bake individual casseroles for 35 to 40 minutes, or until set and lightly browned. (Bake 2½-quart casserole for 15 to 20 minutes longer.)

Makes 4 servings.

*Per serving: 655 calories, 52 g protein, 26 g fat, 52 g carbohydrate, 259 mg cholesterol, 837 mg sodium.*

1.  Preheat oven to 400°F. In large pot of lightly salted boiling water, cook pasta for 8 minutes. Drain pasta; set aside.

2.  Meanwhile, in skillet over medium-high heat, brown beef. With slotted spoon, remove beef to bowl. Discard all but 2 tablespoons drippings in skillet. To drippings in skillet, add onion and chili powder; sauté for 5 minutes, stirring frequently. Add green pepper, garlic and oregano; sauté for 2 to 3 minutes, stirring frequently.

3.  Stir in cooked pasta, browned beef, tomatoes, corn and green chilies. Spoon half of the pasta mixture into 3-quart baking dish and sprinkle with half of the cheese; repeat layering. Bake for 25 to 30 minutes, or until heated through.

Makes 6 to 8 servings.

*Per serving: 617 calories, 38 g protein, 35 g fat, 37 g carbohydrate, 115 mg cholesterol, 551 mg sodium.*

## TURKEY 'N' PASTA PEPPERS

Choose peppers that will stand upright so they don't fall over when filled. (Pictured, pages 206 and 207.)

¼ pound bow-tie pasta
¼ cup olive oil
1 small onion, chopped
1½ pounds turkey cutlets, cut into
    ½-inch pieces
2 to 3 medium cloves garlic, minced
3 tablespoons chopped parsley
2 teaspoons dried oregano
½ to ¾ teaspoon crushed red pepper
½ teaspoon salt
1 can (28 ounces) tomatoes, undrained
6 yellow, red and/or green peppers

1. Preheat oven to 400°F. In large pot of lightly salted boiling water, cook pasta for 5 minutes. Drain pasta; set aside.

2. Meanwhile, heat oil in large skillet over medium-high heat. Add onion; sauté for 3 to 5 minutes, or until tender, stirring occasionally. Add turkey and half of the garlic; cook for 2 minutes, or until turkey loses its pink color, stirring frequently. Remove from heat; stir in chopped parsley, oregano, crushed pepper and salt.

3. Drain liquid from tomatoes into large roasting pan or Dutch oven. Coarsely chop tomatoes. Add pasta and 3 cups of the chopped tomatoes to the turkey mixture. Add remaining garlic and chopped tomatoes to tomato juice in roasting pan.

4. Cut off stem ends of peppers; reserve tops, if you like. Scoop out seeds and ribs from peppers to make hollow cups. Spoon turkey mixture into peppers. Set stuffed peppers in roasting pan; replace pepper tops if using. Cover loosely with lid or aluminum foil. Bake for 50 minutes, or until peppers are tender.

Makes 6 servings.

*Per serving: 337 calories, 31 g protein, 12 g fat, 27 g carbohydrate, 70 mg cholesterol, 532 mg sodium.*

## TASTY TUNA-FILLED SHELLS

We used water-packed tuna because it has less than half the calories of the oil-packed variety. (Pictured, pages 206 and 207.)

20 to 24 jumbo pasta shells (about 8
    ounces)
3 tablespoons butter or margarine
2 medium carrots, diced
½ pound mushrooms, thinly sliced
1 bunch scallions, chopped
3 tablespoons all-purpose flour
3 cups milk
¼ cup tomato paste
2 cans (6½-ounce size) water-packed
    tuna, drained
¼ cup chopped watercress or parsley
2 to 3 tablespoons grated Parmesan cheese
Watercress sprigs (optional garnish)

1. Preheat oven to 350°F. In large pot of lightly salted boiling water, cook pasta for 8 minutes. Drain pasta; set aside.

2. Meanwhile, melt butter in large skillet over medium heat. Add carrots; sauté for 2 to 3 minutes. Add mushrooms and scallions; sauté for 3 minutes. Add flour; cook for 2 minutes, stirring constantly. Stir in milk and tomato paste; cook for 5 minutes, or until sauce thickens, stirring constantly.

3. Remove skillet from heat. Spread 1½ cups of the sauce in bottom of 13-by-9-inch baking dish. Add tuna, chopped watercress

and cheese to sauce remaining in skillet, breaking up tuna with a fork.

4. Stuff shells with tuna mixture; pack closely together in dish. Cover with aluminum foil. Bake for 25 to 30 minutes, or until heated through. Garnish with watercress. Makes 6 to 8 servings.

*Per serving: 279 calories, 11 g protein, 10 g fat, 38 g carbohydrate, 30 mg cholesterol, 225 mg sodium.*

## EASY STUFFED LASAGNA

Layer lasagna in the traditional manner, or try this version. (Pictured, pages 206 and 207.)

16 lasagna noodles
1 pound lean ground beef
1 large onion, chopped
1 jar (26 ounces) spaghetti sauce
1 container (15 to 16 ounces) part-skim ricotta cheese
2 cups (8 ounces) shredded part-skim mozzarella cheese
2 tablespoons grated Parmesan cheese

1. Preheat oven to 350°F. Grease deep 3-quart round baking dish. In large pot of lightly salted boiling water, cook lasagna noodles for 7 minutes. Drain noodles; set aside.

2. Meanwhile, in large skillet over medium heat, brown beef with onion. Drain and discard excess fat; stir in spaghetti sauce.

3. Line prepared baking dish with enough noodles to completely cover, overlapping noodles and letting ends hang over edge.

4. In pasta-lined dish, layer one-quarter of the meat sauce, one-third of the ricotta and one-third of the mozzarella. Top with some of the remaining noodles; cut noodles to fit casserole. Repeat layering with remaining meat sauce, ricotta, mozzarella and noodles, ending with a layer of sauce.

5. Bring overhanging noodles up and over to cover meat sauce. Sprinkle with Parmesan. Cover loosely with aluminum foil. Bake for 35 to 40 minutes, or until bubbling, removing foil during last 15 minutes of cooking. Makes 6 servings.

*Per serving: 710 calories, 41 g protein, 29 g fat, 69 g carbohydrate, 92 mg cholesterol, 955 mg sodium.*

## AMAZING PASTA PIZZA

Unique! (Pictured, pages 206 and 207.)

½ pound thin spaghetti or vermicelli
2 eggs, beaten
⅓ cup grated Parmesan cheese
1 jar (14 ounces) pizza or spaghetti sauce
1 cup (4 ounces) shredded part-skim mozzarella cheese
Additional toppings: green peppers, onions, mushrooms, pepperoni

1. Preheat oven to 400°F. Grease 12-inch pizza pan. In large pot of lightly salted boiling water, cook pasta for 6 minutes. Drain pasta and return to pot; let cool slightly.

2. Toss pasta with eggs and ¼ cup of the Parmesan. Spread pasta mixture in prepared pizza pan; bake for 5 minutes.

3. Spoon pizza sauce over pasta, leaving ½-inch border around edge. Sprinkle with mozzarella, remaining Parmesan and toppings of your choice. Bake for 15 minutes, or until cheese melts and "crust" is firm. Makes 4 servings.

*Per serving (without additional toppings): 406 calories, 22 g protein, 12 g fat, 51 g carbohydrate, 159 mg cholesterol, 705 mg sodium.*

# Pleasing Picky Eaters

*Choose from these sure-to-please recipes with menu suggestions for a balanced meal. Each one is sure to delight the family fussy eater.*

---

## MENU
### *Whole-Wheat Buttermilk Flapjacks*
~~~~~
### *Peanut butter or yogurt*
~~~~~
### *Berries and sliced bananas*
~~~~~
### *Milk*

---

### WHOLE-WHEAT BUTTERMILK FLAPJACKS

These supper pancakes are extra light!

¾  cup whole-wheat flour
¾  cup all-purpose flour
¼  cup wheat germ
3  tablespoons sugar
3  teaspoons baking powder
1  teaspoon baking soda
¼  teaspoon salt
3  eggs
2  cups buttermilk
½  cup cottage cheese
3  tablespoons butter or margarine, melted
1  teaspoon vanilla extract
1  tablespoon salad oil, or as needed
Peanut butter (optional)

1. In large bowl, mix first 7 ingredients until well combined.

2. In medium bowl, beat eggs, buttermilk, cottage cheese, melted butter and vanilla extract until well combined. Add egg mixture to dry ingredients; stir until just combined.

3. Heat large skillet over medium heat; brush with some of the oil. For each flapjack, pour about ¼ cup batter into skillet (see Note); cook for 2 minutes, or until bubbles form on surface and edges are slightly dry. Turn and cook other side for 2 minutes, or until brown. Transfer to an ovenproof plate; keep flapjacks warm in a 200°F oven.

4. Repeat with remaining batter, brushing skillet with oil as necessary. Spread some peanut butter (if using) between flapjacks; drizzle with Honey-Blueberry Sauce (recipe,

Left: *Crunchy Cereal Sundae Dinner (this page).*

page 214). Or top with sliced fresh fruit, honey or maple syrup and vanilla yogurt.

Makes about 16 flapjacks.

*Per flapjack: 117 calories, 5 g protein, 5 g fat, 14 g carbohydrate, 48 mg cholesterol, 258 mg sodium.*

*Note:* For an extra-tempting treat, make a flapjack with your child's initial! Using a small spoon, drizzle about 1 tablespoon batter in skillet to form an initial. (Write initial backward for "N," "K," etc.) Cook for 2 minutes. Pour ¼ cup of batter over the initial to form a flapjack and continue cooking for about 2 minutes (initial will be browner). Turn flapjack and cook other side for about 2 minutes.

## MENU
### *Crunchy Cereal Sundae Dinner\**

### CRUNCHY CEREAL SUNDAE DINNER

Cereal isn't just for breakfast time anymore! This fuss-free dish is a complex-carbohydrate feast that's super for supper. For the most nourishing meal, look for cereal that's low in sugar, fat and salt. (Pictured, left above.)

1 cup dry cereal (or use a mixture—let kids combine a few)
½ cup milk
½ cup fruit-flavor yogurt
½ cup of your child's favorite fruit, sliced
2 tablespoons chopped walnuts or peanuts (optional)

1. Place cereal in serving bowl.
2. Add milk; top with yogurt and fruit. Sprinkle with walnuts, if you like. (Other toppings might include wheat germ, toasted shredded coconut and/or chopped dried fruit.)

Makes 1 hungry kid-size or 1 adult serving.

*Per kid-size portion (with mixture of toasted-oat cereal, bite-size shredded wheat and mixed-grain cereal with nuts and raisins): 383 calories, 14 g protein, 7 g fat, 70 g carbohydrate, 22 mg cholesterol, 319 mg sodium.*

\*This nutritionally balanced meal is fine to serve all by itself!

### GOOD MORNING!

● **Graham Goodies:** Youngsters love graham crackers spread with peanut butter and sprinkled with raisins or shredded coconut. Parents might prefer a sprinkling of crumbled, cooked bacon or grated carrots.

● **Bananas on a Raft:** Toast a slice of whole-wheat bread or cinnamon-raisin bread. While toast is still hot, spread with peanut butter and top with banana slices.

● **Apple Muffins:** Spread a split and toasted English muffin with applesauce. Top with plain nonfat yogurt, wheat germ and a little ground cinnamon.

● **Ricotta Cone:** You overslept? Put a scoop of ricotta or cottage cheese in an ice-cream cone and stud with raisins and walnuts. Hand your child breakfast on her way out the door!

● **Sunshine on a Muffin:** Split a corn muffin; butter and toast. Top each half with some apricot jam and thin slices of cheddar cheese.

## MENU
### Easy Cheesy French Toast
〜〜〜
### Applesauce
〜〜〜
### Milk

### EASY CHEESY FRENCH TOAST

Serve with Honey-Blueberry Sauce (recipe, right), if you like.

¼ cup milk
3 tablespoons grated Parmesan cheese
2 eggs
¼ teaspoon black pepper
4 ounces Muenster cheese, cut into 4 slices
8 slices (cut diagonally ½ inch thick) French bread
2 tablespoons (¼ stick) butter or margarine

1. In shallow dish, combine milk, Parmesan, eggs and pepper; beat with fork until well combined.

2. Put cheese slices between bread slices to make 4 small sandwiches. Dip both sides of sandwiches in egg mixture to coat.

3. Melt butter in large skillet over low heat. Carefully place sandwiches in skillet; cover and cook for 6 to 8 minutes, or until golden brown, turning once and adding more butter if necessary.

Makes 4 kid-size or 2 adult servings.

*Per kid-size portion: 376 calories, 17 g protein, 19 g fat, 34 g carbohydrate, 155 mg cholesterol, 677 mg sodium.*

### HONEY-BLUEBERRY SAUCE

Yummy for topping waffles and French toast.

1 jar (10 ounces) blueberry spreadable fruit
2 tablespoons honey

In small pan over low heat, combine fruit, honey and ¼ cup water; heat through, stirring occasionally.

Makes about 1 cup.

*Per tablespoon: 45 calories, 0 g protein, 0 g fat, 11 g carbohydrate, 0 mg cholesterol, 0 mg sodium.*

## MENU
### Peanut-Butter Club Sandwich
〜〜〜
### Frozen yogurt
〜〜〜
### Fruit juice

### PEANUT-BUTTER CLUB SANDWICH

Something new and tasty to do with that old faithful, PB & J. (Pictured, right.)

6 slices oatmeal or whole-wheat bread
¼ cup peanut butter
4 to 5 teaspoons blackberry spreadable fruit
1 small banana, sliced
½ apple, cored and thinly sliced
4 teaspoons honey

1. Spread 1 slice bread with 1 heaping teaspoon peanut butter, and then with about 2 teaspoons spreadable fruit. Cover with half of banana slices.

2. Spread second slice of bread with 1 heaping teaspoon peanut butter; place on banana slices, peanut-butter side down. Spread top of bread with 1 heaping teaspoon peanut butter; cover with half of apple slices; then drizzle with 2 teaspoons honey.

3. Spread third slice of bread with 1 heaping teaspoon peanut butter; place on apple slices, peanut-butter side down.

4. Repeat with remaining ingredients to make 2 peanut-butter club sandwiches. Cut each sandwich diagonally into quarters. Insert a frilly toothpick in each quarter; remove toothpick before eating.

Makes 4 kid-size or 2 adult servings.

*Per kid-size portion: 267 calories, 8 g protein, 10 g fat, 39 g carbohydrate, 0 mg cholesterol, 354 mg sodium.*

*Above: Peanut-Butter Club Sandwich (facing page).*

---

## MENU
### *Deluxe Banana Split*
~~~~~
### *Raisin or zucchini bread*
~~~~~
### *Milk*

---

### DELUXE BANANA SPLIT

Fresh fruit and creamy cottage cheese make this banana split a delicious—and healthful—dinner treat.

1 small banana
½ cup cottage cheese
½ orange, segmented
½ pear, cored and cut into chunks
¼ cup seedless red grapes, halved
3 tablespoons granola
Ground cinnamon

1. Cut banana crosswise in half; then cut each piece lengthwise into quarters.

2. Divide banana and cottage cheese between 2 cereal bowls. Top each with some orange, pear, red grapes and granola. Sprinkle with cinnamon. (Feel free to add other goodies—try chopped dates or dried apricots, raisins, chopped nuts, sunflower seeds and/or wheat germ.)

Makes 2 kid-size servings or 1 adult serving.

*Per kid-size portion: 197 calories, 9 g protein, 5 g fat, 32 g carbohydrate, 8 mg cholesterol, 218 mg sodium.*

**MENU**

*Make-Your-Own Pizza*

〰〰

*Cucumber slices*

〰〰

*Banana chunks topped
with spreadable fruit and
chopped peanuts*

〰〰

*Milk*

## MAKE-YOUR-OWN PIZZA

Kids choose their favorite toppings and skip what they don't like. (A hint for Mom: Have kids add extra cheese or meat for optimum protein power! Pictured, above.)

1 package (10 ounces) all-ready pizza crust
1 cup No-Yucky-Stuff Spaghetti Sauce (recipe, page 219), or prepared pizza sauce
1 cup (4 ounces) shredded part-skim mozzarella cheese
Assorted toppings: pepperoni, meatballs, ricotta cheese, green and red peppers, Parmesan cheese, mushrooms, diced ham, cooked sausage or bacon, olives

*Left: Make-Your-Own Pizza (facing page).*

1. Preheat oven to 450°F. Lightly grease jelly-roll pan or baking sheet.

2. Unroll pizza crust in prepared pan. Press into a 15-by-10-inch rectangle; cut into quarters. Top each quarter with ¼ cup of the sauce; then with ¼ cup of the cheese. Let kids add their own toppings.

3. Bake on bottom rack of oven for 15 to 18 minutes, or until crust is brown.

Makes 8 kid-size or 4 adult servings.

*Per kid-size portion (without toppings): 148 calories, 6 g protein, 5 g fat, 18 g carbohydrate, 14 mg cholesterol, 335 mg sodium.*

## MENU
### *Mighty Meatball Hoagie*
~~~~~
### *Carrot and celery sticks*
~~~~~
### *Apple slices*
~~~~~
### *Low-fat chocolate milk*

## MIGHTY MEATBALL HOAGIE

A great way to use leftover meatballs.

2  Mini Ketchup Meatballs (recipe, page 218), halved
1  frankfurter bun, halved crosswise
¼  cup No-Yucky-Stuff Spaghetti Sauce (recipe, page 219), or prepared spaghetti sauce
¼  cup (1 ounce) shredded part-skim mozzarella cheese

Preheat oven to 400°F. Place 2 meatball halves in each half of bun; top with sauce, and then cheese. Place on baking sheet and bake for 10 to 15 minutes, or until heated through.

Makes 2 kid-size servings or 1 adult serving.

*Per kid-size portion: 328 calories, 21 g protein, 18 g fat, 20 g carbohydrate, 98 mg cholesterol, 663 mg sodium.*

## BREAKFAST, ANYONE?

● Melon Bowl: Scoop the seeds out of half a cantaloupe. Sprinkle with fresh lime juice and top with a spoonful of ricotta cheese. Serve with a toasted blueberry muffin.

● Crunchy Nosh: Spread a split and toasted bagel with cream cheese. Sprinkle with granola.

● Cheery Cereal: Top your child's favorite cereal with apple slices, peanuts, milk and a little granulated brown sugar.

● Italian Scrambled Eggs: Beat eggs with Parmesan cheese and dried Italian seasoning; cook in a little olive oil—wonderful served with sliced fresh tomatoes.

● Breakfast Bananas: Sauté sliced bananas in a little butter or margarine; sprinkle with cinnamon-sugar. Serve with a dollop of nonfat yogurt and some cinnamon toast.

● Strawberry Croissant: Slice a croissant lengthwise. Spread one piece with ricotta cheese and the other with strawberry jam and press together.

● Fruit 'n' Spice Oatmeal: Prepare instant or regular oatmeal, using fruit juice for the liquid specified on package. Stir in a little ground cinnamon and grated nutmeg.

# MENU
### Mini Ketchup Meatballs
~~~~~
### Alphabet pasta or other
### small pasta
~~~~~
### Frozen fruit bar
~~~~~
### Milk

---

## MINI KETCHUP MEATBALLS

This is a basic recipe to use in a variety of winning ways.

6  strips bacon, cooked and crumbled
   (optional)
2  pounds lean ground beef
2  cups fresh bread crumbs
2  eggs
¼  cup milk
¼  cup grated Parmesan cheese
2  tablespoons chopped parsley
1  tablespoon prepared mustard
¾  teaspoon salt
¾  teaspoon black pepper
½  cup ketchup
1  teaspoon salad oil

1.  Preheat oven to 350°F. In large bowl, mix bacon (if using), beef, bread crumbs, eggs, milk, cheese, parsley, mustard, salt, pepper and ⅓ cup of the ketchup until combined. Shape mixture into 1½-inch balls.

2.  Heat oil in large skillet over medium heat. Add meatballs in batches; cook until browned (no need to cook through).

3.  Place meatballs on large baking sheet; brush with remaining ketchup. Bake for 30 to 35 minutes, or until cooked through.

Serve with Crazy Ketchup Dipping Sauce (recipe follows).

Makes 12 kid-size or 6 adult servings.

*Per kid-size portion: 210 calories, 16 g protein, 13 g fat, 7 g carbohydrate, 84 mg cholesterol, 397 mg sodium.*

## CRAZY KETCHUP DIPPING SAUCE

Simple to prepare—also tastes terrific with hamburgers.

½  cup ketchup
2  tablespoons mayonnaise
2  teaspoons lemon juice
¼  teaspoon black pepper

In small bowl, mix all ingredients until well combined.

Makes about ½ cup.

*Per tablespoon: 43 calories, 0 g protein, 3 g fat, 4 g carbohydrate, 2 mg cholesterol, 200 mg sodium.*

---

### CHEESE SNACKTIME

Keep several kinds of cheese in the fridge so your kids will have the fixings for protein-packed snacks they can make with little or no adult supervision.

● Cheesy Apple Crunch: Spread a rice cake or cracker with apple butter and top with a slice of cheddar cheese.

● Taste of Honey: Spread a graham cracker with Neufchâtel or cream cheese; drizzle with honey.

● Cheese Wrap: Spread slices of ham or turkey with ketchup or mustard; wrap around sticks of string cheese.

● Peach Melba: Spread a toaster corn cake with raspberry jam and then ricotta cheese. Top with well-drained canned peach slices.

## MENU
*Pasta with No-Yucky-Stuff*
*Spaghetti Sauce*

~~~~~

*String cheese*

~~~~~

*Canned pears*

~~~~~

*Milk*

## NO-YUCKY-STUFF SPAGHETTI SAUCE

Little ones will love this mild and smooth-textured sauce. They won't even know there are vegetables in it!

¼ cup (½ stick) butter or margarine
2 medium carrots, chopped
2 medium stalks celery, chopped
1 small onion, chopped
1 small clove garlic, minced
2 cans (28-ounce size) Italian plum
   tomatoes, drained (reserve liquid)
2 teaspoons dried basil
2 teaspoons sugar
1 teaspoon salt
½ teaspoon black pepper
½ teaspoon dried oregano
2 tablespoons chopped parsley (optional)

1. Melt butter in large pot over medium-low heat. Add carrots, celery, onion and garlic; cover and cook for 15 minutes, or until very tender, stirring occasionally.

2. Transfer vegetable mixture to blender or food processor fitted with steel blade; add tomatoes and puree until completely smooth.

3. Return vegetable-tomato puree to pot. Stir in reserved tomato liquid, basil, sugar, salt, pepper and oregano. Increase heat and bring to a boil. Reduce heat to low; partially cover and simmer for 1 hour, stirring frequently. Add parsley (if using) during last 5 minutes of cooking.

4. Serve sauce over pasta, make spaghetti and meatballs (see Note) or use in our Make-Your-Own Pizza or Mighty Meatball Hoagie (recipes, pages 216 and 217).

Makes about 6 cups.

*Per ¼-cup kid-size portion: 36 calories, 1 g protein, 2 g fat, 4 g carbohydrate, 5 mg cholesterol, 224 mg sodium.*

*Note:* For spaghetti and meatballs, prepare Mini Ketchup Meatballs (recipe, page 218) through step 2. In large pot, combine meatballs with 1 recipe No-Yucky-Stuff Spaghetti Sauce; bring to a boil. Reduce heat to low, partially cover and simmer for 30 minutes, or until meatballs are cooked through. Serve over spaghetti.

### YOGURT SNACKTIME

Rich in calcium but low in fat and cholesterol, nonfat yogurt makes a great snack for children and adults alike.

● Apricot Shake: In a blender, whirl equal parts of plain nonfat yogurt and drained canned apricots; add pinches of cinnamon and brown sugar.

● Blackberry Waffle: Mix plain nonfat yogurt with a spoonful of blackberry preserves and a few chopped walnuts. Serve on a toasted frozen waffle.

● No-Cook Fruit Crisp: Stir mixed chopped fresh fruit into vanilla yogurt; top with granola.

● Maple-Graham Crunch: Crumble a few graham crackers into a bowl. Stir in several spoonfuls of plain nonfat yogurt and a little maple syrup; top with raisins.

## MENU
### Dunk 'n' Dip Crispy Chicken Nuggets
~~~~~
### Buffalo Bill Barbecue Sauce
#### and/or
### Tutti-Frutti Sauce
~~~~~
### Grated carrot-raisin salad
~~~~~
### Graham crackers
~~~~~
### Low-fat chocolate milk

## DUNK 'N' DIP CRISPY CHICKEN NUGGETS

Your kids will be crazy about this tasty version of popular fast food. Try serving with one or both of our dipping sauces.

2 eggs
⅓ cup all-purpose flour
⅔ cup plain dried bread crumbs
½ cup crushed potato chips
½ teaspoon black pepper
¼ teaspoon salt
1½ pounds boneless, skinless chicken breasts, cut into 1½-inch chunks
⅓ cup salad oil

1. In shallow dish, beat eggs with 2 teaspoons water. Spread flour in second shallow dish. In third dish, mix bread crumbs, potato chips, pepper and salt.

2. Dredge each piece of chicken in flour, shaking off excess; then dip in egg, letting excess egg drip back into dish. Roll in crumb mixture to coat; place on wire rack.

3. Heat 2 tablespoons of the oil in large skillet over medium heat. Add enough chicken to fit in a single layer without crowding; cook for 5 to 6 minutes, or until browned and cooked through, turning occasionally. With tongs, transfer cooked chicken to a baking sheet lined with paper towels; keep warm in a 200°F oven.

4. Repeat with remaining chicken, adding oil as necessary to skillet. Serve nuggets with Buffalo Bill Barbecue Sauce and/or Tutti-Frutti Sauce (recipes follow).

Makes 8 to 10 kid-size or 6 adult servings.

*Per kid-size portion: 249 calories, 21 g protein, 13 g fat, 12 g carbohydrate, 91 g cholesterol, 207 mg sodium.*

## BUFFALO BILL BARBECUE SAUCE

This sassy sauce is a cinch to prepare!

1 cup chili sauce
2 tablespoons red-wine vinegar
1 tablespoon Worcestershire sauce
1 tablespoon molasses
2 teaspoons prepared mustard
1 teaspoon chili powder

In small saucepan over medium heat, combine all ingredients with ¼ cup water. Bring mixture to a boil; reduce heat to low and simmer for 5 minutes. Let cool slightly before serving.

Makes about 1 cup.

*Per tablespoon: 23 calories, 1 g protein, 0 g fat, 5 g carbohydrate, 0 mg cholesterol, 249 mg sodium.*

## TUTTI-FRUTTI SAUCE

A sweet-and-sour sauce kids will love.

1 can (8¾ ounces) apricot halves or sliced peaches in light syrup, undrained
2 tablespoons apricot jam
2 tablespoons cider vinegar
1 tablespoon prepared mustard

In small saucepan over medium heat, combine all ingredients. Bring mixture to a boil; reduce heat to low and simmer for 5 minutes. Pour into blender or food processor fitted with steel blade; blend until smooth.

Makes about ⅔ cup.

*Per tablespoon: 28 calories, 0 g protein, 0 g fat, 7 g carbohydrate, 0 mg cholesterol, 21 mg sodium.*

## MENU
*Pint-Size Burger Biscuits*

*Steamed green beans*

*Orange segments*

*Low-fat chocolate milk*

## PINT-SIZE BURGER BISCUITS

Here's a special kid's version of a burger.

1 cup all-purpose flour
1½ teaspoons baking powder
¼ teaspoon salt
2 tablespoons butter or margarine
6 slices American cheese, diced
⅓ cup plus 1 tablespoon milk
¾ pound lean ground beef

1. For biscuits: Preheat oven to 450°F. Lightly grease baking sheet. In medium bowl, mix flour, baking powder and salt until well combined. With pastry blender or 2 knives, cut in butter until mixture resembles coarse crumbs. Add cheese and toss until combined. Add ⅓ cup of the milk; with fork, quickly stir just until mixture forms a soft dough and leaves sides of bowl. With floured hands, knead dough 2 to 3 times, or until dough holds together.

2. On lightly floured surface, roll or pat out dough to about ½-inch thickness. With 2½-inch biscuit cutter, cut out rounds; re-roll trimmings and cut out (will make about 6 biscuits).

3. Place biscuits on prepared baking sheet; brush tops with remaining 1 tablespoon milk. Bake for 12 to 15 minutes, or until golden brown.

4. Prepare burgers: Preheat broiler. Shape beef into 6 thin patties; place on broiling rack 3 to 5 inches from heat source. Broil for 4 to 6 minutes, or until of desired doneness, turning once. (If your kids like cheeseburgers, quarter a few extra slices of American cheese; place 1 or 2 quarters on each burger during last minute of cooking.)

5. Split biscuits in half with a fork; place burgers on bottom halves of biscuits. Add favorite condiments and sandwich burgers with biscuit tops.

Makes 6 kid-size or 3 adult servings.

*Per kid-size portion: 310 calories, 17 g protein, 19 g fat, 17 g carbohydrate, 68 mg cholesterol, 579 mg sodium.*

# Food To Grow On

*For growing kids, select from these delicious, easy-to-make recipes that are loaded with body-building vitamins and minerals.*

## OAT 'N' FRUIT CRISP

This breakfast is full of vitamin C, as well as potassium, which helps the heart, nervous system and kidneys. (Pictured, right.)

*Above: Oat 'n' Fruit Crisp (this page).*

1   can (8 ounces) pineapple chunks in juice, undrained
1   medium papaya, peeled, seeded and cut into small chunks
1   medium banana, thinly sliced
1   teaspoon quick-cooking tapioca
½   cup old-fashioned oats
¼   cup (½ stick) butter or margarine, cut into small chunks
2   tablespoons all-purpose flour
2   tablespoons sugar
4   double graham crackers, coarsely crushed

1.  Preheat oven to 375°F. In 2-quart baking dish, combine first 3 ingredients. Sprinkle with tapioca; toss gently until combined.

2.  In small bowl, combine oats, butter, flour and sugar; mix with fingers until coarse crumbs form. Stir in graham crackers; sprinkle mixture evenly over fruit.

3.  Bake for 20 to 25 minutes, or until topping is lightly browned. Serve warm, topped with yogurt, if you like.

Makes 6 servings.

*Per serving: 217 calories, 3 g protein, 9 g fat, 33 g carbohydrate, 21 mg cholesterol, 144 mg sodium.*

## BANANA-BERRY CONES

Serve the gang a sure-to-please treat full of calcium for strong bones as well as infection-fighting vitamin C.

1   cup mixed diced banana and strawberries
1   cup part-skim ricotta cheese
3   tablespoons strawberry all-fruit preserves
4   sugar cones
Colored sprinkles or granola (optional)

1.  In small bowl, mix diced fruit, ricotta and preserves.

2.  Place cones in small glasses to hold them steady; fill with ricotta mixture. Top with sprinkles or granola (if using).

Makes 4 servings.

*Per serving: 179 calories, 8 g protein, 5 g fat, 26 g carbohydrate, 19 mg cholesterol, 112 mg sodium.*

## APPLE-CINNAMON BUCKWHEAT MUFFINS

These muffins are high in vitamin E, which is vital for muscles and red blood cells.

½ cup raisins
¼ cup apple juice
¾ cup buckwheat flour
¾ cup all-purpose flour
¼ cup wheat germ
1 teaspoon baking soda
1 teaspoon ground cinnamon
¼ teaspoon salt
⅓ cup butter or margarine, softened
½ cup packed light-brown sugar
1 egg
1 cup unsweetened applesauce

1. Preheat oven to 375°F. Grease a 12-cup muffin pan or line with paper liners.

2. In small bowl, combine raisins and apple juice; let stand while preparing batter.

3. In medium bowl, mix buckwheat flour, all-purpose flour, wheat germ, baking soda, cinnamon and salt until well combined.

4. In large bowl, with electric mixer on medium speed, cream butter. Add brown sugar and egg; beat until light (mixture may look slightly curdled). With wooden spoon, stir in raisins with juice and applesauce. Add flour mixture; stir just until combined.

5. Spoon batter into prepared muffin cups, filling each three-fourths full. (Fill empty cups halfway with water.) Bake for 25 minutes, or until toothpick inserted in center comes out clean. Serve with Sesame Peanut Butter (recipe follows), if you like.

Makes about 10 muffins.

*Per muffin: 207 calories, 4 g protein, 7 g fat, 34 g carbohydrate, 38 mg cholesterol, 210 mg sodium.*

## SESAME PEANUT BUTTER

Kids will be partial to this protein-packed spread that contains plenty of manganese and magnesium, minerals that help form and strengthen teeth and bones.

½ cup smooth peanut butter
¼ cup sesame seeds, toasted
2 teaspoons honey (optional)

In blender or food processor fitted with steel blade, blend all ingredients until smooth, scraping down sides of blender or processor with a rubber spatula as needed.

Makes about ¾ cup.

*Per tablespoon: 79 calories, 4 g protein, 7 g fat, 2 g carbohydrate, 0 mg cholesterol, 51 mg sodium.*

## ORANGE SMOOTHIE

This quick-fix shake gives kids a yummy dose of calcium, plus phosphorus to help muscles work right.

1 container (8 ounces) peach- or apricot-flavor low-fat yogurt
½ cup orange juice
2 tablespoons nonfat dry milk (optional)
1 tablespoon honey
½ teaspoon vanilla extract
6 ice cubes

In blender on medium-high speed, blend all ingredients until smooth and creamy.

Makes 2 servings.

*Per serving: 180 calories, 5 g protein, 1 g fat, 37 g carbohydrate, 5 mg cholesterol, 67 mg sodium.*

### MOM'S CHICKEN AND DUMPLINGS

This all-time favorite is a great source of niacin, which helps the body metabolize food and maintain a healthy complexion.

Chicken mixture:
2  tablespoons olive or salad oil
1½ pounds boneless, skinless chicken breasts, cut into bite-size pieces
¼  teaspoon black pepper
1  medium onion, finely chopped
2  tablespoons butter or margarine
3  tablespoons all-purpose flour
2  packages or cubes low-sodium chicken-flavor instant bouillon
1  bay leaf
1  package (10 ounces) frozen green peas and carrots, thawed
1  package (10 ounces) frozen corn, thawed

Dumplings:
1  cup buttermilk baking mix
¼  cup chopped parsley (optional)
¾  teaspoon dried sage
½  cup milk

1.  For chicken mixture: Heat oil in large skillet over medium-high heat. Add chicken with pepper in batches; sauté for 5 minutes, or until lightly browned, stirring frequently. With slotted spoon, remove to small bowl.

2.  To drippings in skillet, add onion and butter; sauté for 5 minutes, stirring occasionally. Reduce heat to low; add flour and cook for 5 minutes, or until golden brown, stirring constantly. Add bouillon and bay leaf; stir in 3 cups water. Increase heat to medium; cook for 10 to 15 minutes, or until slightly thickened, stirring constantly. Add browned chicken, peas and carrots and corn; cover and bring to a boil. Reduce heat to low and simmer while preparing dumplings.

3.  For dumplings: In medium bowl, combine baking mix, parsley (if using) and sage. With fork, stir in milk until just combined. Drop batter by heaping tablespoons on top of chicken mixture. Cover and simmer for 10 minutes, or until toothpick inserted in dumplings comes out clean. Discard bay leaf before serving.

Makes 4 to 6 servings.

*Per serving: 455 calories, 38 g protein, 16 g fat, 39 g carbohydrate, 95 mg cholesterol, 477 mg sodium.*

*Note:* For cheesy dumplings, add ¼ cup (1 ounce) shredded cheddar cheese to baking mix before adding milk.

### SUPER STEAK SANDWICHES

Beef is a terrific source of iron, which helps promote growth, and zinc, an aid to digestion and healing.

3  tablespoons reduced-sodium soy sauce
1  tablespoon minced fresh ginger
1  tablespoon oriental sesame oil
1  small clove garlic, minced
1¼ pounds beef top-round steak, trimmed, 1¼ inches thick
Sandwich rolls, sliced tomatoes and lettuce leaves (optional)

1.  For marinade: In large, shallow glass dish, mix first 4 ingredients.

2.  With sharp knife, lightly score both sides of steak; place steak in dish with marinade, turning to coat. Cover and refrigerate for at least 6 hours or overnight.

3.  Preheat broiler. Place steak on broiling rack 4 to 6 inches from heat source. Broil for 12 to 15 minutes for medium-rare, or until

of desired doneness, turning once. Let steak stand for a few minutes before thinly slicing on diagonal, across the grain.

4. If desired, make steak sandwiches with rolls, tomatoes and lettuce, or serve steak slices with Creamy Cucumber and Tomato Salad (recipe, page 226).

Makes 4 to 6 servings.

*Per serving (steak only): 209 calories, 26 g protein, 10 g fat, 1 g carbohydrate, 71 mg cholesterol, 410 mg sodium.*

## A-TO-Z MINESTRONE

This alphabet soup is a tasty place to hide vegetables packed with vitamin K—essential to a healthy circulatory system. (Pictured, right.)

1  tablespoon olive or salad oil
1  large clove garlic, minced
1  medium onion, finely chopped
3  cans (10½-ounce size) low-sodium chicken broth
2  cups vegetable or tomato juice
1  package (16 ounces) frozen mixed vegetables
1  can (15¼ to 16 ounces) red kidney beans, undrained
¾  cup alphabet or other small pasta
1½ teaspoons dried basil
1  teaspoon dried oregano
¼  teaspoon black pepper
Salt to taste
Grated Parmesan or mozzarella cheese (optional)

1. Heat oil in large pot over medium heat. Add garlic and onion; sauté for 5 minutes, or until tender, stirring occasionally. Increase heat to high. Stir in broth, vegetable juice and

*Above: A-to-Z Minestrone (this page).*

frozen vegetables; cover and bring to a boil. Reduce heat to low; simmer for 5 minutes.

2. Stir in remaining ingredients except salt and cheese; simmer uncovered for 10 minutes, or until pasta is tender. Add salt; sprinkle with cheese (if using).

Makes about 8 cups.

*Per 1-cup serving: 178 calories, 8 g protein, 3 g fat, 30 g carbohydrate, 0 mg cholesterol, 485 mg sodium.*

## CREAMY CUCUMBER AND TOMATO SALAD

Eyes, bones, gums and skin all benefit from this salad's shot of vitamins A and C.

2  tablespoons plain nonfat yogurt
2  tablespoons cholesterol-free, reduced-calorie mayonnaise
1  teaspoon brown sugar
1  teaspoon cider vinegar
½  teaspoon reduced-sodium soy sauce
2  medium cucumbers, peeled and cut into small chunks
1  pint cherry tomatoes, halved

In serving bowl, mix first 5 ingredients until well combined. Add cucumbers and tomatoes; gently toss with yogurt mixture.

Makes 4 to 6 servings.

*Per serving: 35 calories, 1 g protein, 1 g fat, 5 g carbohydrate, trace cholesterol, 49 mg sodium.*

## CAMPFIRE PORK 'N' BEANS

Our lean version of a kid's classic is full of thiamine (vitamin $B_1$), which promotes good muscle tone, and riboflavin (vitamin $B_2$), which maintains healthy skin.

2  tablespoons olive or salad oil
1  medium onion, finely chopped
1  pound pork cutlets
1  can (16 ounces) vegetarian baked beans in tomato sauce
2  tablespoons ketchup
1  tablespoon brown sugar
1  tablespoon cider vinegar
1  teaspoon dry mustard

1. Heat 1 tablespoon of the oil in medium skillet over medium-high heat. Add onion; sauté for 3 to 5 minutes, or until tender, stirring occasionally. With slotted spoon, remove onion to bowl.

2. Add remaining 1 tablespoon oil to skillet; heat until very hot. Add pork (in batches, if necessary). Cook for 2 to 3 minutes, or until browned, turning once. Add pork to onion in bowl.

3. Reduce heat to low. To drippings in skillet, stir in remaining ingredients until well combined. Return pork and onion to skillet; spoon bean mixture over pork and onion. Cover and simmer for 5 to 10 minutes, or until pork is cooked through.

Makes 4 servings.

*Per serving: 351 calories, 29 g protein, 14 g fat, 30 g carbohydrate, 77 mg cholesterol, 604 mg sodium.*

## CAPTAIN HOOK'S FISH STICKS

This recipe is rich in iodine—essential to the thyroid gland, which controls body metabolism—and selenium, a mineral that works with vitamin E to keep tissue healthy.

¼  cup cholesterol-free, reduced-calorie mayonnaise
¼  cup milk or buttermilk
1  tablespoon prepared mustard
⅔  cup seasoned dried bread crumbs
⅓  cup cornflake crumbs
1½  pounds cod or flounder fillets (use thick fillets), cut into 4-by-1-inch pieces

1. Preheat oven to 450°F. Generously grease jelly-roll pan or baking sheet.

2. In shallow dish, mix mayonnaise, milk and mustard until smooth. In second shallow dish, mix bread crumbs and cornflake crumbs. Dip each piece of fish into mayonnaise mixture, and then into crumb mixture

to coat; shake gently to remove excess crumbs. Place fish in prepared pan.

3. Bake for 12 to 15 minutes, or until fish sticks are golden brown and flake easily. Serve with ketchup or tartar sauce and lemon wedges, if you like.

Makes 6 servings.

*Per serving: 240 calories, 23 g protein, 9 g fat, 15 g carbohydrate, 56 mg cholesterol, 583 mg sodium.*

## TASTY TUNA TAMALES

Give kids a boost of iodine, selenium and vitamin D with these Mexican roll-ups.

1 can (6½ ounces) water-packed tuna, drained
2 tablespoons plain nonfat yogurt
2 tablespoons cholesterol-free, reduced-calorie mayonnaise
¾ teaspoon ground cumin
6 (7-inch) flour tortillas
¼ cup prepared mild salsa
3 ounces Monterey Jack cheese, cut into 6 slices

1. In bowl, mix first 4 ingredients.
2. Heat large skillet over medium heat. Add 1 tortilla; heat for 15 seconds on each side, or until just pliable. Remove to work surface. Spoon 2 teaspoons salsa in center of tortilla; top with about 2 tablespoons tuna mixture and 1 slice cheese. Fold up bottom edge of tortilla to cover part of filling; then fold in the sides. Fold top of tortilla down like an envelope to enclose filling. Roll tortilla over and press gently to flatten slightly. Repeat with remaining tortillas and filling.
3. Reduce heat to low; place filled tamales in skillet, seam-sides down. Cook for 2 to 3

minutes, or until lightly browned and heated through, turning once.

Makes 6 servings.

*Per serving: 217 calories, 15 g protein, 5 g fat, 25 g carbohydrate, 24 mg cholesterol, 497 mg sodium.*

## MAUI WOWIE SWEET POTATOES

A meal in itself with plenty of vitamin A to help the body build and repair tissue.

2 medium sweet potatoes
⅓ cup milk
1 tablespoon butter or margarine
1 cup (4 ounces) shredded Monterey Jack cheese
½ cup canned crushed pineapple in juice, undrained
½ teaspoon salt
¼ teaspoon grated nutmeg
Assorted toppings: shredded coconut, chopped nuts, brown sugar

1. Preheat oven to 350°F. Scrub potatoes; pierce with a fork in several places. Bake for 1 hour, or until tender.
2. Cut potatoes lengthwise in half. Scoop out centers, leaving a shell about ¼-inch thick. In large bowl, combine scooped-out potato, milk and butter. With potato masher or fork, mash until smooth. Stir in cheese, pineapple, salt and nutmeg.
3. Refill potato shells with potato-cheese mixture; place in medium baking dish. Let kids add their favorite toppings. Bake for 15 minutes, or until heated through.

Makes 2 to 4 servings.

*Per serving (without toppings): 270 calories, 9 g protein, 12 g fat, 31 g carbohydrate, 36 mg cholesterol, 478 mg sodium.*

# Lunchbox Express

*Here is the game plan to fix a week's worth of lunches: First, prepare the basic filling and freeze filling in a tightly sealed container. As needed, thaw filling and add extras (from chart, page 231). Or make sandwiches by assembly-line method and freeze them.*

## SMOKY HAM-AND-CHEESE SPREAD

This tangy mixture makes enough to freeze for 10 sandwiches.

½ pound smoked ham, cut into chunks
½ pound mild cheddar or American cheese, cut into chunks
1 jar (3½ ounces) roasted red peppers, drained
3 tablespoons mayonnaise
1 tablespoon milk
1 scallion, cut into 2-inch pieces

In blender or food processor fitted with steel blade, process all ingredients until almost smooth.

Makes about 2½ cups.

*Per ¼-cup serving: 155 calories, 10 g protein, 12 g fat, 1 g carbohydrate, 37 mg cholesterol, 492 mg sodium.*

*To freeze:* Place in tightly sealed container and freeze. Thaw in the refrigerator. When thawed, add an additional tablespoon of mayonnaise.

*Right: (Clockwise from top right) Chunky, Chewy Brownies (page 235), Oatmeal Date-Nut Cookies (page 234), sandwiches made of Sliced Meat Loaf with Herbed Cheese Topping (page 232), Basic Salmon Salad (page 230), Basic Chicken Salad (page 230) with apricots and Brie.*

## REDUCED-CHOLESTEROL EGG SALAD

Removing half of the egg yolks in this recipe reduces cholesterol—not flavor!

12  hard-cooked eggs, peeled
2  small stalks celery, diced
2  tablespoons cholesterol-free, reduced-calorie mayonnaise
2  tablespoons sunflower seeds
1  tablespoon plain low-fat yogurt
1  tablespoon minced fresh dill, or 1 teaspoon dried dillweed
2  teaspoons Dijon mustard
½  teaspoon salt
½  teaspoon black pepper
¼  teaspoon paprika

1.  Cut 6 of the eggs in half; remove and discard yolks. Finely chop whites and remaining whole eggs.
2.  In medium bowl, mix chopped eggs with remaining ingredients. Stir mixture until well combined.
Makes about 3 cups.
*Per ½-cup serving: 135 calories, 10 g protein, 9 g fat, 3 g carbohydrate, 274 mg cholesterol, 363 mg sodium.*
*Note:* Do not freeze egg salad—freezing makes cooked egg whites rubbery.

## BASIC CHICKEN OR TURKEY SALAD

This simple recipe is great for easy-freezer sandwiches. Check our chart (right) for great extras you or the children can add at lunchtime. (Pictured, pages 228 and 229.)

2½  cups diced cooked chicken or turkey
2  tablespoons mayonnaise
2  tablespoons plain low-fat yogurt
½  teaspoon salt
½  teaspoon black pepper

In medium bowl, mix all ingredients until well combined.
Makes about 2½ cups.
*Per ½-cup serving: 177 calories, 21 g protein, 10 g fat, 1 g carbohydrate, 66 mg cholesterol, 314 mg sodium.*
*To freeze:* Place in tightly sealed container and freeze. Thaw in the refrigerator. When thawed, add an additional tablespoon of mayonnaise or yogurt.

## BASIC SALMON OR TUNA SALAD

This quick-fix version of a traditional recipe makes almost a week's worth of frozen sandwich fillings. (Pictured, pages 228 and 229.)

2  cans (6½- to 7½-ounce size) water-packed salmon or tuna, drained
3  tablespoons mayonnaise
2  tablespoons chopped scallions
2  teaspoons grated lemon peel
1  teaspoon lemon juice

In medium bowl, mix all ingredients until well combined.
Makes about 2 cups.
*Per ½-cup serving: 183 calories, 24 g protein, 9 g fat, 1 g carbohydrate, 41 mg cholesterol, 352 mg sodium.*
*To freeze:* Place in tightly sealed container and freeze. Thaw in the refrigerator. When thawed, drain off any excess liquid, and add an additional tablespoon of mayonnaise.

# Brown-Bag It!

*Need new ideas for lunch? Here's an easy-to-follow single-serving sandwich chart.*
*Check the EXTRAS column for delicious additions to the basic fillings.*

| Sandwich | Filling | Bread/Wrapper | Extras |
|---|---|---|---|
| Lettuce Packets | Smoky Ham-and-Cheese Spread | Leaf lettuce (top leaves with ham spread and roll into packets) | ● Coarsely ground black pepper ● Chopped parsley |
| Zesty Ham & Cheese | Smoky Ham-and-Cheese Spread | Rye bread | ● Capers ● Watercress |
| Tortilla Roll-Up | Smoky Ham-and-Cheese Spread | Flour tortilla | ● 1 tablespoon salsa ● Chopped cilantro or parsley ● Olive slices |
| Spicy Egg with Cheese | Reduced-Cholesterol Egg Salad | Mini or regular bagel | ● Cucumber slices ● Monterey Jack cheese with jalapeño peppers |
| Tarragon-Egg | Reduced-Cholesterol Egg Salad | French bread | ● Chopped tarragon ● Red-pepper slices ● Chicory or fresh spinach |
| Egg and Avocado | Reduced-Cholesterol Egg Salad | Pumpernickel or black bread | ● Avocado slices ● Chopped olives |
| Chicken with Apricots and Brie | Basic Chicken or Turkey Salad | Kaiser roll | ● Dried apricots or pears ● Brie slices ● Romaine or leaf lettuce |
| BBQ Chicken | Basic Chicken or Turkey Salad | Whole-wheat hamburger bun | ● 1 tablespoon BBQ sauce ● Deli coleslaw |
| Tropical Chicken | Basic Chicken or Turkey Salad | Toasted English Muffin | ● Pineapple tidbits ● Chopped pecans |
| Curried Chicken | Basic Chicken or Turkey Salad | Cracked-wheat bread or toasted frozen waffles | ● 1 tablespoon chutney ● Chopped walnuts ● Diced apple ● ¼ teaspoon curry powder |
| Oriental Chicken | Basic Chicken or Turkey Salad | Croissant | ● Snow peas ● Diced water chestnuts ● 1 teaspoon sesame oil |
| Crunchy Salmon and Radish | Basic Salmon Salad | Pita bread or kaiser roll | ● Radish slices ● Alfalfa sprouts |
| Dilled Salmon or Tuna | Basic Salmon or Tuna Salad | Pumpernickel or black bread | ● Chopped dill ● Avocado slices |
| Seafood-Stuffed Shells | Basic Salmon or Tuna Salad | Cooked jumbo shells or manicotti | ● Chopped basil ● Diced tomato ● Diced mozzarella cheese |
| Capered Tuna | Basic Tuna Salad | Mini or regular bagel | ● Capers ● Red-onion slices ● Coarsely ground black pepper ● Alfalfa sprouts |
| Greek Salmon or Tuna | Basic Salmon or Tuna Salad | Pita bread | ● Feta cheese ● Cherry tomatoes ● Chopped oregano ● Cucumber slices |
| Super Hero | Sliced Meat Loaf with Herbed Cheese Topping | Hero roll | ● 2 tablespoons sour cream or mayo mixed with 2 teaspoons horseradish ● Arugula ● Tomato slices |
| Hearty Meat Loaf | Sliced Meat Loaf with Herbed Cheese Topping | Pumpernickel or whole-grain bread | ● String cheese ● Sliced gherkins ● Mayo ● Ketchup |
| Meat Loaf Croissant | Sliced Meat Loaf with Herbed Cheese Topping | Croissant | ● Thinly sliced Brie or Port du Salut cheese ● Cucumber slices ● Dijon mustard |
| Meat Loaf with Chili Mayo | Sliced Meat Loaf with Herbed Cheese Topping | Sliced peasant or sourdough bread | ● 1 tablespoon chili sauce mixed with 1 tablespoon mayo ● Bibb lettuce ● Red-pepper slices |
| Fruited Ham 'n' Cream Cheese | Cream Cheese and Fruit Spread | Raisin bread | ● Smoked ham or turkey slices |
| Fruity Cutouts | Cream Cheese and Fruit Spread | Raisin bread (cut out with cookie cutters) | ● Banana slices |

## SLICED MEAT LOAF WITH HERBED CHEESE TOPPING

Great for dinner—then slice and freeze any leftovers for a ready-made lunch. (Pictured, pages 228 and 229.)

Meat loaf:
1½ pounds lean ground beef
½ pound lean ground pork
⅔ cup seasoned dried bread crumbs
⅓ cup prepared spaghetti or tomato sauce
1 egg
1 large clove garlic, minced
1 medium onion, finely chopped
1 medium tomato, chopped
1 teaspoon dried oregano
½ teaspoon salt

Topping:
2 tablespoons seasoned dried bread crumbs
1 tablespoon grated Parmesan cheese
1 teaspoon dried basil
½ teaspoon dry mustard

1. Preheat oven to 350°F. For meat loaf: In medium bowl, mix all ingredients except topping until just combined. Press mixture into 9-by-5-inch loaf pan.

2. For topping: In small bowl, mix all ingredients; sprinkle over meat loaf. Bake for 1 hour, or until cooked through. Refrigerate until well chilled before slicing.

Makes about 8 servings.

*Per serving: 290 calories, 24 g protein, 16 g fat, 11 g carbohydrate, 104 mg cholesterol, 542 mg sodium.*

*To freeze:* Wrap each meat-loaf slice individually and freeze until ready to use.

## CREAM CHEESE AND FRUIT SPREAD

This luscious spread can be made a week ahead and refrigerated (do not freeze).

½ cup chopped mixed dried fruit (pitted dates, apricots, raisins)
½ cup orange juice
1 package (8 ounces) cream cheese, softened
¼ cup chopped walnuts
1 tablespoon grated orange peel
½ teaspoon ground cinnamon

1. In small saucepan over medium-high heat, bring dried fruit and orange juice to a boil. Reduce heat to low; simmer for 5 minutes, or until fruit is softened. Remove from heat; cool completely.

2. In medium bowl, mix fruit mixture with remaining ingredients. Stir until well combined.

Makes about 1½ cups.

*Per ¼-cup serving: 206 calories, 4 g protein, 16 g fat, 13 g carbohydrate, 42 mg cholesterol, 115 mg sodium.*

## SIMPLE STUFFED PEARS

This fruit-and-cheese combo makes a delicious light lunch or healthful dessert.

2 ounces Camembert or Brie cheese, softened
2 tablespoons sliced almonds, toasted
2 tablespoons diced apple or other fruit
2 pears, cored

1. Remove rind from cheese. In small bowl, mix cheese, almonds and apple.

2. Stuff pears with cheese mixture. Wrap individually in plastic wrap and refrigerate until ready to eat.

Makes 2 servings.

*Per serving: 237 calories, 8 g protein, 12 g fat, 28 g carbohydrate, 20 mg cholesterol, 240 mg sodium.*

## GRANOLA POPCORN JACKS

A short baking time in the oven makes this great snack extra crisp.

¼ cup honey
¼ cup (½ stick) butter or margarine
½ teaspoon ground cinnamon
8 cups unsalted popcorn (about ⅓ cup unpopped corn)
½ cup unsalted peanuts
½ cup chopped mixed dried fruit (pitted dates, apricots, pears)
½ cup shredded coconut, toasted

1. Preheat oven to 350°F. In saucepan over medium-high heat, bring honey, butter and cinnamon to a boil. Reduce heat to low and simmer for 8 minutes; stir occasionally.

2. In large bowl, combine popcorn, peanuts, dried fruit and coconut. Gradually pour honey mixture over popcorn mixture, tossing constantly with a spoon. Spread mixture on ungreased nonstick baking sheets.

3. Bake for 10 minutes, stirring popcorn occasionally. Cool completely before placing in an airtight container or bags. Popcorn will keep for up to 1 week.

Makes about 9 cups.

*Per cup: 180 calories, 3 g protein, 11 g fat, 21 g carbohydrate, 14 mg cholesterol, 65 mg sodium.*

## PEANUT-BUTTER SENSATIONS

Kids of all ages love peanut butter! Here are some delicious sandwich ideas to take you beyond the classic PB & J.

● Mix peanut butter with grated carrot and a handful of raisins; then spread on slices of whole-wheat bread or spoon into a pita.

● Spread chunky peanut butter on a slice of black bread; top with cucumber slices, thinly sliced smoked turkey or ham and another slice of bread.

● Make a mixture of equal parts peanut butter, crushed pineapple and chopped celery; stir in a little honey and sandwich between rice cakes.

● Spread chunky peanut butter on hearty oatmeal bread; top with some applesauce, a little freshly grated nutmeg and another slice of bread.

● Spread peanut butter on thin slices of challah or white bread; cover with sliced strawberries and sprinkle with ground cinnamon.

● Mix peanut butter with finely chopped dried fruit such as pitted dates, pears or apricots; slather onto a split corn muffin.

● Combine peanut butter with finely chopped walnuts, pecans or almonds and a little honey or jam; then spread the peanut butter mixture on cracked-wheat or date-nut bread.

● Fill celery stalks with a mixture of peanut butter, whipped cream cheese and chopped raisins; or spread the mixture on whole-wheat crackers or slices of bread.

● Stir together peanut butter and grated apple; then spread on slices of cinnamon-raisin bread.

● Make a mixture of equal parts peanut butter and trail mix; then spread on a toasted bagel or English muffin.

● Spread peanut butter on a toasted frozen waffle or slice of raisin bread; top with crumbled cooked bacon, banana slices and another waffle or slice of raisin bread.

## GOLDEN OATIE BARS

Stock the cookie jar with our chewy, low-sugar version of the granola bar.

Vegetable cooking spray
2½ cups rolled oats (old-fashioned or
    quick cooking)
½ cup chopped mixed dried fruit
½ cup chopped walnuts
6 tablespoons (¾ stick) margarine or
    butter, melted
¼ cup sugar
¼ cup honey
1½ teaspoons ground cinnamon
1 teaspoon vanilla extract
2 eggs, beaten

1. Preheat oven to 350°F. Lightly coat 9-inch square baking pan with cooking spray.

2. In large bowl, mix all ingredients until well combined. Press mixture firmly in prepared pan. Bake for 30 minutes, or until golden brown and firm. Cool completely before cutting into small bars. Will keep in an airtight container for up to 1 week.

Makes about 15.

*Per cookie: 172 calories, 4 g protein, 9 g fat, 21 g carbohydrate, 37 mg cholesterol, 65 mg sodium.*

● Because nuts contain oil, they can turn rancid over time. The best way to keep nuts fresh? Simply wrap them airtight and place them in the freezer. Add frozen nuts directly to cookie batters and other recipes—they'll defrost in no time. Nuts will keep for up to a year in the freezer.

## OATMEAL DATE-NUT COOKIES

These nutritious goodies are spiced with ginger and chock-full of fiber. (Pictured, pages 228 and 229.)

1 cup all-purpose flour (or use part flour,
    part oat bran)
1½ to 2 teaspoons ground ginger
1 teaspoon baking soda
¼ teaspoon salt
¾ cup (1½ sticks) butter or margarine,
    softened
¾ cup packed dark-brown sugar
1 egg
1 teaspoon vanilla extract
2 cups old-fashioned oats
1 cup chopped pitted dates
1 cup chopped walnuts

1. Preheat oven to 350°F. In small bowl, mix flour, ginger, baking soda and salt until well combined. In large bowl, with electric mixer on medium speed, cream butter with sugar until light and fluffy. Beat in egg and vanilla extract. Reduce speed to low; beat in flour mixture until just combined. With wooden spoon, stir in oats, dates and walnuts until combined. Drop cookie dough by tablespoons onto ungreased baking sheets, about 2 inches apart.

2. Bake for 12 to 15 minutes. (For a chewier cookie, bake for 12 minutes; for a crisper cookie, bake for 15 minutes.) Cool slightly on baking sheets; then remove to wire racks and cool completely. Cookies will keep for 2 to 3 weeks if stored in an airtight container, or up to 3 months in the freezer.

Makes about 3 dozen.

*Per cookie: 119 calories, 2 g protein, 6 g fat, 14 g carbohydrate, 18 mg cholesterol, 81 mg sodium.*

## CHUNKY, CHEWY BROWNIES

Loads of chocolate and pecans make these yummy. (Pictured, pages 228 and 229.)

1¾ cups granulated sugar
½ cup (1 stick) butter or margarine, softened
⅓ cup dark corn syrup
1 teaspoon vanilla extract
⅛ teaspoon salt
3 eggs
1⅓ cups all-purpose flour
4 squares (1-ounce size) unsweetened chocolate, melted and cooled slightly
1¼ cups chopped pecans
Confectioners' sugar

1. Preheat oven to 350°F. Lightly grease 13-by-9-inch baking pan.

2. In large bowl, with electric mixer on medium speed, beat granulated sugar, butter, corn syrup, vanilla extract and salt until just combined. Add eggs, and then flour; increase speed to high and beat for 2 minutes. Add chocolate; beat until well combined. With wooden spoon, stir in pecans, reserving some to sprinkle on top. Spread batter in prepared pan; sprinkle with reserved pecans.

3. Bake for 40 minutes, or until toothpick inserted in center comes out almost clean. Cool completely; then sprinkle lightly with confectioners' sugar. Cut into small bars.

Makes about 2 dozen.

*Per brownie: 200 calories, 2 g protein, 11 g fat, 26 g carbohydrate, 45 mg cholesterol, 63 mg sodium.*

## BROWN-BAG TIPS

### The Deep Freeze

● When preparing frozen sandwiches, use dense-textured bread, such as whole wheat, which won't get soggy when thawed. Wrap each half individually, freeze and use within two weeks.

● Spread bread completely with a little butter, margarine or peanut butter to prevent filling from soaking into bread. (Don't use mayonnaise, salad dressing or jelly—these will make frozen bread soggy.)

● Use masking tape or freezer labels to list the contents, quantity, date and any special instructions for frozen salads and spreads; for example: "Add 1 tablespoon mayonnaise or yogurt when thawed."

### Quality Control

● Keep sandwiches cool by packing them in the lunchbox with a container of frozen juice, a bag of frozen cookies, or frozen grapes, peaches or plums. By lunchtime, everything will be ready.

● Batches of frozen fillings should be thawed in the refrigerator—not on the counter—to avoid health problems.

● For a super-fresh, non-soggy sandwich, pack lettuce leaves, sliced tomatoes and other extras separately. Add them to your sandwich when you're ready to eat.

### Perfect Planning

● Keep fillings simple; use prepackaged foods if you're pressed for time and purchase juice containers and snack packs in advance.

● Pack lunchboxes the night before and store in the refrigerator. Note: Foods that lose crispness when chilled, such as cookies and crackers, should be added in the morning.

● Let your children help plan menus and make sandwiches. Lunch will be more fun for kids if they've been involved in the preparation.

# Recipes for Junior Chefs

## (Ages 7 and Up)

*Put aprons on the kids and let them make their own snacks. These easy recipes are perfect for young chefs.*

### BANANA-RAMA SMOOTHIES

Always make sure the top of the blender is in place before turning it on, and never try to stir a shake with a spoon while the blender is running. (Pictured, right.)

1  large banana
½  cup orange juice
¼  teaspoon vanilla extract
¾  cup milk
2  tablespoons nonfat dry milk
6  ice cubes
Utensils: measuring cup and spoons, blender, 2 tall glasses

1. Peel the banana. With your hands, break the banana into chunks. Put the banana, orange juice, vanilla extract, milk and dry milk in the blender. Put the lid on the blender and turn it on high speed. Blend until the mixture is smooth.

2. Put the ice cubes in the tall glasses, and then fill them with the fruit shake. You can substitute any of your favorite fruit juices for the orange juice, if you like.
Makes 2 servings.
*Per serving: 161 calories, 6 g protein, 3 g fat, 29 g carbohydrate, 14 mg cholesterol, 69 mg sodium.*

### ORANGE-PINEAPPLE YOGURT DELIGHTS

For a special snack, try this cool treat.

1  can (11 ounces) mandarin oranges
1  can (8 ounces) pineapple chunks in juice
6  ice cubes
1  container (8 ounces) vanilla-flavor low-fat yogurt
2  tablespoons nonfat dry milk
¼  teaspoon ground cinnamon
Utensils: strainer or colander, can opener, large spoon, blender, measuring spoons, 2 tall glasses

1. Set the strainer or colander in the sink. Carefully open the cans of mandarin oranges and pineapple with the can opener. Empty the fruit into the strainer to drain.

2. Spoon the fruit into the blender. Add the ice cubes, yogurt and dry milk. Put the lid on the blender and turn it on medium-high speed. Blend until the mixture is smooth and creamy. Pour the drink into the tall glasses and sprinkle with the cinnamon.
Makes 2 servings.
*Per serving: 275 calories, 8 g protein, 2 g fat, 61 g carbohydrate, 6 mg cholesterol, 109 mg sodium.*

### FAST FRUIT FIZZIES

Pour apple juice into an ice-cube tray and freeze for "juice" cubes. (Pictured, right.)

½  cup fresh strawberries
2  ice cubes
¾  cup apple juice
½  cup seltzer or club soda
Utensils: strainer or colander, measuring cups, paper towels, blender, 2 tall glasses

*Above: Fast Fruit Fizzies (facing page), Banana-Rama Smoothies (facing page).*

1. Set the strainer or colander in the sink. Pull any green leaves off the strawberries. Put the strawberries in the strainer and rinse quickly under cold running water. Let the strawberries drain; then pat dry with the paper towels.

2. Put the strawberries, ice cubes and apple juice in the blender. Put the lid on the blender and turn it on medium-high speed. Blend until the mixture is smooth. Add the seltzer and blend for 5 to 10 seconds. Pour the fizzies into the tall glasses.

Makes 2 servings.

*Per serving: 55 calories, 0 g protein, 0 g fat, 14 g carbohydrate, 0 mg cholesterol, 3 mg sodium.*

## STRAWBERRY-PEACH PARFAIT

You can use any other favorite canned fruit.

1  cup fresh strawberries
1  can (8 ounces) sliced peaches in light syrup
1  container (8 ounces) lemon- or vanilla-flavor low-fat yogurt
2  teaspoons honey
2  tablespoons chopped peanuts
Utensils: strainer or colander, measuring cup, paper towels, fork, 2 mixing bowls, can opener, measuring spoons, large spoon, 2 stemmed glasses, 2 spoons

1. Set the strainer or colander in the sink. Pull any green leaves off the strawberries. Put the strawberries in the strainer and rinse quickly under cold running water. Let the strawberries drain; then pat dry with the paper towels. Using the side of the fork, cut each strawberry into 2 pieces and put in one of the mixing bowls.

2. Carefully open the can of peaches with the can opener and empty into the strainer to drain. Using the side of the fork, cut each peach slice into 2 pieces. Add the peaches to the mixing bowl with the strawberries and toss the fruits together. Put the yogurt and honey in the second mixing bowl and stir with the large spoon.

3. Put a spoonful of the yogurt mixture into the bottom of each of the stemmed glasses. Spoon some fruit over the yogurt. Continue layering the yogurt and fruit until they are used up. Sprinkle the top of each parfait with some chopped peanuts.

Makes 2 servings.

*Per serving: 272 calories, 8 g protein, 6 g fat, 51 g carbohydrate, 5 mg cholesterol, 73 mg sodium.*

# Snacktime Specials

*Gather your kids in the kitchen to make these terrific treats! Just remember—as long as snacks are not scheduled too close to mealtime, they won't spoil little appetites.*

## VEGETABLE HIDEAWAY PIZZA POCKETS

Vegetables are fun to eat when they're served up in these easy-to-make pockets!

1  loaf Italian bread
1  medium carrot, grated
1  medium zucchini, grated
1  medium tomato, diced
¾  teaspoon dried Italian seasoning
1  cup (4 ounces) shredded part-skim mozzarella cheese
½  cup prepared pizza sauce

1. Preheat oven to 350°F. Cut bread crosswise into 4 pieces; cut each piece lengthwise in half. Make "pockets" by hollowing out the center of the bread.

2. In medium bowl, combine carrot, zucchini, tomato, Italian seasoning and ½ cup of the cheese. Layer each pocket with some vegetable mixture; then pizza sauce and remaining cheese. Place pizza pockets on baking sheet, cheese-side up. Bake for 20 minutes, or until heated through.

Makes 8 servings.

*Per serving: 172 calories, 8 g protein, 3 g fat, 28 g carbohydrate, 9 mg cholesterol, 385 mg sodium.*

## CRUNCHY TORTILLA CHIPS

These oven-baked treats are much lower in fat and salt than the commercial variety.

12  corn tortillas

Preheat oven to 400°F. Cut tortillas into quarters; place in a single layer on baking sheets. Bake for 12 minutes, or until crisp. Remove to wire racks to cool. Store chips in an airtight container.

Makes 48 chips.

*Per chip: 17 calories, 1 g protein, 0 g fat, 3 g carbohydrate, 0 mg cholesterol, 13 mg sodium.*

## LONE STAR BEAN DIP

A hearty, high-fiber dip that's great with the Crunchy Tortilla Chips (recipe, above).

1  can (15¼ to 16 ounces) red kidney beans, rinsed and drained
2  tablespoons dried minced onion
1  tablespoon cider vinegar
1  teaspoon chili powder
1  teaspoon ground cumin
2  tablespoons plain low-fat yogurt

1. In medium bowl, combine beans, onion, vinegar, chili powder and cumin. With electric mixer on low speed, beat until all the beans are mashed into a paste. Add yogurt; beat until well combined.

2. Serve dip at room temperature, or heat by microwaving on High for 1 minute. Serve with cut-up raw vegetables or tortilla chips. Store dip in refrigerator for up to 1 week, tightly covered.

Makes 1⅓ cups.

*Per tablespoon: 20 calories, 1 g protein, 0 g fat, 4 g carbohydrate, 0 mg cholesterol, 77 mg sodium.*

## FINGER-LICKIN' NACHOS

This Tex-Mex snack is a hit with kids.

12 Crunchy Tortilla Chips (recipe, left)
⅓ cup Lone Star Bean Dip (recipe, left)
¼ cup prepared mild salsa
¼ cup (1 ounce) shredded Monterey Jack
   cheese

1. Preheat oven to 350°F. Place chips on a baking sheet. Top chips with dip; drizzle with salsa and sprinkle with cheese.
2. Bake for 10 minutes, or until heated through. (To cook in microwave: Place nachos in microwaveproof dish and microwave on High for 1 to 2 minutes.)
Makes 12 nachos.

*Per nacho: 36 calories, 2 g protein, 1 g fat, 5 g carbohydrate, 2 mg cholesterol, 109 mg sodium.*

## CREAMY PEANUT BUTTER FONDUE

Half the fun of this is in the dipping.

⅓ cup creamy peanut butter
⅓ cup unsweetened applesauce
⅓ cup apple juice
4 slices cinnamon-raisin or whole-wheat
   bread
¼ cup spreadable fruit or jam
1 large apple, cored and thinly sliced
1 banana, cut into bite-size chunks
8 strawberries
1 orange, peeled and sectioned

1. In small bowl, with electric mixer on low speed, beat peanut butter and applesauce until well combined. Add apple juice; beat until smooth. Spoon into small serving bowl.
2. Make 2 sandwiches, using bread slices and spreadable fruit; diagonally cut each sandwich into quarters to form triangles.

3. Arrange sandwich triangles and fruit around peanut butter fondue. Dip sandwiches and fruit in fondue.
Makes 4 servings.

*Per serving: 323 calories, 8 g protein, 12 g fat, 52 g carbohydrate, 1 mg cholesterol, 192 mg sodium.*

## FROSTY BANANA POPS

You'll need lollipop sticks to make these frosty treats. If kids can't eat all the banana pops at one time, wrap each leftover pop separately in plastic wrap and freeze for another time. (Kids 7 and up could make this without Mom's help.)

1½ cups pecan halves, or 8 whole graham
   crackers
1 container (8 ounces) vanilla-flavor low-
   fat yogurt
1 teaspoon ground cinnamon
2 large bananas

1. Place pecan halves or graham crackers (pick your favorite) in plastic bag. With rolling pin, crush pecans and remove crushed pecans to a plate; set aside.
2. In medium bowl, combine yogurt and cinnamon. Peel bananas and cut into halves with the side of fork. Press lollipop sticks into the 4 banana pieces. Holding stick, dip each banana in yogurt mixture, and then roll in crushed pecans until banana is completely coated. Place bananas on baking sheet and place in freezer for at least 1 hour.
Makes 4 servings.

*Per serving: 380 calories, 7 g protein, 28 g fat, 31 g carbohydrate, 3 mg cholesterol, 39 mg sodium.*

# Cook-Together Cookie Collection

*Festive cookies are a cinch to make with this collection. Choose from Cutout Cookies (below), Six-Way Shortbread Rounds (page 244) and Fun-Dough Creations (page 246). Creating the cookies is as much fun as eating them!*

# Cutout Cookies

### BROWN-BUTTER DOUGH

Butter that has been lightly browned in a saucepan gives this dough a deep, rich color and taste.

3½  cups all-purpose flour
¾  teaspoon baking soda
½  teaspoon grated nutmeg
¼  teaspoon ground allspice
¼  teaspoon salt
1  cup (2 sticks) unsalted butter
1  cup sugar
1  egg
½  cup buttermilk

1. In large bowl, mix first 5 ingredients until well combined.

2. Melt butter in medium saucepan over medium-low heat. Cook for 5 to 6 minutes, or until lightly browned and no longer bubbling, being careful not to burn.

3. Add browned butter to flour mixture; with electric mixer on low speed, beat until well blended. Beat in sugar, egg and buttermilk until just combined.

4. Divide dough into two pieces. Flatten each piece slightly and wrap in plastic wrap. Refrigerate for 3 hours or freeze for 1 hour, or until firm. (If preparing dough to make Frosty Snowflakes or Holiday Pony Pops, knead some cocoa powder into dough before chilling; see step 1 of those recipes.)

### GRANDMA'S GINGERSNAP DOUGH

The more ginger you add to this dough, the "hotter" the cookies will be.

1¾  cups all-purpose flour
½  cup whole-wheat flour
2 to 3 teaspoons ground ginger
1  teaspoon ground cinnamon
½  teaspoon baking soda
½  teaspoon salt
¼  teaspoon ground cloves
10  tablespoons (1¼ sticks) unsalted
    butter, softened
1  cup sugar
1  egg
1½  tablespoons grated orange peel
1½  tablespoons honey

1. In medium bowl, mix first 7 ingredients until well combined.

2. In large bowl, with electric mixer on medium speed, cream butter with sugar until light and fluffy. Beat in egg, orange peel and honey. Reduce speed to low; beat in flour mixture until just combined.

3. Divide dough into two pieces. Flatten each piece slightly and wrap in plastic wrap. Refrigerate for 2 hours or freeze for 30 minutes, or until firm.

## HOLIDAY PONY POPS

Use a heart-shape cookie cutter, garlic press and lollipop sticks to make these adorable treats. (Pictured, right.)

1 batch Brown-Butter Dough
  (recipe, left)
2 tablespoons unsweetened cocoa
  powder
About 22 miniature semisweet
  chocolate chips

1. Prepare dough and divide into 2 pieces as recipe directs; knead cocoa into 1 of the pieces before chilling as directed.

2. Preheat oven to 350°F. On lightly floured surface, with floured rolling pin, roll dough, 1 piece at a time, to about ¼-inch thickness; keep remaining dough chilled.

3. With 3-inch heart-shape cookie cutter, cut out about 11 cookies for pony heads. Reserve dough scraps; keep chilled. Place hearts on ungreased baking sheets, spacing far enough apart to allow for lollipop sticks. Push a lollipop stick about 1 inch into rounded edge of each heart. Cut ¾-inch tip off pointed bottom of hearts. Cut tips in half for pony ears; set aside. Repeat with remaining dough to make about 22 ponies (keep chocolate and plain dough scraps separate).

4. Press reserved dough scraps through new or well-scrubbed garlic press to make strands for pony manes. Tear strands into short lengths; attach to pony heads. (We used a contrasting color of mane to pony heads.) Arrange reserved pony ears on top; press pieces together firmly to fuse when baked. Press chips into dough for eyes.

5. Bake for 13 to 15 minutes, or until set. Cool slightly on baking sheets; with wide spatula, carefully remove to wire racks and

*Above: (Clockwise from bottom) Snow Babies (page 242), Holiday Pony Pops (this page), Frosty Snowflakes (page 243), Christmas Tweety Doves (page 242).*

cool completely. Tie a short length of ribbon around each lollipop stick, if you like.

Makes about 22.

*Per cookie: 188 calories, 3 g protein, 9 g fat, 25 g carbohydrate, 32 mg cholesterol, 63 mg sodium.*

## SNOW BABIES

Kids will enjoy cutting out and decorating these scrumptious goodies. Store cookies between layers of wax paper in a tin or other airtight container. (Pictured, page 241.)

1 batch Brown-Butter Dough or
   Grandma's Gingersnap Dough (recipes,
   page 240)
Food coloring
3 tubes prepared white decorating
   icing
About ⅔ cup shredded coconut
Snowflake décors

   1. Prepare dough as recipe directs.
   2. Preheat oven to 350°F. On lightly floured surface, with floured rolling pin, roll dough, 1 piece at a time, to about ⅛-inch thickness; keep remaining dough chilled.
   3. With 3-to 4-inch gingerman or teddy-bear cookie cutter, cut out cookies for snow-baby bodies. (If using teddy-bear cutter, trim off ears.) With 1-inch round cookie cutter or soda-bottle cap, cut out *same number* of rounds for faces. Place cookie bodies and faces on separate ungreased baking sheets, about 1 inch apart. Repeat with remaining dough and rerolled chilled scraps.
   4. Bake cookie bodies for 10 to 12 minutes, or until set; bake cookie faces for 4 to 6 minutes. Cool slightly on baking sheets; then carefully remove to wire racks and cool completely.
   5. To paint eyes and mouths on cookie faces, use a toothpick dipped in food coloring. To paint cheeks, dilute red food coloring with a little water and paint on with a small brush.
   6. Place some white icing into several small cups; tint with several different colors of food coloring. Spread some colored icing over 1 cookie body; press a cookie face onto body to attach. Pipe white icing around outside edge of face; press some coconut onto icing for trim on snow baby's "hood." Add snowflake décors for buttons. Repeat with remaining cookies; let stand until icing sets.
   Makes about 3 dozen.
   *Per cookie: 161 calories, 2 g protein, 7 g fat, 23 g carbohydrate, 20 mg cholesterol, 42 mg sodium.*

## CHRISTMAS TWEETY DOVES

Kids can use a bright bakable glaze to paint these birds their favorite colors. (Pictured, page 241.)

1 batch Brown-Butter Dough or
   Grandma's Gingersnap Dough (recipes,
   page 240)
About 32 miniature semisweet chocolate
   chips
About 32 blanched slivered almonds
3 egg yolks
Food coloring
1 tube prepared decorating icing

   1. Prepare dough as recipe directs.
   2. Preheat oven to 350°F. On lightly floured surface, with floured rolling pin, roll dough, 1 piece at a time, to about ⅛-inch thickness; keep remaining dough chilled.
   3. With 2-inch round cookie cutter, cut out 8 circles. Cut each circle in half for dove wings; place on ungreased baking sheets, about 1 inch apart. With 3-inch round cookie cutter, cut out 10 circles. Cut 8 in half for dove bodies; place on separate ungreased baking sheets, about 2 inches apart. Cut remaining 2 circles into 8 pieces each

(like pie wedges) for dove tails. Attach a tail to flat side of each dove body. Press pieces together firmly to fuse when baked. Repeat with remaining dough for a total of about 32 doves. (We made bite-size cookies from the dough scraps. Chill scraps; then cut out with small heart, star or canapé cutters.)

4. Press chocolate chips into dough for eyes. Break almond slivers in half; attach 2 halves to each dove for beaks.

5. To paint doves, place each egg yolk in a separate small cup. Add ¼ teaspoon water to each cup, beating until smooth. Add drops of different food coloring to each cup; paint glaze on cookies with small brush. If paint starts to dry, mix in a few drops of water.

6. Bake dove wings for 8 to 10 minutes, or until set; bake bodies for 10 to 12 minutes. Cool slightly on baking sheets; then carefully remove to wire racks and cool completely. Squeeze a little icing onto underside of each dove wing; press wings onto dove bodies to attach. Let stand until set.

Makes about 32.

*Per cookie: 151 calories, 2 g protein, 7 g fat, 20 g carbohydrate, 42 mg cholesterol, 44 mg sodium.*

### FROSTY SNOWFLAKES

Use readily available cookie cutters to create fanciful snowflakes. (Pictured, page 241.)

1 batch Brown-Butter Dough (recipe, page 240)
2 tablespoons unsweetened cocoa powder
2 tubes prepared white decorating icing

1. Prepare dough and divide into 2 pieces as recipe directs; knead cocoa into 1 of the pieces before chilling as directed.

2. Preheat oven to 350°F. On lightly floured surface, with floured rolling pin, roll dough, 1 piece at a time, to about ⅛-inch thickness; keep remaining dough chilled.

3. Use a variety of cookie cutters to cut out snowflake centers and points: For snowflake centers, cut out cookies with 2- to 3-inch round, star, snowflake, diamond and/or square cookie cutters. For snowflake points, cut out small shapes with canapé cutters or other tiny cookie cutters.

4. Place snowflake centers on ungreased baking sheets, about 4 inches apart. Attach points to centers to create snowflakes; press pieces together firmly to fuse when baked. Use any combination of shapes and sizes and contrasting colors of dough—no snowflake need be the same as any others. (Or just use a star or snowflake cookie cutter instead of combining shapes, if you like.) Repeat with remaining dough and rerolled chilled scraps.

5. Bake for 10 to 12 minutes, or until set. Cool slightly on baking sheets; then with wide spatula, carefully remove to wire racks and cool completely. Use icing to pipe snowflake design on top of each cookie; let stand until icing sets.

Makes about 5 dozen.

*Per cookie: 85 calories, 1 g protein, 4 g fat, 12 g carbohydrate, 12 mg cholesterol, 23 mg sodium.*

◆ Keep dough scraps chilled—if left at room temperature, dough becomes difficult to roll.

# Six-Way Shortbread Rounds

*Right: Six-Way Shortbread Rounds all dressed up with toppings (see suggestions).*

### BASIC SHORTBREAD

Here, our simple cookie recipe with luscious variations, plus lots of dipping and sandwich suggestions.

**2 cups all-purpose flour**
**¼ teaspoon salt**
**1 cup (2 sticks) unsalted butter, softened**
**¾ cup sifted confectioners' sugar**

1. Preheat oven to 350°F. In small bowl, mix flour and salt.

2. In large bowl, with electric mixer on medium speed, cream butter with sugar until light and fluffy. With wooden spoon, stir in flour mixture until just combined.

3. On lightly floured surface, with floured rolling pin, roll dough to about ¼-inch thickness. With 2-inch round or scallop-edge cookie cutter, cut out cookies; place on ungreased baking sheets, about ½ inch apart. Gather scraps, reroll and cut out (chill scraps if dough is too soft to roll).

4. Bake for 15 to 18 minutes, or until very lightly browned around edges. Remove to wire racks and cool completely. You can serve the cookies plain or decorate as desired (see the following Dipping and Sandwich Suggestions).

Makes about 3 dozen.

*Per basic shortbread cookie: 78 calories, 1 g protein, 5 g fat, 7 g carbohydrate, 14 mg cholesterol, 16 mg sodium.*

**Shortbread Variations (pictured, right):**
● **Sugar-and-Spice:** Follow basic shortbread recipe, adding ½ teaspoon ground cardamom, ½ teaspoon ground cinnamon and ¼ teaspoon grated nutmeg to flour in step 1.
● **Christmas Cocoa:** Follow basic shortbread recipe, decreasing flour to 1¾ cups and adding ⅓ cup unsweetened cocoa powder to flour in step 1.
● **Lemony Poppy Seed:** Follow basic shortbread recipe, adding 2 tablespoons poppy seeds and 2 tablespoons grated lemon peel to butter-sugar mixture in step 2.
● **Crispy Coconut:** Follow basic shortbread recipe, adding ¾ cup shredded coconut to butter-sugar mixture in step 2.
● **Georgia Pecan:** Follow basic shortbread recipe, adding 1 cup finely chopped pecans (or other nuts) to butter-sugar mixture in step 2.

---

● Always use the correct cup when measuring ingredients. Liquid cups, usually glass or plastic, have a pouring spout. Place the cup on a flat surface, add the liquid and check at eye level. Measuring cups for dry ingredients, which are generally metal or plastic, should be filled to the top and then leveled off. When measuring flour, lightly spoon it into the measuring cup and then level off—never scoop flour out of the container. Brown sugar should be packed very firmly in the cup.

## Dipping and Sandwich Suggestions

If you'd like an extra-special shortbread cookie, whip up a chocolate or peanut-butter glaze. Use it for dipping, decorating and making instant cookie sandwiches. Here's how: Over low heat in small, heavy saucepan, stirring constantly, melt ½ cup semisweet-chocolate chips, white-chocolate chips or peanut-butter chips with some solid vegetable shortening—use 1½ teaspoons shortening for semisweet chocolate; 2 teaspoons shortening for white chocolate; and 3 teaspoons shortening for peanut butter.

● **Single Dip:** Dip each cookie half in warm glaze.

● **Nutty Double Dip:** Coat half of each cookie in warm glaze; immediately dip glaze-covered portion into chopped nuts (pistachios, pecans, peanuts, walnuts, macadamias or almonds).

● **Treat-Topped:** With knife, dab a bit of warm glaze on top of cookie; sprinkle with sliced almonds, toasted shredded coconut, chopped candied cherries, colored sprinkles or sugar crystals.

● **Shortbread Swirls:** For a pretty feather effect, spread warm glaze over cookie; then drizzle or pipe thin parallel lines of a different-color glaze over first glaze. Pull a toothpick several times crosswise through lines, alternating the direction that you pull to form a feather pattern.

● **Dip and Roll:** Dip edges of cookie in warm glaze; then roll in nonpareil candies, colored sprinkles or sugar crystals, toasted shredded coconut or chopped nuts.

● **Chocolate Zigzags:** Dip fork into warm white-chocolate glaze; then drizzle glaze over cookie in zigzag pattern. With another fork, drizzle a semisweet-chocolate zigzag in opposite direction.

● **Crystal Drizzles:** Dip fork into warm glaze; then randomly drizzle lines of glaze over cookie. Sprinkle with green or red sugar crystals.

● **Jam Sandwich:** Spread about ½ teaspoon jam or warm glaze on bottom of a cookie; sandwich with another cookie. Dust with a little confectioners' sugar.

# Fun-Dough Creations

## BASIC FUN-DOUGH

We give seven ideas for cookies kids can shape and decorate themselves.

3¼  cups all-purpose flour
½  teaspoon baking soda
¼  teaspoon salt
1  cup (2 sticks) unsalted butter or
    margarine, softened
½  cup granulated sugar
¼  cup packed light-brown sugar
1  teaspoon vanilla extract
1  egg

1. In medium bowl, mix flour, baking soda and salt until well combined.

2. In large bowl, with electric mixer on medium speed, cream butter with granulated sugar and brown sugar until light and fluffy. Beat in vanilla extract and egg. Reduce speed to low; beat in flour mixture until just combined. Wrap dough in plastic wrap; refrigerate for 1 hour or freeze for 30 minutes, or until firm.

3. Preheat oven to 350°F. Shape dough into 1-inch balls (see suggestions that follow to form cookies into various shapes). Place shaped cookies on ungreased baking sheets, about 1 inch apart.

4. Bake for 15 to 20 minutes, or until very lightly browned. Cool slightly on baking sheets; then remove to wire racks and cool completely.

Makes about 60 1-inch balls of dough.

*Per cookie: 61 calories, 1 g protein, 3 g fat, 7 g carbohydrate, 12 mg cholesterol, 18 mg sodium.*

**Fun-Dough Variations:**

● **Cocoa Fun-Dough:** Follow basic fun-dough recipe, decreasing the flour to 2¾ cups and adding ½ cup unsweetened cocoa powder to flour in step 1.

● **Green and Red Fun-Dough:** Follow basic fun-dough recipe, dividing dough in half before chilling. Knead about 12 drops of green food coloring into half of dough; knead about 12 drops of red food coloring into other half of dough. Wrap each half separately in plastic wrap; chill as directed.

*Right: (Clockwise from top left) Fun-Dough Suggestions (facing page), Crystal Trees, Tiny Teddies, Merry Mice, Magic Mushrooms, Dandy Candy Canes, Bright Holiday Wreaths, Crazy Caterpillars.*

## Fun-Dough Suggestions
### (Pictured, below)

**Crazy Caterpillars:** Make a row of 4 fun-dough balls; press together firmly to fuse when baked. Brush 3 balls with beaten egg white; then sprinkle with green- or red-tinted shredded coconut (toss with a few drops of food coloring). Attach red shoestring licorice for legs and cinnamon red-hot candies or miniature chocolate chips for eyes and/or nose. Bake as directed.

**Merry Mice:** Shape 1 ball of plain or cocoa fun-dough into oval; make a slight point at 1 end for head. Attach a piece of red shoestring licorice for tail; confetti décors for eyes and nose; and pine nuts for ears. Bake and cool as directed.

**Tiny Teddies:** Use 1 ball of cocoa fun-dough for body; shape smaller balls for legs, arms, head, ears and nose. Press together firmly to fuse when baked; brush with beaten egg white. Attach confetti décors for eyes, nose and/or buttons. Decorate body with nonpareil candies or décors. Bake and cool as directed.

**Magic Mushrooms:** Shape 1 ball of cocoa fun-dough into mushroom cap and 1 ball of plain fun-dough into stem; press together firmly to fuse when baked. Brush cap with beaten egg white and decorate with chocolate sprinkles. Bake and cool as directed.

**Dandy Candy Canes:** Roll 1 ball of red-tinted fun-dough and 1 ball of plain fun-dough into two 6-inch ropes. Place ropes side by side and twist together; pinch ends to seal. Curve 1 end to form candy cane. Brush with beaten egg white and sprinkle with crushed peppermint candies. Bake and cool as directed.

**Crystal Trees:** Roll 2 balls of green-tinted fun-dough into two 6-inch ropes. Roll 1 ball of plain fun-dough into 6-inch rope. Shape each rope into an upside-down V; curl ends up to form branches. Arrange branches to form a tree (see photo). Shape 1 ball of plain fun-dough into triangular tree trunk and attach to tree; press together firmly to fuse when baked. Brush branches with beaten egg white; sprinkle with colored sugar crystals. Bake and cool as directed.

**Bright Holiday Wreaths:** Roll 1 ball of green-tinted fun-dough and 1 ball of plain fun-dough into two 6-inch ropes. Place ropes side by side and twist together. Bring ends together to form a wreath; pinch ends together to seal. Decorate with chopped gumdrops or other nonmelting candies; bake and cool as directed.

# Index

# Contributors

## RECIPE DEVELOPERS

Robert Farrar Capon, Rena Coyle,
Sandra Lounsbury Foose, Claudia Gallo,
Jean Galton, Sandra Rose Gluck,
Katja Goldman, Mary Goodbody,
Carol Guthrie, Lori Longbotham,
Pat Messing, Catherine Paukner,
Joanna Pruess, Miriam Rubin,
Susan Spedalle, Helen Taylor-Jones,
Elizabeth Terry, Leslie Weiner,
Elizabeth Wheeler, Olwen Woodier,
Marianne Zanzarella.

## PHOTO PROP AND FOOD STYLISTS

Adrienne Abseck, Betty Alfenito,
Randi Barritt, Laurie Jean Beck,
Anita Calero, Bob Chambers,
Linda Cheverton, Mary Ann Clayton,
Anne Disrude, Anne Egan, Rick Ellis,
Joanne Furtak, Carol Gelles, Laura Hart,
Dora Jonassen, Francine Matalon-Degni,
Nancy Micklin, Hannah Millman,
Deborah Mintcheff, Gina Parker,
Catherine Paukner, Denise L. Rowley,
Helen Taylor-Jones, Marianne Zanzarella.

## PHOTOGRAPHERS

Al Clayton, pages 98, 99, 102, 104, 107,
 108-109, 110, 111, 113, 115, 124-125,
 127, 128.
Dennis Galante, pages 163, 173.
Beth Galton, pages 171, 184, 194, 204.
Julie Gang, page 237.
Richard Jeffery, pages 116, 117, 120, 123.
Peter Johansky, pages 6-7, 8, 10, 15, 17,
 19, 28, 32, 37, 38, 39, 41, 43, 46, 51,
 53, 54, 58, 64, 222, 225, 228-229.
James Kozyra, pages 13 and 35.
Rita Maas, page 81.
Judd Pilossof, pages 26 and 77.
Jerry Simpson, pages 89, 90, 92, 118, 130,
 131, 133, 137, 138, 144, 147, 149.
Michael Skott, pages 160-161, 166-167,
 169, 191, 195, 199, 245, 246, 247.
Mark Thomas, pages 45, 66-67, 72, 82-83,
 94, 152-153, 157, 170, 175, 178, 201,
 206-207, 209, 241.
Marty Umans, pages 212, 215, 216.
Lou Wallach, page 181.
Lisa Charles Watson, cover and pages 12,
 22, 24, 29, 49, 56.
Elizabeth Watt, pages 69 and 79.